Comparative Government and Politics

To Samuel Edward Finer.

Born 22 September 1915, youngest son of Max and Fanny Finer

Married Ann, 1949 (marriage dissolved 1975); married Catherine, 1977 – two sons (Jeremy and Josiah), one daughter (Jessica)

Educated Holloway School, London; Trinity College, Oxford, BA (Oxon) 1st Class Hons. Modern Greats (PPE), 1937; 1st Class Hons. Modern History, 1938; MA (Oxon) 1946, D.Litt. 1979; Sen. George Webb-Medley Scholar, 1938–40

Served War, 1940–46; Captain Royal Signals, 1945

Lecturer in Politics, Balliol College, Oxford, 1946–49; Junior Research Fellow, Balliol College, Oxford 1949–50; Professor of Political Institutions, University of Keele, 1950–66; Professor of Government, University of Manchester, 1966–74; Gladstone Professor of Government and Public Administration, University of Oxford, 1974–82; Deputy Vice-Chancellor, University of Keele, 1962–64; Visiting Professor and Faculty Member, Institute of Social Studies, The Hague, Netherlands, 1957–59; Visiting Professor in Government; Cornell University, 1962; Hebrew University, Jerusalem, 1969; Simon Fraser University, BC, 1976; Europe University Institute, Florence, 1977; Stanford University, 1979; Hong Kong University, 1980; Visiting Schweitzer Professor, Columbia University, 1982

Chairman, Political Studies Association of UK, 1965–69; FRHistSoc. DU Essex, 1982, FBA 1982

Comparative Government and Politics

Essays in honour of S.E. Finer

Edited by
Dennis Kavanagh and Gillian Peele

HEINEMANN
LONDON

WESTVIEW PRESS
BOULDER, COLORADO

Heinemann Educational Books Ltd
22 Bedford Square, London WC1B 3HH

LONDON EDINBURGH MELBOURNE AUCKLAND
HONG KONG SINGAPORE KUALA LUMPUR
NEW DELHI IBADAN NAIROBI JOHANNESBURG
EXETER (NH) KINGSTON PORT OF SPAIN

British Library Cataloguing in Publication Data

Comparative government and politics.
  1.   Comparative government
  I.   Kavanagh, Dennis II. Peele, Gillian
  III. Finer, S.E.
  320.3   JF51

ISBN 0-435-83470-3

Published in the United States of America 1984
by Westview Press, Inc
5500 Central Avenue
Boulder, Colorado 80301
Frederick A. Praeger, Publisher

ISBN 0-8133-0094-0 (U.S.)

Printed in Great Britain.

288 564

Contents

Contributors

Alan Angell, Fellow St. Antony's College, Oxford, previously colleague of S.E.F. at Keele University

Jean Blondel, Professor of Government, Essex University, previously colleague of S.E.F. at Keele University

Hugh Berrington, Professor of Politics, Newcastle University, previously colleague of S.E.F. at Keele University

Vernon Bogdanor, Fellow and Tutor in Politics, Brasenose College, Oxford

Hans Daalder, Professor of Politics, Leiden University, previously colleague of S.E.F. at European University Institute, Florence

Jack Hayward, Professor of Politics, Hull University, previously colleague of S.E.F. at Keele University

Dennis Kavanagh, Professor of Politics, Nottingham University, previously colleague of S.E.F. at Manchester University and European University Institute Florence

Donald MacRae, Professor of Sociology, London School of Economics, previously colleague of S.E.F. at Oxford

George Moyser, Lecturer in Government, Manchester University, previously colleague of S.E.F. at Manchester

Geraint Parry, Professor of Government, Manchester University, previously colleague of S.E.F. in same department

Gillian Peele, Fellow and Tutor in Politics, Lady Margaret Hall, Oxford

David Robertson, Fellow and Tutor in Politics, St. Hugh's College, Oxford

Preface

This volume of essays is presented to Professor Sammy Finer. The volume is an expression of the affection and esteem with which his friends and former colleagues regard him and his work. It was originally hoped to mark the occasion of his retirement in 1982 from the Gladstone Chair of Government and Public Administration at Oxford. A late start has meant that we have missed that date.

We had a difficult task in deciding which friends to invite to write a chapter for volume. To have invited even a small proportion of the potential contributors would have made the book too large. Our first principle of selection was to invite contributions from persons who had been colleagues of Sammy's, at Oxford (1946–50), Keele (1950–66), Manchester (1966–74), Oxford (1974–82), and the European University Institute in Florence (1977). Individual contributors chose their own topics. But we encouraged each one to address a theme about which Sammy Finer has written. The chapters in the volume cover such topics as pressure groups, the military, political parties, elites, political leaders, political participation, coalitions, constitutions and the state of political science. Such a list gives an indication of the wide range of Sammy Finer's interests and expertise.

The essays themselves reflect the range of modern comparative government. Just as Professor Finer himself stimulated research in a number of areas but established no rigid school or sect within political science, the authors represent different sub-fields of the discipline and have their own methodological biases. Two features give the collection unity and a common focus. First, all the essays are comparative – not in the sense that they necessarily all deal with more than one country but rather in the sense that they all employ insights and understandings derived from the general exploration of political systems. Secondly, all of the essays are on themes that continue to concern modern practitioners of political science and as such are inevitably ones which Professor Finer himself has taken up in his writings.

Two essays in the collection are somewhat different from the others. Hans Daalder's examination of the state of modern political science offers a *tour d'horizon* which we hope will enable the reader to understand some of the developments in the subject alluded to in other essays. Dennis Kavanagh's personal account of Professor Finer and his career is designed to give the reader some idea of the colourful character to whom this collection is dedicated. Doubtless many other friends and colleagues could have produced alternative favourite stories and 'Finerisms'. We hope that the reader will at the end of the day feel that he has learnt something more both about British political science and about one of its major post-war figures.

Dennis Kavanagh
Gillian Peele

1 Personality, Politics and Government: S.E. Finer*
Dennis Kavanagh

British political science has had few contributors of real distinction. Bagehot was a founding father; Bryce and Barker were among the pioneers; Laski and Brogan came in a later generation; then perhaps Bill Mackenzie and Oakeshott. But if one asks who, in subsequent generations, could join that roll-call, the name of Sammy Finer stands out.

Sammy Finer's achievements as a political scientist are notable, both for their breadth and depth. The historian who wrote about Chadwick and public health in the nineteenth century is also the political scientist who analysed Early Day Motions in the House of Commons and the diverse behaviour of military dictators. The careful analyst of constitutions is also the political stirrer, who, with his attack on adversary politics, contributed to a real change in our thinking about the British party system and the ways of Westminster. The theorist who edited the work of Siéyès and Pareto is also the teacher who could provide lucid textbooks on local government, public administration and comparative government. During his academic career the study of politics and government has been transformed and, as a mark of this specialisation, become fragmented. Yet in an age of specialisation Finer has been not only a notable synthesizer of diverse approaches and subjects, he has also ranged freely and successfully across the discipline.[1]

Finer's parents, Max and Fanny Finer, came to England as Jewish immigrants from Romania in 1900. He was born in London in 1915, following two brothers and three sisters. His mother was 42 when she gave birth to Sammy, and the nearest sibling was already 9 years old. Psychologists have their theories about the personalities of first-born,

* I would liked to thank a number of Sammy Finer's former colleagues for comments on this chapter. I would also like to thank my colleagues at Nottingham, J.S. McClelland and Peter Morris, for their suggestions.

and of the last born. Sammy – 'I came out of the blue' – did not suffer a lack of affection or attention: rather the opposite. After attendance at Holloway School he won an Open Scholarship to Trinity College Oxford. He graduated with a first in PPE in 1937 and was then persuaded to try to do the Modern History School in a year – 'the best piece of academic advice I have ever had'[2] – and gained another first. The major influence on the young Sammy appears to have been his older brother, the remarkable Herman Finer, then a lecturer in government at the London School of Economics. Sammy's early ambition was 'to be like my brother'. When Sammy eventually had the chance to do research in 1938 it was an earlier remark of Herman's which prompted him to choose Chadwick for his research topic. Herman Finer, eighteen years older than Sammy, was eventually lost to Chicago in the 1940s. But that was not before he had produced a stream of outstanding books, including *The Theory and Practice of Modern Government*, a massive work which, amid the sparse pre-war literature, was like a bible to teachers of politics. Herman was a difficult act for anybody to follow and many younger brothers would have been terrified to follow in his footsteps. There was mutual admiration, not enmity, between the brothers. It is possible, however, to see in Sammy's work a similar interest in comparative government and a determination to leave as large a mark on the subject as the encyclopaedic Herman.

After war service in the Middle East Sammy returned to Oxford and Balliol as a lecturer and then Junior Research Fellow. His first book, *A Primer of Public Administration*, was published in 1950, and then his magisterial study of *The Life and Times of Sir Edwin Chadwick* in 1952. He was also working in the field of local government and eventually produced (with J.P.R. Maud) *Local Government in England and Wales* in 1953, which long remained a standard text. In 1950 he went to the newly founded University of Keele in Staffordshire, where A.D. Lindsay, his old Master at Balliol, was the founding Vice-Chancellor. The chair to which Finer was appointed was originally designated as one in Local Government and Administration, tailor-made for him at the time. But it was soon changed to Political Institutions, a change which better reflected Sammy's range and depth. He remained at Keele until 1966 and was deputy Vice-Chancellor between 1962 and 1964. This period saw him complete his famous study of pressure groups, *Anonymous Empire* (1958), as well as *Private Industry and Political Power* (1958), *Backbench Opinion in the House of Commons*, with his Keele colleagues Bartholomew and Berrington (1961), and *Man on Horseback* (1962). He also found time to edit *Siéyès: What is the Third Estate?* (1963), and the sociological writings of Pareto (1966).

In 1966 he succeeded W.J.M. Mackenzie as Professor of Government at Manchester University. He remained there for eight productive years, and his 600-page *Comparative Government* was published in 1970. In 1974 he returned to Oxford and a Fellowship at All Souls as Gladstone Professor of Government and Public Administration, the most prestigious post in the field. While there he edited *Adversary Politics and Electoral Reform* (1975), which grew out of his influential *New Society* article, 'In defence of deadlock',[3] which was followed by *The Changing British Party System 1945–79* (1980). He retired from the Chair, but from little else, in 1982. In addition to the above posts he has also held numerous visiting professorships at universities in North America, Western Europe, Hong Kong and Israel.

Over the years he has poured forth dozens of scholarly articles and contributions to books as well as doing radio talks and various short 'think pieces'. Finer has never been short of ideas, mostly good ones, and never seemed to lack the ability to carry them through. A humane, energetic, amused, erudite approach permeates his various works. The processes of government are full of paradox and it has been part of his genius to perceive – and even occasionally to enhance – the quiddities of politics. In his academic writing he has sometimes restrained the impish humour which, in a profusion of anecdotes, delights lecture audiences and friends. Thus his remark to students: 'Politicians are not as clever or as charismatic as you or me; particularly me.' Or his dismissal of a distinguished American political scientist's attempt to integrate various political science approaches into one all-encompassing model, 'He is trying to be the U-Thant of the profession.' Or, again, his alternative title for R.T. McKenzie and Allan Silver's *Angels in Marble*, a study of working-class Conservatives in England, *The Anatomy of Alf Garnett*, or the suggested substitute *Arsenic and Old Hat* for Marcuse's *One-Dimensional Man*.

A festschrift is a tribute to scholarship, an attempt to assess and add to what a learned man has given to his subject. But it cannot ignore the man. It is inevitable that subjective assessments of Sammy as a person will vary. But surely those who know him well will agree that he is a man of strong opinions. He has always been impatient with what he regards as 'cant' or 'pussy-footing'. He has not suffered fools gladly nor discussants who took time to labour the obvious. In seminars he might show more interest in his doodling (if these survive they will form an impressive collection) than in what others were saying. But he could still be relied upon to make an enlightening intervention. Along with his impatience and quickness of mind goes great energy, exuberance and loyalty – to friends, institutions, Israel and his subject.

He has always been an elegant and striking dresser. He appreciates bright shirts and ties. Is there a touch of Disraeli, of whom he once wished to write a biography? The drab surroundings of Dover Street in Manchester in the early 1970s were often lightened by the appearance of the 'charismatic dandy'.[4] In the best Oxford tradition he is also a great talker, intense, engaged, argumentative, witty and unleashing a stream of 'Finerisms'. One colleague, who shared a hotel room with him at a conference, remembers falling asleep with Sammy's voice still declaiming. He woke the next morning to hear the voice talking again, and perhaps wondered if it had ceased while he was asleep!

Sammy Finer's contribution to the political science goes far beyond his own considerable writing. There is a tendency among some academics to disparage the work of the outstanding scholar by claiming that he must have neglected his teaching or administrative duties (more often the converse is true). Sammy was of course a brilliant teacher and lecturer – even on an 'off-day' – not least of first-year undergraduates. But he was also an effective chairman of two outstanding departments, Political Institutions at Keele, and then Government at Manchester. His preferred style in both places was not to involve himself in administrative detail but to delegate to colleagues and to concentrate on larger matters. This was a judicious use of his talents but he was lucky to have cooperative colleagues.

At both Keele and Manchester he recruited to the subject some of the most promising available talent. At Keele he was a pioneer; at Manchester he took over from W.J.M. Mackenzie; he left both as major centres for the study of politics and government. A high proportion of current professors of politics in Britain have at some time served under him. At Manchester in particular he arrived at a time when the departure of Mackenzie to Glasgow and many staff to chairs elsewhere meant that there was a major task of rebuilding the department. He made some judicious senior appointments, including Denis Austin and Ghita Ionesco, to provide ballast to a department which was top-heavy with assistant and very junior lecturers. As well as attracting able people, he also, by personal example and stimulus, helped the less talented to excel.

At Oxford the structure (particularly the Gladstone Professor's lack of patronage and resources) and the college system gave him less opportunity to shape the discipline. But in teaching and in friendly advice he has continued to pour forth ideas and to launch students into fruitful paths of research. As ever, he was a great draw for students.

In addition to his duties as a departmental head and member of various university senates he has also been a Deputy Vice-Chancellor, an active Fellow of All Souls, and has left a considerable imprint on the character and politics of each of the institutions that he has graced. He was Chairman and later President of the Political Science Association. He has been active in the International Political Science Association (he was offered the Presidency), the Institute of Jewish Affairs, the Police Board, and the editorial board of *Government and Opposition*.

Of Sammy it could fairly be said that he was, and is, a born teacher. He has always loved lecturing, preferably to large audiences. Before big lectures his practice was to wind himself up like a prize-fighter or actor (not bad analogies for the physical effort and rhetorical skills which he employed in lectures). But even with small audiences he would still give his best. (At the European University Institute in Florence, in 1977, he gave masterly seminars in comparative politics to a handful of graduate students whose command of the English language was unsure). He was able to strike a rapport with his audience, was stimulated by the contact, and this communicated itself to students ('feedback', 'I suppose', or 'I slew them this morning'). He might start his lectures hesitantly, but would soon gather steam. He liked to announce a clear theme at the outset (always an 'important' one, as he would tell the audience), and lectured in an analytical step by step manner. He was fond of using projectors, diagrams, and anecdotes. It was all put over with great dash, in vivid language and with a full array of theatrical gestures. He was curt about lecturers who would not, in his own words, 'articulate' – 'bloody mumblers'.

During his eight-year stint at Manchester he always gave the first-year lectures in government each Tuesday and Thursday to more than four hundred students drawn from various subjects. Many of them later regarded the lectures as one of the most stimulating experiences of their student days. In December 1973, lectures were frequently being cancelled because of the power cuts which were being made at the time of the coal miners' work to rule. After one cancellation, Sammy sat his students down in a large open space and lectured in the semi-darkness. Some passers-by and at least one university porter stopped in curiosity and joined the audience. The lectures later formed the basis of his massive *Comparative Government*.[5]

Some other fine teachers have skilfully communicated by being allusive, or understating a case, or merely sketching a line of argument. This was not for Finer. He would master a subject, arrive at conclusions and would then want to hammer them home. This was the purpose of study and of communication. What gave his lectures their impact was that they were so clearly the work of somebody who had thought and cared about the subject. Sammy's skill as a communicator rests first and foremost on his mastery of the subject he was considering. Students had no doubt that they were in the presence of authority.

But Finer's sense of commitment to the subject and his arresting language also helped. He has always had a marvellous feel for languages (he can still sing the Romanian songs he learned as a child). If he heard a striking expression or word he would repeat it lovingly. Students and colleagues had to broaden their vocabulary to keep up with Sammy; various Victorian and Edwardian terms mixed harmoniously with the latest Beatles-age slang and colloquialisms. At times there was a touch of Professor Edgeworth about him.* He spoke different idioms – 'simultaneously', he would claim. The three-page preface to his *Comparative Government* begins with a quotation from Hippocrates, has a Latin aphorism and ends with some lines from Tennyson. An introductory page of his *Man on Horseback* reprints a few bars of music in Italian from Mozart's *Don Giovanni* and ends with a quotation from Dante. A person reading or listening to him is quickly made aware of his sense of fun; Sammy practises seriously the playful science (*Die Frolich Wissenschaft*).

Finer has also been interested in the correct use of political terms and is an enemy of semantic confusion. It was fitting that his contribution to the special twenty-fifth anniversary issue of the journal *Political Studies* is entitled 'Vocabulary of political science'. He was always sceptical about the intellectual gains which were claimed for the new concepts and terms in the behavioural approach. He never shared the vogue for Talcott Parsons or David Easton's use of 'systems' in the 1960s – 'it's all in Pareto and Herbert Spencer you know'. Like his great friend Giovanni Sartori, he thought that progress would come through careful definition of terms and clear and consistent use of concepts rather than imitation of the natural sciences. Throughout his work there is a concern with definitions and making clear what exactly he is writing about.** He wanted to convince but even more to be understood. The first page of his *Comparative Government* offers a definition, in this case of government. The very first sentence of *Adversary Politics* defines his subject:

---

* I recently read an article of his which dismissed a book by Habermas as 'inspissated'. Who else would use such a word in such a context? I was reminded of this: 'Professor Edgeworth, of All Souls, avoided conversational English, persistently using words and phrases that one expects to meet only in books. One evening, Lawrence returned from a visit to London, and Edgeworth met him at the gate. "Was it very caliginous in the Metropolis?" "Somewhat caliginous, but not altogether inspissated", Lawrence replied gravely.' Robert Graves, *Goodbye to All That* (Cape, London, 1929) p.246.

** He would agree with Bagehot's complaint about political discourse that every generation leaves a series of inapt words.

Briefly the adversary system is a stand-up fight between two adversaries for the favour of the lookers-on.

On page 2 of *Anonymous Empire* the lobby is defined:

Wherever in this book I use the term 'the lobby', I shall mean: The sum of organisations in so far as they are occupied at any point in time in trying to influence the policies of public bodies in their own chosen direction; though (unlike political parties) never themselves prepared to undertake the direct government of the country.

His essay on pressure groups and political participation starts:

By 'political participation', I stipulate:
sharing in the framing and/or execution of public policies.[6]

His chapter on the role of the military and the growth of the state begins with a sub-heading: 'Terminology', and he ends his article on 'The vocabulary of political science' in 1975 as follows:

Just as institutions exist to channel and contain its [political activity's] surge and flow, so an appropriate, exact, and specific vocabulary is required to channel and contain and so make comprehensible the multifarious variety of the elements comprehended in its study.[7]

It did not concern Sammy that the study of politics would not be a science (in the sense of having universal laws), or value-free. But he has not been like a number of other British political scientists. For a number of years leading British political scientists have often bemoaned the state of the discipline, complained about its lack of status compared to other social sciences, and generally apologised for its lack of apparent relevance or usefulness to practical politicians and civil servants. A sense of modesty and self-criticism have their place. But at times the breast-beating and defeatism have been overdone. This was not Finer. Whatever he was working on, he has always thought it was worthwhile. He did not regard the study of moral and political theory as the core of the discipline. He did not content himself with 'the pursuit of intimations', which would have given him too passive a role.

He mastered – and was never captured by – the various models and schools of American political science that proliferated in the 1950s and 1960s. Students struggled to keep up with games theory, communications theory, general systems theory, rational choice, functionalism, and elite theory. Indeed, at his prodding, Manchester in 1970 started a course in contemporary political analysis for third-year students and post-graduates. But he was sceptical that these tools would make the study of politics more scientific. I would guess that he is similarly sceptical about the current vogue for public policy and for being 'useful' and 'relevant', in the narrow sense in which those terms are frequently used today. Yet at all times, as Vernon Bogdanor notes in his chapter, Sammy has been up-to-date with a changing discipline. He has never lost his interest or his enthusiasm for reaching out intellectually while avoiding being captured by 'fads', and there have been a good few of those.

Sammy is something of a political sociologist in the grand tradition of Weber and Aron. He joins the study of politics and government to broader social, economic and cultural factors, and is a comparative scholar *par excellence*. But what is crucial to understanding Sammy's work is that he has never been a reductionist. He repudiated the fashion for explaining political phenomena via economics, sociology or whatever. Hence his suspicion of Marxism and so much mainstream American political science and behaviouralism in the 1960s and 1970s. A particular target was Talcott Parsons' model of the political process: inputs, black-box, outputs. In this model the government and political institutions were reduced to a mechanism, a black box, which 'converted' inputs from the environment. In this new vocabulary the state disappeared only to reappear as a political system. The approach resulted in a shift of emphasis from the political institutions and government to the environment. He would have none of it: the state was the most significant form of association. This analysis was most elegantly presented in an article in *Government and Opposition* in 1969.[8] But Finer is not a dry, formal, legal institutionalist. He would accept some of the criticisms of the lifelessness of some members of this school (cf. his dismissal of continental political jurists, 'they continue their barren rituals, make a desert and call it "politology"').[9] He sees institutions as representing patterns of behaviour, and has never lost sight of the political aspects of the process and institutions of government. He is interested in explanation. I cannot improve on his own statement of what he was about:

> When I reflect on what I have been doing in my work, it seems, at the end of the day, something that I can express variously as: *interpreting* a body of factual knowledge; or, if you will, making a *pattern* out of it; as most simply and probably most comprehensibly, *making sense* out of it.[10]

The study of institutions can seem to hover uncertainly between history and journalism. Sammy Finer was firmly grounded in the Oxford history school as well as in politics. But though he has studied history, he writes mainly as a contemporary political scientist, aware that different techniques are needed for different approaches. Indeed, his best work is in areas in which history and political science interact. From history he drew a range of knowledge, across time and space, which he has often dipped into like a vast data bank. He has always been able to illustrate or refute general propositions about social behaviour. He was properly dismissive of much of the literature on political development in the 1960s. This concentrated on the problems of state and nation-building in the new states of Africa and Asia. But it was often written by people who lacked a sense of history and, in particular, a sense of how the great states of Europe had emerged. He joined a team of distinguished scholars, led by Charles Tilly and Gabriel Almond in 1970, and produced a masterly essay on the role of the military and its relations to the emergence of states. The study showed that the problems of state-building in Europe in the past centuries had indeed been very different from those of contemporary states. In a personal retrospect Sammy has claimed that his historical background gave him a perspective 'without which the study of politics would have been barren *a priorism* or an empty set of mechanical computations'.

Sammy's strengths as a teacher are reflected in his writings. His books are not only read but highly readable. They are free from jargon and suffused with his own vitality and personality. He has also been able to invest potentially dry subjects with interest: consider his study of Chadwick or his early works on local government and public administration. These works demonstated his flair and his ability to draw out the important issues.

Finally, one has to acknowledge the enormous range of his knowledge. This is obvious not only in the sheer diversity of his writings (certainly comparable with that of brother Herman), but also in the way in which he frequently draws in broader historical and comparative material to enrich a single case study. His study of Britain in his *Comparative Government* ends with a discussion of Pareto optimality which is linked to immobilism in British government. A point in his study of pressure groups is enlightened by a reference to J.C. Calhoun's *Disquisition on Government* (1853). A point in *Man on Horseback* is illustrated by a reference to the 1936 Spanish *Supplement* to the *Enciclopedia Universel*. Indeed, it is interesting that, in spite of Herman's influence, his own background in history, and his war service, Sammy confined his research to strictly English subjects before *Horseback* (published when he was 47).

His style of work has been to immerse himself in a subject; to read and think about a subject and talk about it obsessively. When organising the material, he is fortunate in his ability to write quickly and, enviably, without innumerable improving drafts. With sleeves literally rolled up and sustained by an endless supply of cigarettes and an occasional swig of whisky ('liberally diluted with water, you will note'), he has always been able to drop extraneous matters and concentrate on the task in hand. His history tutor at Oxford later recalled that he had never had a student who could assess exactly the amount of work required to get an alpha on each paper, and then proceed to do exactly that and no more. (But how else could one have gained a first in history in one year?) His particular talent has been to perceive emerging patterns in his data quickly. He once referred to this as the ability to make 'an intuitive leap' from the data to analysis, interpretation and explanation. He would not have had much respect for Bryce's injunction 'what is wanted are facts, more facts'. He has not sought to be a macro-theorist but tried to fashion theories of the middle range, based on observations of real-world political phenomena.

Finer's work has never required large research grants or teams of research assistants. He has worked on one collaborative venture but generally he has been a lonely scholar. There is no Finer 'school' or 'approach'. Americans and some West Europeans enjoy 'workshops' or colloquia where, it is said, 'ideas interact', or people 'dialogue'. I do not think Sammy really enjoyed many of these. In academic life, he was not a 'groupie'.

To understand Sammy's contribution to the subject one has to remember that in the 1950s political studies in Britain were mostly non-comparative, atheoretical, and showed little interest in other countries apart from France and the United States. Developments in American political science at the time, particularly the application of social science techniques, found few echoes in Britain. Before 1950 it was not possible to take a degree in politics alone and most university courses in the subject combined a study of 'the British constitution', narrowly defined, with a study of the writings of major political theorists. One critic recalled that, 'warmed-over facts with a topping of *Times* editorialising seemed to be the formula at Oxford in the fifties'.[11] Academic political science was a small, intimate world, largely centred on Oxford and the London School of Economics. The Political Studies Association, a professional body for teachers and researchers in the field, was established in 1950. It had around 100 members at the end of its first year, and grew slowly over the next decade. Few of the teachers had a degree in politics. D.N. Chester, the first chairman of the P.S.A. recalled in 1975 that:

> it was comparatively easy for, say, a modern historian to become a well-accepted teacher of politics quite quickly. All that was needed, in addition to the knowledge of British, American and French history they already possessed, was the reading of a dozen or so standard works and an interest in contemporary affairs.[12]

When Sammy returned to Oxford in 1974, the study of politics had changed greatly. The expansion and creation of new universities in the 1960s and 1970s and the encouragement of the social sciences produced a marked increase in the number of students and lecturers involved in politics courses. Membership of the P.S.A. rose to more than 700 by 1976. The study of politics became more professional and more specialised. There was an outpouring of books and articles about British politics and the politics of many other states. My own view is that the study of politics has made great strides over the past thirty years. It is more rigorous, more often based on first-hand research, and most topics have now acquired their own shelves of studies.

It is beyond the scope of this introduction to provide an assessment of Sammy's writings, but some things may be said. He has been a great innovator in post-war British political science. Sammy was not drawn to the well-worn grooves of academic British political science – local government, Parliament as an institution, Prime Minister and Cabinet, elections and voting, etc. His imagination enabled him to open up new areas. He was the first British political scientist into the field of pressure groups, into using Early Day Motions to study the values and behaviour of MPs, and into military intervention. These areas had been neglected before Sammy turned to them. Herman Finer, indeed, had dismissed the case for studying pressure groups in Britain, because of the strength of the political parties: 'There is hardly a loophole through which a lobbyist can slide to extort concessions.'[13]

Sammy has been able to use typologies and models to reduce the disorder of real world data, the number of cases, and to make general statements. He has used the language of variables, relationships and associations applied to political phonomena. In *Comparative Government* he wanted to break away from the country by country approach. What was needed, he claimed, was a conceptual framework which would allow one to classify countries and make comparisons. This interest in patterns and models may have been encouraged by his youthful and short-lived liking for Marxism ('everything suddenly became clear') and his study of Pareto. He introduces his own typology with a defence of the form. It:

> (a) covers all the known varieties of governmental forms, with (b) the most economical set of distinctions, so as to (c) provide the receiver with what he at any rate, regards as a satisfactory basis for explaining what forms arise in what given circumstances and, (d) hence, has some power of predicting what vicissitudes or alterations a given form may undergo should circumstances change in named respects.[14]

He differentiated the forms of government on three dimensions: the extent to which the public is involved, the *participation-exclusion* dimension; the extent to which the rulers regard or disregard the concerns and values of the public, the *order-representativeness dimension*; the basis of public compliance with the government, the *coercion-persuasion dimension*. He then developed categories and sub-categories to locate the 150 different states in his typology. It is an impressive achievement in summarising and systematising.

In *Horseback* there is a typology which interrelates the levels of political culture, characteristics of this culture, typical methods of military intervention, and levels to which this intervention is pressed.[15] The essentials of a complex subject are condensed into a single page diagram. In his study of the changing role of the armed forces (or what he calls its 'format', including the criteria of military service, size, composition and stratification), in state-building (territorial consoli-dation, specialised personnel, and recognition of its integrity by other states), he distills a mass of historical and comparative data to identify clusters of variables or cycles. These include, *inter alia*, the economy-technology format, stratifiction format, beliefs format and the extraction-coercion cycle. His argument proceeds by way of statements about the links between the cycles and showing the different ways they interacted and the consequences for state and nation-building in France, England and Prussia-Germany. The interrelations are all laid out in clear diagrams. Again, it is an example of his use of case studies and the comparative method as a way of uncovering relationships and producing limited generalisations.[16]

Sammy Finer has not been unaffected by his close study of Pareto. He has similarly wanted to get behind theories, political formulae and constitutional facades. Hence his scepticism about the facile way the influential Dicey presented the role of Benthamite ideas on policy in the nineteenth century.[17] He can be scathing about Dicey's generalities on other matters also.[18] W.J.M. Mackenzie, in his *Politics and Social Science*, has noted the concern of the early twentieth-century elitists, like Pareto, Michels and Mosca, to locate 'the truth behind the truth', and the resultant interest in military and bureaucratic elites and pressure groups. Interestingly, Finer has done important work on each of these 'new' and 'non-constitutional' phenomena.[19] He has also been successful in questioning, modifying and, on occasion, overturning, the conventional wisdom of the day. This was most manifest in his debunking of the textbook idea that ministerial responsibility entailed a minister's resignation whenever he could be shown to have made a serious blunder. This was backed by 'a veritable canon' of parliamentary '*obiter dicta*', before Finer dismissed it in 1956 in his *Public Administration* article, 'The individual responsibility of ministers'.

Other observers may take a different view of a person's strengths and regard them as weaknesses. In spite of his achievements or, perhaps, because of them, Sammy has been a controversial figure in the political science profession. Critics may claim that his very range, over countries and time, involves a sacrifice of depth; that his enthusiasm has led him to start hares or make over-ambitious claims for some of his work, e.g. on Early Day Motions, or for his typology in *Comparative Government*. His quick mind, ready wit and phrase-making skills could make him intolerant of the pedestrian. To be worthy was often, in his world, also to be dull. Even his friends would grant the element of truth in these comments. I can hear him say 'So what?' These were the costs of his being a ginger element, an institutionalised stimulus.

Some academics have sought a prominent role in public life – Laski, Cole and Max Beloff, Finer's immediate predecessor as Gladstone Professor, have been obvious cases. But Sammy has generally refrained from extending his academic role into the political arena and has certainly never wanted to be a political party man. He has never been an uncritical admirer of the British political system. The rosy view of the British political system which dominated the discipline until the mid-1970s could not count Sammy amongst its supporters. Passages in *Anonymous Empire*, *Comparative Government*, let alone *Adversary Politics*, all show a scepticism about many of the assumed virtues and benefits of the British system. In recent years, however, his sense of despair at the political system, and particularly the political parties, has encouraged him (in his books on the British party system) to advocate proportional representation and various other reforms. His critique of the much admired two-party system in Britain was quite new. In the post-war debate on 'what's wrong with Britain' it was frequently the party leaders who diagnosed and prescribed. Here was a shift of emphasis in which the party system, particularly the interaction of the Conservative and Labour parties, was indicted as a cause of some of the problems and a barrier to their resolution. Earlier on he was in two minds about the role of pressure groups. Readers of an article he wrote in the *Listener*, 'In defence of pressure groups', may have been bothered to read him also write 'Why pressure groups are sapping our civic energy' in the NALGO journal, *Public Service*, around the same time.[20]

A careful reader of his work will, however, note a number of continuities over the years. He ended his study of pressure groups, for example, by calling for more openness, for

'Light! *More* light.'

to be cast on what was 'faceless, voiceless, unidentifiable', in brief, anonymous! Twenty years later his study of the party system ends on a populist note, in which the political parties' monopoly of decision-making will be broken by the introduction of referendums and initiatives. The public are to be mobilised against the elite of party activists.

A *festschrift* is not an obituary. This book was conceived as a tribute to Sammy Finer on his retirement and we are discussing the themes he has written about. But there is more to come. It is characteristic of the man that he should celebrate his formal freedom not only by taking up two visiting professorships but also by buying a word processor and setting off with the modest(!) goal of writing a comprehensive history of government from the earliest times to the present. We cannot think of any other person who could undertake this task. We shall await this – and much more – from his pen with eager anticipation.

Notes

1. For a list of publications, see pp. 000.
2. S.E. Finer, 'Political science: an idiosyncratic retrospect of a putative discipline', *Government and Opposition*, 1980, p. 347. A number of the unattributed quotes in this chapter are drawn from this article, or from my own recollections of conversations with him.
3. *New Society*, 5 September 1974.
4. The term is that of Peter Hennessy (*Times Higher Education Supplement*, 15 February 1974).
5. The lectures were first delivered at Keele.
6. 'Groups and political participation' in G. Parry (ed.), *Participation in Politics* (Manchester University Press, Manchester, 1972), p. 58.
7. *Political Studies*, 1975, p. 254.
8. 'Almond's concept of the "political system": a textual critique'.
9. 'Political science: an idiosyncratic retrospect . . .', p. 351.
10. Ibid., p. 363.
11. B.M. Barry, 'The strange death of political philosophy', *Government and Opposition*, 1980, p. 278.
12. 'Political studies in Britain: recollections and comments', *Political Studies*, 1975, p. 163.
13. *Theory and Practice of Modern Government* (Methuen, London, 1969, 4th edn.), p. 463.
14. pp. 39–40.
15. p. 168.
16. In C. Tilly (ed.), *The Formation of National States in Western Europe* (Princeton University Press, Princeton, 1975).
17. 'The transmission of Benthamite ideas' in G. Sutherland (ed.), *Studies in the Growth of Nineteenth Century Government* (Allen & Unwin, London, 1972).

18. Thus, on Dicey's attempt to explain why conventions are binding: '. . . one of the (albeit undeservedly) famous works on the Constitution, Dicey's *Introduction to the Study of the Law of the Constitution* (1885) was a typically perverse attempt' (*Comparative Government*, p. 147).
19. W.J.M. Mackenzie, *Politics and Social Science* (Penguin, London, 1967), p. 64.
20. *The Listener*, 7 June 1956, pp. 751–2 and *Public Service*, June 1956, p. 161.

Publications of S.E. Finer

Books: sole author

MONOGRAPHS

A Primer of Public Administration (Frederick Muller Ltd), 1950
The Life and Times of Sir Edwin Chadwick (Methuen), 1952
(reprinted, 1960, 1980)
Anonymous Empire: A study of the Lobby in Great Britain (Pall Mall),
1958 (2nd edn., 1966)
Private Industry and Political Power (Pall Mall), 1958
The Man on Horseback: the Role of the Military in Politics (Pall Mall),
~~1962~~ (2nd edn. 1976, 3rd edn. [Hebrew] 1983)
Comparative Government (Allen & Unwin), 1970 (reprinted 1974, and
each other year subsequently)
The Changing British Party System (1945–1979) (American Enterprise
Institute), 1980

EDITED, INTRODUCED AND PRESENTED

Siéyès: What is the Third Estate? (Pall Mall), 1963
Vilfredo Pareto: Sociological Writings (Pall Mall), 1966 (reprinted 1975)
Five Constitutions (Penguin), 1979

Books: jointly authored

Local Government in England and Wales (with Lord Redcliffe-Maud)
(Oxford University Press), 1954
Backbench Opinion in the House of Commons (with D. Bartholomew
and H.B. Berrington) (Pergamon), 1961
Adversary Politics and Electoral Reform (ed.) (Anthony Wigram), 1975

Sections, or chapters contributed to collective volumes

'Interest groups and the political process in Great Britain' in *Interest
Groups in Four Continents*, ed. by H. Ehrmann, (Pittsburgh
University Press), 1958, pp. 117–43
'The Politics of Great Britain' in *Modern Political Systems: Europe*, ed.
by R.C. Macridis, (Prentice-Hall), edns. 1963, 1968, 1972, 1978, 1983
'Development: the political climate' in *Development – the Western
View*, ed. by C.A.O. van Nieuwenhuijze, (Mouton, the Hague),
1972 pp. 228–57

'Groups and political participation' in *Participation in Politics*, ed. by
G. Parry, (Manchester University Press), 1972 pp. 57–79
'The transmission of Benthamite ideas' in *Studies in the Growth of
Nineteenth Century Government*, ed. by G. Sutherland, (Allen &
Unwin), 1972, pp. 11–32
'State – and nation-building in Europe: the role of the military' in *The
Formation of National States in Western Europe*, ed. by C. Tilly,
(Princeton University Press), 1975, pp. 84–163
'The military and politics in the Third World' in *The Third World*, ed.
by W.S. Thompson, (Institute for Contemporary Studies, San
Francisco), 1973, pp. 65–98; 2nd edn; 1983, pp. 75–114
'Faces of Europe: the civil servants and bureaucrats' in *The Faces of
Europe*, ed. by Sir A. Bullock, (Phaedon Press, Oxford), 1980,
pp. 363–75
'The morphology of military regimes' in *Soldiers, Peasants and
bureaucrats*, ed. by R. Kolkowicz & Korbowski, (Allen & Unwin),
1982, pp. 281–310

Articles (over 5000 words)

'Patronage and the public service', *Public Administration*, 1952
pp. 329–58
'The teaching of politics in the university, *Universities Quarterly*,
1953, pp. 44–54
'The political power of private capital', *Parts I and II*, *Sociological
Review*, 1955, pp. 279–294, 1956, pp. 5–30
'The individual responsibility of ministers', *Public Administration*,
1956, pp. 377–96
'The anonymous empire', *Political Studies*, 1958, pp. 16–32
'Research in political science in Great Britain', *Politische Forschung*,
(Band 17), 1960, pp. 22–37
'Military and society in Latin America', *Sociological Review*,
(Monograph 1), 1967, pp. 133–51
'Pareto and plutodemocracy', *American Political Science Review*,
1968, pp. 440–50
'Almond's Concept of the "Political System": a textual critique',
Government and Opposition, 1969, pp. 3–21
'The political power of organized labour', *Government and
Opposition*, 1973, pp. 391–406
'Patrons, clients, and the state', *Atti dei convegni Lincei, Accademia
dei Lincei*, Rome, 1973, pp. 165–86
'Statebuilding, state boundaries and border control', *Social Science
Information*, 1974, pp. 79–126

'The vocabulary of political science', *Political Studies*, 1975, pp. 122

'Special interest groups', *Encyclopaedia Britannica*, 1978, pp. 445–50

'Militari e politica nel terzo mondo', *Rivista Italiana di Scienza Politica*, 1980, pp. 5–50

'Political science: an idiosyncratic retrospect of a putative discipline, *Government and Opposition*, 1980, pp. 346–63

'Perspectives in the world history of government', *Government and Opposition*, 1983, pp. 3–22

IN *NEW SOCIETY*

Military take-over bidders, Volume 6, number 162, 4 November 1965.

The present discontents: in defence of deadlock, Volume 29, number 662, September 1974.

The unions and power, Volume 31, number 664, February 1975.

The politics of language, Volume 31, number 649, 13 March 1975.

Taxation and revolt, Volume 32, number 654, 17 April 1975.

One and indivisible [state-formation in Europe], Volume 32, number 659, 22 May 1975.

The Israelis' dilemma, Volume 33, number 666, 10 July 1975.

The moving target [ministerial responsibility], Volume 33, number 669, 31 July 1975.

The mind of the military, Volume 33, number 670, 7 August 1975.

The fetish of frontiers, Volume 33, number 673, 4 September 1975.

Manifesto moonshine [the doctrine of the mandate], Volume 34, number 683, 13 November 1975.

Uncertain trumpets [military take-overs], Volume 34, number 688, 11 December 1975.

On terrorism, Volume 35, number 694, 22 January 1976.

The year of corruption, Volume 35, number 699, 26 February 1976.

Big and beautiful? [size and democracy], Volume 36, number 740, 1 April 1976.

Party names, party games [nomenclature of political parties], Volume 36, number 709, 6 May 1976.

Left, right, and rhetoric, Volume 36, number 714, 10 June 1976.

The second oldest trade [mercenaries], Volume 37, number 719, 15 July 1976.

Canada's mosaic, Volume 37, number 724, 26 August 1976.

Kinds of democracy, Volume 37, number 729, 23 September 1976.

Onward and downward? [The concept of 'decline'], Volume 38, number 734, 28 October 1976.

Another catch 22 [constitutionalism and dictatorship], Volume 38, number 739, 2 December 1976.

Waiting for lefty [Italian politics], Volume 40, number 757, 7 April 1977.

A law and its meaning [the Brezhnev Constitution], Volume 41, number 772, 21 July 1977.

The triumph of entropy [the future for Britain], Volume 42, number 789, 17 November 1977.

IN *THE LISTENER*

In defence of pressure groups, 7 June 1956.
Taxing people is wrong, 3 November 1977.
The invisible strikers, 24 November 1977.

2 British Government: The Paradox of Strength*
Hugh Berrington

'So they go on in strange paradox' charged a backbench Conservative critic of the Baldwin government, 'decided only to be undecided, resolved to be irresolute, adamant for drift, solid for fluidity, all powerful to be impotent.'[1]

Constitutional commentators are still divided as to whether the executive in modern Britain is too strong or too weak. A strong executive is held to be one which, because of the scope of its power, and the consistency and size of its backing in the legislature, can achieve its goals without difficulty; a weak executive appears to be one with limited legal authority, dependent, when taking aciton, on the concurrence of other constitutional organs, and/or lacking a consistent majority in the legislature. Writers in the individualist tradition of Dicey, such as Keeton, and even socialists, such as Crossman,[2] have emphasised the enormous power of the executive. Others, more recently, have noted the weakness of modern British government. There may be a sense in which both schools are simultaneously right. The thesis which is advanced here is that the weakness of modern British government springs from its apparent strength; its defects stem from what many have regarded as its chief virtues. The weakness does not lie primarily in the failings of the country's leaders, or in the shortcomings of its people. The incapacity stems from the country's political institutions, not from any one branch of government such as Parliament, or the executive, but from the network of institutions, and the interaction between those institutions which we call 'the British system of government'.

Mrs Thatcher's administration, in its resolution and strength of purpose, is unusual amongst post-war governments; the temperament of its leader coincided with certain changes, possibly short-lived, in the

* I am grateful to David Hine, Charles Rowley, Peter Jones and Rod Hague for their helpful comments on earlier drafts of this article.

political environment. It would be rash to assume that the political circumstances that facilitated Mrs. Thatcher's mode of leadership will survive for long.

Teachers of British government, explicitly and implicitly, often extol the virtues of the Westminster model – the British pattern of government – and compare it with the forms of government in the United States or the French Fourth Republic, usually to the disparagement of the last two. British government, it is said, combines a capacity for decisive action with responsiveness to the popular will; it makes possible the implementation of a coherent programme in which all the different parts fit together.

Other countries, especially those with numerous parties or with a separation of powers, or federalism, are contrasted unfavourably with the British model. The supreme virtue of the British pattern lies, it is said, in its avoidance of the fragmentation of power found in federal states or in countries with a functional division of powers. The unitary form of government maintains a high degree of territorial concentration of power, and the fusion of executive and legislature prevents deadlock or obstruction at the centre.

In turn, the Single-Member, Simple-plurality electoral formula fosters the growth of a disciplined two-party system and, like the fusion of legislative and executive powers, makes it easy to focus responsibility. When things go wrong, voters know whom to blame. Two parties offer rival programmes to the electors; the victor obtains a monopoly of power for four or five years, ensuring the coherent implementation of its manifesto, and with it the forging of the direct chain from citizen to government.

Foreign observers, especially Americans, have long admired parliamentary government in Britain. A long line of commentators, from Woodrow Wilson, through Lowell, to Beer, have extolled the virtues of the British system of government, whilst in 1950, a committee of the American Political Science Association in its report *Toward a More Responsible Two-Party System* published a set of prescriptions for the United States which obviously owed much to British experience.[3]

The system enjoys wide support in Britain too, and political scientists have tended to supply the rationalisations for it which are dear to politicians of both left and right. It is broadly congenial to those twin and rival elements of the British political culture – deference to authority and the supremacy of the popular will. The model finds favour amongst both moderate left and much of the British right. Social Democrats (using this term to indicate those reared in the tradition of British Fabianism or the American New Deal) like it because it facilitates the execution of a broad-ranging programme of reform. A strong state makes possible economic intervention and planning and the development of social services. Expositors of the old Tory tradition like it because it emphasises executive authority and executive strength.[1]

Of course, this pattern has had its detractors. It is notable, however, that the only coherent and sustained critiques have been of the excessive strength of the state, and more particularly, of the power of the executive. A disciplined two-party system within a sovereign parliament makes, it is alleged, for a dangerously powerful executive; and the absence of an entrenched bill of rights enables politicians, and by proxy, civil servants, to trample on individual liberties. Hence, in recent years there have been renewed demands for a written constitution which would limit the sovereignty of Parliament, for the establishment of specialist parliamentary committees to expose the executive to greater and more informed challenge, for proportional representation which would make it unlikely that one party would exercise untrammelled legislative power, and for a second chamber with strong powers, which would be able the better to resist a majority in the House of Commons. Such proposals nearly always start from the presumption that government in general, or the executive, or a majority in the Commons has too much power. The argument presented here is the contrary and highlights a paradox; governments in Britain are, in some ways, not too strong, but too weak. First, however, let us look a little more closely at those features of our political institutions that provoke fears that government in Britain is over-powerful.

The sovereignty of Parliament
British government is characterised by the concentration of sovereign power in the Queen in Parliament. The absence of any legal limits to the ultimate power of Parliament (except in so far as these have been imposed by Britain's adherence to the EEC), the lack of a written constitution laying down boundaries on the legal competence of the Queen in Parliament, set British government apart from most of the other major democracies in the world.

The Second Chamber
Within the sovereign Parliament one element, the second chamber, is remarkably weak. The House of Lords has limited authority, modest functions, restricted powers and a composition which through its very anomalies, inhibits the chamber from exercising those few powers left to it.

Fusion, not separation, of powers
Legislature and executive are closely linked, with an important element

of common membership and this fusion contrasts with the pattern in the United States, where there is an almost total separation between the two branches.

A disciplined two-party system
More important, though, than the formal links between executive and Parliament is the two-party system, whose significance is greatly increased because party discipline is strong.* British government would work very differently if Members of Parliament behaved with as little reference to party as do members of the American Congress. The fusion of executive and legislature, coupled with the two-party system as it has worked for most of the last 100 years, creates an identity of interest and feeling between the executive and the majority in the House of Commons. The party system brings the executive and the legislature into an almost automatic concert, so giving a superficial justification to the charge that Britain is 'an elective dictatorship'.

Local government
Elected local councils are subordinate to central government – using this term in the broad sense – in a number of ways. Local councils are creatures of the national Parliament; their functions can be changed, their powers circumscribed, their boundaries re-drawn, and they themselves can be abolished, by Act of Parliament. In their day-to-day working, local councils are subject to a series of controls, some specific, some general, exercised by the central departments.

Nationalised industries
The boards of nationalised industries are appointed by Ministers, and the industries are subject to open Ministerial control in certain functions, such as investment programmes. More importantly, Ministers influence the boards in numerous ways not spelt out by Parliament, through day-to-day persuasion. In many instances, command, rather than influence, would be a more appropriate term.[5]

The range of functions of the state
The twentieth century has seen an enormous extension of the functions of the state, carrying government into fields hitherto remote from its reach. It is this extension of state functions which has helped to prompt some of the vociferous calls for a written constitution and the establishment of a strong, independent second chamber.

* See p. 33 below for reference to the recent erosion of party discipline in Parliament.

With hindsight, it seems odd that the political and constitutional implications of extensive economic intervention by governments have, except on the individualistic right, been barely discussed. It has simply been assumed that a constitution and a political system, appropriate to the *laissez-faire* economy of the nineteenth century should be suitable for the twentieth. Critics of the collectivist state have overwhelmingly fastened on the dangers of adding to the state's functions and powers; commentary about the effect of these changes in weakening the state has been largely parenthetical.

Once governments assume explicit responsibility for the economic well-being of their citizens, the relationship between material interest groups and government is transformed. Governments are apt to be judged by the criterion of economic well-being, which tends to make governments dependent on the producer groups whose acquiescence, if not cooperation, is essential:

> First, what has taken place is not a simple extension of the powers and functions of the state, but a complex intermingling of public and private. It is worth noting that this is contrary to what many expected. . . . It [the State] is not involved simply as master, although ultimately it has power to coerce. In practice, there is a great and important diffusion of power, and this is important for the work of the Civil Service.[6]

Apparent power, real weakness

Most commentators have stressed the power of the executive in modern Britain; in recent years however, some, such as Brittan, King and Beer,[7] have been struck by the impotence of government, though only Brittan has referred explicitly to the constitutional structure as a source of that incapacity. The apparent powers of government, which derive from the political institutions and the structure of the parties, conceal real weakness; indeed this apparent power does more than conceal the weakness; it is a partial cause of it, perhaps the main cause.

At this point, for the purposes of greater clarity and simplicity it is necessary to distinguish between two kinds of power – power with reference to other branches or institutions of government, including the political parties, and the power of the total complex of government organs over other groups. There is the power of the executive over all the agencies of government, and the power of government over society. In essence, the message of this article is that the first kind of power will not necessarily go hand-in-hand with power over society and that there may even be an inverse relationship between the two kinds of power.

British government is not in practice the vehicle for coherent implementation of the majority will implied by the institutional forms.

Twenty-five years ago, S.E. Finer in his *Anonymous Empire*[8] recalled
J.C. Calhoun's distinction between the *numerical* majority and the
concurrent majority. Britain was even then, Finer averred, ruled by a
concurrent majority, with organised interests able to impose their
vetoes or pursue their policies, through the form of Cabinet government: 'it should be our task', wrote Finer, 'to strengthen the numerical
majority as against the concurrent majority'. However, after asking
how we can strengthen the authority of the numerical majority he
admitted that

> we run into an almost insoluble difficulty. The present system by which the
> lobby has formed a symbiosis with Parliament and the Civil Service has the
> supreme merit of bringing the interested parties into policy-making. By this
> very same token, while bringing the interested parties in, it shuts the general
> public out.[9]

The supreme defect of the contemporary political system lies in two
features of the executive: the executive has an apparently high, and
institutionally almost uncircumscribed, capacity to act, and is highly
exposed to organised groups. Power is as power does – and as power is
able. The significance of the seemingly vast powers of the British
executive depends upon the will and on the political ability to use
them. 'The thicker the hay', said Alaric the Goth when warned of the
numbers and apparent military strength of the effete defenders of
Rome, 'the easier it is mowed.'[10] The powers of the executive become,
not the artillery trained upon the economic interest groups, so much
as the primary target of these groups. Two parties, working under the
first-past-the-post electoral formula strive feverishly to accumulate
enough support, in a sufficient number of constituencies, to obtain a
parliamentary majority. That majority, once installed, is subject only
to curbs outside the formal institutions. The majority is organised and
cohesive; the power it wields through the House of Commons and
through (and under) the Cabinet is not effectively shared with other
institutions; for these reasons, that majority and its leaders can never
plead either legal incapacity or political helplessness as grounds for
failing to give the interest groups what they want. The strength of a
post-war British government may be likened to that of a medieval
knight, whose body was protected by thick armour, except at one
point – the heart.

The rise of organised interest groups
A distinctive mark of our society is the myriad of highly-organised
groups on whose cooperation, or at least, acquiescence, governments
depend for the carrying out of their policies. Before examining the

relationship between material interest groups and government let us take a further look at the groups themselves.*

Spontaneous groups

The practice of interest groups seeking state intervention on their behalf is hardly new. We have only to think of wool merchants or fishermen in medieval England; more recently, in the nineteenth century, quite apart from the rising groups of manual workers, British and American farmers and railway users lobbied the legislature and executive for concessions. Groups of this kind are *spontaneous*. They arise naturally out of producer relationships in the context of the market. Their membership is defined by the particular function they perform. Farmers grow wheat, miners dig coal, weavers make cloth.

Artificial groups

The second type of material interest group has, in contrast, been created by the action of the state. Council house tenants, whose very existence depends as a group on decisions taken by the state, are a pure example of this kind. Less clearcut but still good examples are afforded by professions such as teachers and social workers. Although such groups would certainly exist, in different form, without the intervention of the state, it is unlikely that they would have achieved their present scale without it. In contemporary Britain such groups have been largely defined by the state, and given their identity by it.

The distinction is not absolute. Some groups are essentially 'artificial' but may have a natural spontaneous clientèle – groups such as private sector tenants and old-age pensioners. Both are examples of pre-existing groups which, though they have some basis for shared aims apart from that conferred by the state, have a community of interest which has been hardened by the patronage of the state. There is a spectrum, at one end of which we have purely spontaneous, and at the other wholly artificial, groups.

* In this discussion the use of the term 'material interest groups' excludes those numerous groups often called 'cause' or 'promotional' groups, that campaign to further a specific policy which does not confer immediate material benefits on the group members themselves. There is a distinction between the British Medical Association, or the Transport and General Workers Union, on the one hand, and the Campaign for Nuclear Disarmament and the Society for the Protection of the Unborn Child, on the other. The latter groups are not engaged in the productive process and though their activities often influence political decisions, their relationship with government is essentially different from that of the material interest groups.

By its own actions the state creates or fosters organised groups which in turn impose demands upon the state – or, to quote Samuel Beer's pithy dictum, 'The lobby may create the program – but the program creates the lobby.'[11]

Government and interest groups: costs and benefits

The nature of the relationship between government and interest groups is shaped partly by the form of the institutions of government. In the United States, political decision-making is dispersed amongst the three branches of government at federal level – President, Congress and the courts – and further divided between the centre and the states. Interest groups have to spread their activity over numerous and diverse organs. Pressure group activity in the United States tends therefore to be highly *visible*; much of it takes place at levels which cannot escape publicity. In Britain, political decision-making is heavily concentrated within the executive, and much of it takes place behind closed doors. The greater visibility of pressure group activity in the United States has led some observers to infer that pressure groups are more powerful in America than in Britain. Such a judgement confuses ostentation with power. American pressure groups certainly tend to be much more *conspicuous* than those in Britain. They are not thereby more powerful.

British governments do, in fact, continuously give way to pressure groups. Some governments have been more responsive than others, and some – like Mrs Thatcher's – more discriminating – but the fact of concession is undeniable. The question naturally arises why governments – often backed by a substantial majority in Parliament, and able, because of that support to summon vast legal authority to their help – do so often give way to interest groups? The answer lies partly in the country's political culture, the nature of which stands in contrast to the character of the formal institutions. British political culture, especially the elite political culture, lays stress on consensus, on conciliation, on compromise, if need be at the expense of consistency and effectiveness. Interest groups can often, therefore, hope to achieve their aims through discussion, usually at official level. Failure to meet interest groups' demands too may have perhaps unintended, incidental but still unpleasant results. If firms go bankrupt, in an industry hit by foreign competition, workers will lose their jobs.

There is more to it, though, than a political culture which puts excessive weight on conciliation and compromise. The partnership between state, labour and capital has been a feature, if often blurred, of most advanced industrial democracies since the end of the Second World War. This partnership, known variously as corporatism and neo-corporatism, depends for its effectiveness on widespread consensus or, failing such consensus, a state strong enough to curb those groups that reject the rules. British politics has seen a series of such attempts at partnership since 1945 – the 'wage-freeze' era under Cripps and (briefly) Gaitskell from 1947 to 1951, the establishing of the National Economic Development Council under Macmillan in 1961/62, the Wilson government's National Plan of 1965, the Heath government's initiative of 1972, and, for a more limited partnership between government and trade unions, the Wilson/Callaghan administration's Social Contract. All but the last of these initiatives have been based on a wish to reach agreement between the three elements – state, capital and labour – about the development of the economy and in particular about the way increases in national income are to be allocated. Political leaders are concerned about economic growth both because of a general sense of civic spirit and because of their belief that they will be judged primarily at the next election on their economic record. In Britain these attempts at partnership have never survived for long. Britain before Thatcher was an example, not of corporatism but of corporatism which failed.

If, however, interest groups meet opposition from government – whether from officials or ministers – they can often invoke sanctions of considerable severity. Such sanctions, which ultimately derive their effectiveness from the political imperative that politicians have to win re-election, can be divided into two kinds – direct and indirect.

Direct sanctions
Sanctions of this kind draw their force from the threat that significant electoral groups can make, to inflict reprisals on candidates of the governing party at the next election. Politicians may fear that cohesive, substantial groups will cast their votes for other parties.

'I had made up my mind', wrote Harold Macmillan of the annual agricultural price review in March 1957, 'to go for the "agreed" settlement in spite of the embarrassment about milk . . . . But really, we have so much trouble coming to us that we must try to have some friends and preserve the firm agricultural base of the party, in the House and the country.'[12] Sam Beer, in his seminal article, 'Pressure groups and parties in Britain', published in 1956 refers to a 'recent' Chancellor of the Exchequer as saying 'the farmers are the swing vote'.[13]

A more recent example comes from Joel Barnett, Chief Secretary to the Treasury in Mr Callaghan's government, who recounts a problem affecting textile imports. 'I next heard that Edmund Dell had phoned the Prime Minister on Sunday, but had got a flea in his ear, as I had made the Prime Minister fully aware, not only of the problems of the industry but also of the number of marginal seats in Lancashire. The outcome was that we did manage to achieve some further reduction in imports of cotton cloth.'[14]

Both these examples are of groups – farmers and cotton workers – that are concentrated in a limited number of constituencies. There are, however, other groups such as old age pensioners, capable of exerting strong electoral pressure, which are widely dispersed across the country, but whose very size makes them electorally important despite their dispersion.

The fear that public employees, or specific categories of them, would be sufficiently numerous or concentrated to exert electoral pressure was once openly expressed. Lowell, in his classic *The Government of England* first published in 1908, said there had been constant complaints about pressure being brought to bear on MPs, and through MPs on the government, by postal and revenue officials. 'Owing to the concentration of government employees in London the pressure upon the metropolitan members is particularly severe.' The only effective remedy, thought Lowell, was the disfranchisement of government employees – a solution too drastic to commend itself either in his day or ours.[15] The general problem, though, remains.

Nevertheless, this kind of direct electoral sanction is almost certainly less important than the indirect electoral sanctions wielded by interest groups. Indeed, politicians often exaggerate the *objective* importance of such groups. The significance attached to the farmers' vote after the Second World War seems eccentric, in the light of the small size of the group and its concentration in fairly safe seats and it is surprising that Beer should have cited the description of the farmers as the 'swing vote' without further comment. Moreover, though groups like the old age pensioners may be *capable* of exerting heavy electoral pressure they may fail to do so. Survey evidence shows that support for one's party becomes stronger with age, so limiting the likelihood of change.

However, it is what politicians *think* is important which influences their behaviour, not what is *objectively* important. It is not reality which guides men's behaviour but their perceptions of reality. If politicians believe that farmers or old age pensioners can be wooed in sufficient numbers to make a significant difference to the outcome of an election they are likely to court such groups.

Indirect sanctions

Government and organised groups are in a continuous relationship. Groups want concessions – often a wage increase, perhaps a tariff, or a subsidy, or government purchases. Governments want the cooperation of the groups in order to run a range of sophisticated services such as hospitals and schools, to give security to employees and to offer a high and rising standard of living. Governments are faced with a perpetual dilemma. If they resist group demands they face a disruption of services, a loss of production, the extinction of jobs, perhaps a run on the pound. If they give way, they can buy short-term harmony at the price of certain medium or long-term consequences – a decline in competitiveness, a rise in inflation, an increase in unemployment, a deteriorating balance of payments. Governments have to weigh the long-term costs of giving way against the short-term costs of resistance.

Let us postulate for the moment that the only motive a politician has is to win votes. The politician's eyes are fixed upon the next general election. To stand up to the groups, to reject their demands, means risking a disruption of services or production which may, in turn, entail a loss of votes. Barbara Castle said that when Roy Jenkins was Chancellor of the Exchequer he told her, as the Secretary of State for Employment and Productivity, that 'it was OK to deny the municipal busmen their £1 pay increase without productivity strings, but that I must not drive the ships' clerks with their much bigger claim to the point of a strike that would hit our exports'.[16]

There are two glaring examples of the dilemma facing governments in their conflicts with interest groups – the conflict between Mr Heath and his colleagues and the National Union of Mineworkers in late 1973 and early 1974, and that in early 1979 between Mr Callaghan's government and the public service unions. Such governments were faced with a trade-off; they had to estimate how many votes they would lose or gain by resisting the group demands, and also how many votes would be gained, or lost, by giving way. Given the narrow margin of votes between the two main parties at most elections, politicians are likely to be highly sensitive to the risk of losing even a little support. As Samuel Beer put it, referring to the 'tightly knit, competitive political party', 'Keenly on the scent of votes and pressed sharply by its rival in the chase, it probes every neglected thicket in the political landscape.'[17]★

The decision of a vote-maximising government will therefore depend on the perceived electoral costs and benefits of alternative courses of action. Note, once again, the importance of politicians' perceptions. Thus, Harold Macmillan thought that the skill of the Minister of Labour

★ Joel Barnett observes that during the 'Winter of Discontent' Local Authority Associations (then Conservative-controlled) insisted on the Government's committing itself to financing 61 per cent of any pay increase to local council workers 'before they would agree, as employers, to endorse a pay offer to end the strikes. They knew they had us over a barrel, in that we wanted to end the politically damaging strikes. . . .'[18]

in settling a 'ridiculous and very widespread strike' in engineering would redound to the credit of his government[19] but feared upsetting the farmers. Some of Edward Heath's advisers favoured going to the country during the dispute with the miners in 1973/74; although Mr Heath lost the election, those colleagues who had pressed for an election could plausibly argue that if the election had been held three weeks earlier than it was, the Conservatives would have won.*

This model of the politician as a single-minded vote maximiser may well be much too crude. Top politicians may not be quite as obsessively concerned with re-election if only because of the pressure of events, and the administrative milieu in which so many decisions are made. We can improve the model by incorporating the notion of psychic costs and benefits. Here a politician behaves as he does because he incurs certain psychic gratifications from so doing, or dissatisfaction from not so doing. 'There was a sort of collective guilt complex round the Cabinet table which led to expenditure on "employment measures" that were far from being cost-effective', wrote Joel Barnett, describing his experience in the 1974–9 Labour government.[21] The nurses, and with a Labour government, the miners are examples of interest groups which can clearly profit from such feelings. The notion is, of course, very broad and can encompass a wide range of behaviours.†

We are postulating therefore that in the politician's mind there exists some sort of balance-sheet, not always clearly articulated, which shows the advantages and drawbacks, both electoral and psychic, of different courses of action. On this model, politicians will resist interest groups if the satisfactions, both psychic and those accruing from the perceived electoral advantages, outweigh the costs. We can postulate that the pluses and minuses of different decisions will be entered in each cell,

---

* Both Fay and Young in their *The Fall of Heath* and Douglas Hurd in *An End to Promises* argue that Heath was unwilling to exploit the confrontation with the miners for electoral benefit and that when he did decide to call an election it was more for a new mandate to meet the general long-term problems created by the sharp rise in the price of oil than to meet the immediate situation in the coal industry.[20]

† Note the comment in Joel Barnett, *op.cit.* 'Two examples serve to emphasise the point. One relates to the nurses, whose pay claims have given successive Governments great headaches; David Ennals made the customary defence of a higher settlement. The nurses were "unique" and "everybody loves them".'

Contrast this with the more cynical admission by Richard Crossman: 'A more recent example is the decision on nurses' pay, where our response was, partly at least, due to the proximity of the election.'[22]

Mr Heath's reluctance to call an early election during the conflict with the miners in 1973/74 is another instance.

and the politician will act according to the net benefit or net cost which he perceives.[23]

	Resist interest group	*Accede to interest group*
Perceived electoral benefits		
Perceived electoral costs		
Psychic benefits		
Psychic costs		

The problem of ungovernability

The danger confronting a democratic government is that the sum total of demands placed upon it may be unrealistically high. The aggregate of demands may be more than the system – any system, whether capitalist, or socialist – is physically capable of meeting given the current level of technical knowledge. Difficulties have been exacerbated by the unrealistic perceptions that leaders of interest groups and their followers have of the size of the 'national cake' – a lack of realism often encouraged by competitive vote-bidding.*

Unrealistic perceptions of the size of the national cake are a special instance of a more general kind of misperception – i.e. belief that

---

* Most of the examples of producer groups cited here have been of trade unions, not of business organisations. This choice arises partly out of the more conspicuous character of trade union pressure which means that more examples are available; partly because the *direct* electoral sanctions of the business lobby are so limited in scope; partly because additional incomes obtained by trades unionists through the exercise of industrial power are more likely than additional business profits to be devoted to consumption. However, the general thrust of the argument does not mainly depend on which side of industry the producer groups belong to. Moreover, some groups are essentially of a vertical nature with both employers and workers making the same demands.

governments can cope with an indefinitely increasing range of functions. As Anthony King has observed, this leads government into an increasing range of dependency relationships.[24] The greater the number of separate groups governments rely on for the successful fulfilment of governmental functions, the greater the probability that any one group will fail to comply.

The contradiction between the vast apparent powers of modern British governments and their seeming inability to achieve their goals has been aptly summarised by Lord Hailsham.

> So far we are left with a paradox. Since the sixteenth century and except in time of war, never has a government possessed more power than it has today. Never has it spent more money, employed a greater army of people, imposed so many regulations, passed so many laws, raised so much in taxation, operated in so many spheres, or exercised a wider patronage.
>
> Yet, at the same time, never does it seem, at least for so many years, to have commanded so little loyalty and perhaps imposed so low a standard of obedience.[25]

Lord Hailsham, following a traditional right-wing stance, has called for a written constitution to protect the individual against the excessive power of the executive. Nowhere, however, though he condemns what he describes as the abuse of trade union power, does he explicitly recognise that the modern problem is, in at least one very important sense, the weakness of the state. The nearest he comes to this position is in censuring the Social Contract between the Labour government and the trade unions, implying that a restriction on the powers of government would, *ipso facto*, limit the power of the trades unions.[26]

Causes of the real weakness of the state
The causes of the real weakness that coincides with apparent strength are found in four features:

(1) *Executive and party political omnipotence*
The basic weakness of the state in relation to organised groups is that these groups know that governments can, in the short term, always deliver what is being exacted from them. There are no hindrances of either a legal or party-political kind which limit the apparent power of government to meet the demands of interest groups.

Even the decline of party discipline since 1966, so meticulously chronicled by Philip Norton,[27] does not seriously impair the ability of a government with a majority in the House of Commons to get its way in the division lobbies. Samuel Beer noted that 'strong' parties often meant 'weak' pressure groups, and that party discipline could enable a party to hold its majority against a group demand. 'But if a "strong" party', he went on, 'can in this way more effectively resist group demands, so also it can more effectively yield to the them. . . . It can control what promises will be made in its name and, once having made them, it can deliver the legislative votes needed to honour them.'[28] Every pressure group knows that the government has no excuse derived from constitutional incapacity, no evasion based on political inability, for not giving the group what it wants. As Bob Jessop, writing from a Marxist standpoint, has put it,

> as the State acquires increased autonomy as a precondition of effective intervention to establish, maintain, or restore conditions necessary to accumulation, it also gains the means to disrupt and undermine these same conditions.[29]

Government control over nationalised industries affords a specific example of the way in which executive power is abused for electoral or more broadly political purposes. 'In the late 1960s and during the 1970s government has become more interventionist', said the NEDO study of 1976, 'reflecting not only the increasing use of the public corporations as a means of implementing macro-economic policy but also the pressures of . . . particular sectional interests.' 'The pressures on government to exercise influence on board and management decisions', said the NEDO team elsewhere in their report, 'have almost certainly increased over the last decade . . . the increasing aspirations of major interest groups – trade unions and consumer bodies in particular – have ensured that government becomes more involved whatever the inclination of individual Ministers and civil servants.' After noting that non-statutory price interventions by government had caused great resentment within the industries, the study observed that government was involved in one way or another in the bargaining process and that this was widely expected by the main participants. '. . . a few corporations particularly object to the way in which government has on more than one occasion negotiated separately with trade unions, when management was negotiating on lines agreed earlier with the government.' The study went on to add that management had in some cases claimed that the eventual settlement was higher than necessary because government had intervened in this way.[30]

The very concentration of power and responsibility in the hands of the government is often praised as the supreme virtue of the British constitution. In fact, this concentration is the *central* weakness of modern British government. It is not that governments endowed with so much seeming power will exercise tyranny; it is rather that governments so placed will be incapable of resisting the importunities of interest groups. To adapt Lord Acton's famous phrase, 'Power exposes: absolute power exposes absolutely.'

(2) *The extension of the functions of the state*

Paradoxically, the more a democratic state extends its range of functions, the weaker it becomes. It needs to rely more and more on the acquiescence, if not the active cooperation, of groups with specialised skills. It is therefore highly vulnerable to threats of non cooperation in the form of strikes, works-to-rule, withholding of information. The more the state tries to do, the more strategically placed is each group whose cooperation the state needs.[31] As a civil servant, Richard Wilding, puts it

> as the scope of the Government's involvement in the life of the country gets wider and wider, the more the Government has to rely on the willingness of people who are not its employees to do what it wants done. There is a sense in which, contrary to the general belief, as Government intervention expands, the power of the Government (ministers and civil servants together) actually diminishes; . . . . Certainly my own feeling, and I suspect that of many of my colleagues, is not a consciousness of growing Government power, but of diminishing power.[32]

(3) *Dependence on popular election*

Of course, the state's reliance on the cooperation of interest groups would be much less were it not for the dependence of the executive on popular election, and the normal structure of civil liberties. The powers available to the executive are very large and, but for the sanction of democratic elections, recalcitrant groups could be coerced or harassed into some kind of compliance. A programme of enforced obedience might not be an efficient way of running the economy, but it would protect the state from serious disruption of services. An authoritarian state able to impose conformity would no longer have the imperative need to placate the interest groups.

It is the mechanism of periodic elections, with the threat of expulsion from office, which makes governments so responsive to interest groups.

(4) *The electoral system*

The fourth feature of our contemporary institutions which weakens the state lies in the particular form of popular election. The 'first-past-the-post' formula working in single-member constituencies intensifies both the direct, and the indirect, electoral sanctions.

The direct sanctions are enhanced by the concentration of particular groups in a relatively small number of seats. Such groups may be either consumers or producers. The 'first-past-the-post' formula magnifies the strength of strategically located groups. So in July 1969 the Cabinet considered the closure of the Central Wales Railway. 'This', wrote Richard Crossman,

> is a parody of a railway and there is an overwhelming case for permanent closure next January, because otherwise we will have to pay a £300,000 subsidy. . . . Roy half-heartedly stood out, I stood out with Dick Marsh, but round the table the others were in favour of the £300,000 subsidy, because three seats were in danger in Central Wales.[33,34]

However, as argued earlier, the direct electoral sanctions, i.e. the votes wielded by resentful groups, are less important than the indirect electoral sanctions. Governments which stand up to interest groups may forfeit their cooperation, so making it harder for governments to satisfy public opinion. Mr Wilson always claimed that the seamen's strike of 1966 blew the government 'off course'. Mr Heath's government was severely damaged by the miners' strike of 1972 and destroyed by that of 1974. Mr Callaghan's government might well have survived but for the Winter of Discontent.

In standing-up to interest groups then, governments incur costs. This would be true whatever kind of electoral system is used. The costs, however, under PR are *proportionate* to the loss of support; under our electoral system they are normally multiplied by a factor of between two and three. A party which loses 1 per cent of the vote to its opponents loses not 1 per cent but from 2 to 3 per cent of the seats. Small movements of votes are usually reflected in relatively large transfers of seats.* An electoral cough is magnified into a parliamentary roar. Governments, therefore, must be responsive to the threat of even a slight loss of support nationally.

However, it is not the two-party system, or the Single Member, Simple Plurality formula in themselves, which expose the democratic state to excessive group demands. A different kind of two-party system, with neither party having much ideological identity or displaying much cohesion in the legislature would provide a considerable defence against the particular threats posed by interest groups in Britain. Similarly, the

---

* In the earlier part of the post-war period a 1 per cent swing in votes from one major party to the other implied a transfer of 18 to 20 seats – about 3 per cent of the total number of seats in Parliament. During the 1970s this figure declined and by the end of the decade was between 10 and 12. After the 1983 election it may be that the exaggerative power of the Single Member, Simple Plurality mechanism has declined further. However, judged by most of the post-war period such a situation is abnormal. I am grateful to John Curtice for the advice about 1983.

Single Member, Simple Plurality mechanism would present little difficulty if, given two parties, one of them were in a semi-permanent majority or if the geographical distribution of opinion threw up a multi-party, rather than a two-party, pattern of representation. The British problem arises because the two main parties are normally so evenly balanced in popular support; the electoral system can turn a small movement of votes into a parliamentary landslide. Between 1950 and 1979, the popular lead of one party over the other in a general election was never more than 8 per cent – and was usually considerably less. Governments in Britain normally have a precarious electoral base.

This sense of vulnerability is increased because of the adversary nature of the political system, itself largely a product of the electoral regime. Political leaders have to choose between being the hammer of government, or the anvil of opposition. A British election normally confronts politicians with an all or nothing choice, between the (apparent) absolute power of government and the oblivion, even if temporary, of opposition.

None of these institutional defects would matter if the necessary norms of restraint were better internalised. The apparent decline of deference, however, and the failure to compensate for this decline by greater self-discipline on the part of group members and voters have revealed the vulnerability of the state. Yet the political culture does not develop in an institutional void. The institutions have themselves hindered the growth of norms of self-restraint, and have fostered the ethos of compromise amongst the elite, precisely because the weakness of government to outside pressure is so apparent. This weakness not only encourages the more powerful groups to press extreme claims but obliges more inherently responsible groups to do so, to avoid their members losing out.

There is no way in which a democratic state can be entirely insulated from the pressures of interest groups, even if it were desirable to make the attempt. Bargaining between government and interest groups will occur in any democratic regime, no matter what particular form its institutions take. What the institutions (including the electoral system) do is to influence the terms on which negotiation takes place.

Cumulative surrender

Governments, then, seem to be judged in large measure, by voters' perceptions of their material well-being. Governments that appear to fail, that cannot deliver, are highly vulnerable, a susceptibility increased by the electoral system.

Once it begins, the process of surrender tends to be cumulative, and follows a Hobbesian logic, as groups that have hitherto abided by the implicit rules of the game discover that they are disadvantaged by their own self-restraint. It is not simply that pressure is seen to pay; it is that the acquiescent also suffer. Modern British government works under chronic siege. Moreover, each victory of the interest groups, whether the demand be justified on its merits or not, diminishes the authority of government for the future, and with it its power. Paradoxically the more governments give way so as, by buying peace, to strengthen their standing with the electorate, the more they undermine their capacity to continue to do those things – provide a higher standard of living, better social services, less unemployment – which voters value. The essence of government lies in the willingness to confront special interests when necessary in defence of the general interest. In the early 1970s the term confrontation became one of abuse. One of the most serious developments up until 1979 was a decline in the willingness of governments to resist the interest groups.

The concessions, furthermore, that governments make to the groups are usually only apparent. Governments, at the price of further inflation, can confer an illusory benefit and gain peace until the next pay round. What they cannot do is to make one section better off by more than the growth of GDP, without taking more from other groups. It is the ultimately self-defeating character of many interest group claims that has been one of the worst features of post-war political development in Britain.

The combination then of unlimited authority and popular election is a recipe, not so much for strong and coherent government, as for near paralysis, for what Beer calls 'pluralistic stagnation',[35] a condition exacerbated by the first-past-the-post method of election.

The response of the politicians

Let us then consider in summary form the specific institutional conditions which have enhanced the power of interest groups in post-war Britain. These are: (i) the legal omnipotence of Parliament; (ii) the effective control of that Parliament by an executive resting on the support of a disciplined party majority; (iii) the Single Member, Simple Plurality electoral system; and (iv) a highly competitive party system reflected in near equality of support for the two main parties.

Between 1945 and say 1980 Britain was characterised by all four conditions. Nevertheless, it is obvious that some governments are less responsive than others to interest groups. Indeed, the behaviour of the Thatcher government from 1979 to 1983, and its striking re-election victory in 1983, seem to contradict the argument of this chapter. The answer lies partly in Mrs Thatcher's personality, but also in the suspension, which may be temporary, of the fourth condition. For most of Mrs Thatcher's first term the official opposition was weak, and did not seem a credible contender for power, a judgement borne out by the results of the 1983 election.

Governmental fears of losing the next election are likely to be much diluted if the chief opposition party is bitterly divided within itself and unable even to maintain, let alone increase, its vote. For brief periods the Liberal/SDP Alliance posed a manifest threat but it did not offer a sustained challenge; just when it seemed that the Alliance might be re-emerging as a major force after a slump in its ratings in early 1982, the Argentinians occupied the Falkland Islands, giving Mrs Thatcher the chance to restore her popularity. A Government which could ride so high in the opinion polls three years after the beginning of the Parliament was uniquely placed to stand firm. Mrs Thatcher's personal interpretation of the political environment coincided with the objective features of that environment.

It is easy, however, to exaggerate the extent to which the Thatcher government stood firm. Mrs Thatcher did not resist the interest groups indiscriminately. Indeed, this allegedly inflexible leader was much more selective than most prime ministers. Thus, she showed considerable wariness of the miners. The NUM were allowed to breach the pay norm in 1981 and 1982 and more significant still, at the first sign of trouble over the proposed closure of pits in 1981, the Government backed down. It gave way to British Leyland in 1980, doubtless aware of the damage that the collapse of this strategically situated enterprise could do to the Conservatives in the numerous marginals of the West Midlands.[36]

It is, of course, true that the Thatcher government showed a willingness to ride out strikes not demonstrated by earlier administrations and more often than not, it won such strikes. In its contests with the Iron and Steel Trades Confederation, the NUR and ASLEF, it was not the Government but the union which gave in. Here, however, the government benefited enormously from what, since the end of the Second World War, was an unprecedentedly high level of unemployment. Britain paid a high price for industrial peace. Even were we willing to incur such a cost, there could be no certainty that the electorate would tolerate such high unemployment for long.

In the last resort it is the perceptions that politicians have of the electorate's reaction which count. If politicians believe that voters will respond favourably to firm, unyielding leadership, at no matter what personal cost to each voter, vote-maximising politicians will have no rational motive for giving way. Mrs Thatcher's greater willingness to confront the interest groups was based on perceptions of electoral reaction which differed from those of most of her predecessors; in turn these different perceptions seem to derive from differences in temperament.

The threat of calling a general election against the demands of an interest group is not an easy one to carry out successfully. It is the government which has to run for re-election, not the interest group. This enshrines an important point; even when the interest group is blamed by the voters, it is the Government which is likely to bear the odium for the consequences.[37] The full results of a strike often follow a long and complex chain of events, and may occur long after the strike itself.

The support of public opinion then is a capricious and sometimes fragile weapon for governments in their struggles with interest groups. Governments armed with such apparently vast powers, but exposed to the ordeal of frequent popular elections are an easy quarry for assertive interest groups. The unlimited legal competence of British government, and its extensive political powers, give it a limitless area for retreat. British government has often resembled a Hobbesian state presiding over an anarchic society.

Foreign experience
It is notable that most comparative appraisals of interest group/government relationships rest on the internal organisation of the interest groups, not on that of government. Simple comparisons between democracies with institutional forms and party structures like those of Britain, and those with a greater dispersion of legal authority and multi-party systems or proportional representation are not likely to be conclusive, because of the large number of variables which shape the relationship between the two sides. Thus, in some countries cultural factors may give governments greater autonomy; in others, trade union density may be lower or the economy less exposed to the leverage of particular groups. Any attempt to make inferences by comparison would have to be on a scale far exceeding the boundaries of this essay. The aim of this article is to emphasise certain institutional features widely believed to confer strength on British government which probably weaken it. Different patterns of governmental institutions, and different electoral mechanisms will alter the form of relationship between government and pressure groups. There is clearly vast scope for enquiry here; what is crucial is that it should not be assumed by facile reference to, say, Italian experience that the British model of concentrated powers and two parties is more consistent with 'strong' government than other forms.

The question arises whether Britain's vulnerability is a consequence of her large public sector, rather than of her form of government. Perhaps it is the smaller public sector, rather than the political institutions, which accounts for what seems to be the greater immunity from interest group pressures of other democratic countries. The problem with this formulation is that it is hard, in post-war societies where governments intervene extensively in the economy, to distinguish a clear boundary between the public and private sectors. The Labour government was blown 'off-course' in 1966, by a strike in the private sector, that of the seamen's union. Contraction of the public sector, therefore, is in itself no solution, so long as governments seek to achieve such goals as a high level of employment and a balance of payments surplus.

The remedies

Constitutional change

Three possible prescriptions suggest themselves. One obvious solution, congenial to neo-liberals, is privatisation. Nationalised industries could be sold off, and welfare functions could be performed by private or voluntary bodies, with individuals insuring themselves against sickness and other hazards with some publicly financed fallback schemes. An alternative to the denationalisation of industries in some fields might be the transfer of such industries to workers' co-operatives, operating under carefully defined market rules.

To many, however, the first solution would be objectionable on grounds of principle. If public ownership of industry remains, and if welfare policies continue to be made on a national basis there must be some change in control. What is necessary is to insulate some of the economic functions of the state from influence by the government of the day. The defect of the nationalised industries and similar bodies is that they are too easily controlled by the government. The Government could be held accountable by the NUM in 1974 because the Government could constrain the National Coal Board in so far as the Board did not breach the counter-inflation statutes, and could, if the NCB wished to make an offer in breach of the law, push through Parliament a bill changing the law.

Further examples from the Heath government illustrate the vulnerability of governments which are very powerful in relation to other formal institutions. Thus, the government sometimes adopted, as a means of unhooking itself, the expedient of an inquiry, undertaken by a High Court judge (e.g. the miners' strike of 1972); on one occasion, when there was the likelihood of a strike against the Industrial Relations Bill because of the imprisonment of some workers, a hitherto virtually unknown public officer, the Official Solicitor, suddenly materialised to enable the men to be released.[38] Governments can only be strengthened (or, what amounts to the same thing, interest groups can only be weakened) if there are some things beyond the legal competence, or the political reach, of the executive.

What this implies is the adoption of some kind of formal curb on the powers of governments and parliamentary majorities. What is required is a written constitution, entrenching the independence of certain specified public services, in some areas of their work, whether they be social welfare agencies or nationalised industries. Decisions on some questions at any rate must be put beyond the reach of Ministers and beyond that of simple parliamentary majorities.

A written constitution, then, is needed, not to confer rights, not to increase the area of apparent popular control, but to limit that control. The aim is to strengthen government by seemingly weakening it. We limit the apparent powers of the state, we reduce the functions of government, to enable governments to carry out more effectively the functions that are left.

What is envisaged here is a large complex of public bodies administering public services or nationalised industries, whose work is insulated, except in certain carefully designated areas, from government intervention. Such bodies could either be appointed or elected, or chosen by a mixture of both methods. Because the aim is to diffuse the activities of interest groups there is positive virtue in developing a series of *ad hoc* authorities with different, overlapping geographical boundaries, with different forms of election and with boards or committees serving for different terms of office.

The NEDO report on nationalised industries called for a Policy Council for each industry which would largely protect the industry from political interference. Such an approach seems to be similar in spirit to the measures suggest here – though the lack of entrenched powers for the Policy Councils might lead to an erosion of their independence.[39]

Such a step, it will be objected, will diminish accountability. What needs to be asserted is that 'accountability' in some fields is spurious. In practice, accountability does not mean accountable to 'the public', but to the 'interested publics', to special publics such as rail commuters, council house tenants, workers in nationalised industries. Some way must be found of ensuring that boards carrying out certain economic or welfare functions are insulated from 'the people' in much the same way as we protect judges from popular pressure. If certain industries and services are to be publicly run, some functions, at least, must be put outside the scope of normal electoral politics.

A written constitution whose primary purpose was to identify certain economic activities, and to protect them from executive or legislative interference, would make strange reading. Its subject matter would jar oddly with the normal stuff of constitutions but this may be because so many constitutions fail to identify the most sensitive areas of government control. The functional role of the state, i.e. the co-ordination of the great producer interests, has become one of the most crucial tasks of modern government. The new functions of government impose new problems, and constitutions should reflect this change.

Such changes will have many drawbacks. At its best, the British constitution does work, in the manner claimed by its panegyrists; the entrenchment of clauses relating to the administration of public economic and welfare agencies would certainly impair the unitary control, and the coherence of policy, which the concentration of power makes possible. Unfortunately, the constitution is at its best less and less often. We need to weigh the handicaps imposed by a written constitution of the kind proposed with the disadvantages which accrue from our present form of government. As Hobbes, writing to assert that sovereign power should be absolute, put it, 'The condition of man in this life shall never be without inconveniences.'[40]

Electoral reform

The issue of electoral reform has already been discussed – though more from the angle of the disadvantages of the present system than from the benefits of reform.

The crucial failing of the present electoral system is the way in which small net movements of votes are magnified into large movements of seats. Up to the early 1970s a 1 per cent swing of votes usually meant, not a 1 per cent transfer of seats, but a 3 per cent change. A party that loses support at a general election suffers a *special* penalty. It is this triple or double forfeit which helps to encourage the triviality and mendacity of our electoral politics. No party leader has any electoral incentive to take the long view. Virtue always incurs some cost; in British politics, political virtue incurs a double or treble cost.

A second consequence of our electoral system is that it offers all or nothing. Political power is concentrated in the leadership of the majority party; the minority have only the sterility and frustration of opposition to look forward to. Adversary politics crystallises the alternatives in the starkest way whilst the electoral system magnifies the risks facing political leaders.

Proportional representation would reduce the incentive governments have to respond to outside pressure. If multi-member constituencies with the single transferable vote were adopted, interest groups would no longer exercise disproportionate power. Their votes would be more spread out – 2000 votes in an electorate of 300,000 would count for less than in a constituency of 60,000.* The ability of 2000 voters to swing a seat would be greatly weakened.

The psychological effect on politicians of the new method could be considerable. Bidding for votes would continue – but strategically-located votes would no longer have the same force. What counts ultimately are the perceptions of politicians. Presumably, after a time-lag, these perceptions will adjust to the new electoral framework.

James Madison, writing in support of the proposals for the new federal constitution, found in the increase in size one of the strongest arguments for an American federation:

> Extend the sphere, and you take in a greater variety of parties and interests

and even more pertinently

> . . . as each representative will be chosen by a greater number of citizens in the large than in the small republics, it will be more difficult for unworthy candidates to practise with success the vicious arts by which elections are too often carried.[41]

A possible consequence of PR with STV, however, is that candidates of the same party, bidding for early preferences against one another, would espouse the claims of particular groups. Even this competition however would be on a personal, and not a party, basis. The dispersion of pressure group activity amongst six hundred members would go far to limit group power.

The Additional Member system, similar to that used in West Germany, dilutes the electoral power of small groups even more effectively. No matter how many seats a party wins, under the first-past-the-post formula, its total representation will depend on the number of votes it obtains at regional, or national, level – not on the distribution of its votes. Each vote will count for one; no vote will have a special strategic value.†

Governments elected under PR, although usually weaker in relation to the House of Commons, would be strengthened against outside interest groups. First, any loss of support a government incurred as a

---

* In a five-member constituency, with an electorate of 300,000 the electoral quota, assuming a turnout of 75 per cent would be 37,501. In a single-member constituency of 60,000 and 75 per cent turnout the quota cannot be more than 22,751 and would probably be substantially less.

† This is not strictly true in West Germany since a party which gains more seats than it is due under the first-past-the-post formula at regional level keeps these extra seats. The number of excess seats is likely to be small and doubtless some correction could be devised to cancel even this excess.

result of resisting interest groups would be reflected in a proportionate and not an exaggerated loss of seats. Secondly, assuming that relations between the larger parties do not have the acrimony found in Italy, a coalition government with, say, 60 per cent of the votes could accept the loss of say 3 or 4 per cent and still continue in office. Governments would no longer rest on such a precarious margin of support.

Such changes would go far to strengthen government, in the prosecution of a more limited range of functions than it has at present. Interest group activity would be diffused over a much wider range of institutions, and would thereby become more visible; an interest group would no longer be able, by coercing the executive, to ensure the mobilisation of all branches of government on its behalf.

It may be objected that the Callaghan government's experience during the Winter of Discontent in early 1979 runs counter to this thesis. The Government had lost its overall majority and was dependent for its parliamentary survival on the support of minority parties. There can be little doubt that the government was severely handicapped in dealing with the interest groups because of its precarious parliamentary position. Governments, it might seem, are stronger in negotiating with interest groups when backed by a robust parliamentary majority.

This plausible view, however, ignores the institutional context of 1979. The Callaghan government was in a weak situation because if an election occurred it would have been (and was) fought under the first-past-the-post electoral system. The government lacked strength precisely because single-party governments lacking a majority are the exception in Britain, and not the norm.

Conclusion
Such changes would not be without costs. At its best the British system of government does display the merits claimed for it; at its best, it does focus responsibility, it does enable the electorate to hold government accountable for a wide range of actions, it does permit the enactment of a programme informed by a unifying philosophy. These merits, however, have increasingly become less evident; governments have been unable to implement their manifestos, and have not been able to impose coherent programmes of legislation. Vacillation, inconstancy, and muddle have been more the hallmarks of successive British governments since 1950. Whatever faults the changes propounded here would reveal, they are unlikely to be as damaging as those from which the country now suffers.

British government has been praised for its strength and its responsiveness – the latter deriving from the constant possibility, and empirically the actual occurrence, of alternations of power between two parties. Paradoxically, such alternation of power, so often proclaimed as a prominent merit of the system is inconsistent with the system's other alleged virtue – strong government.

Notes

1. Winston Churchill, *Parliamentary Debates*, 12 November 1936, Vol. 317, col. 107.
2. G.W. Keeton, *The Passing of Parliament* (Benn, London, 1952) and R.H.S. Crossman in *Introduction* to Walter Bagehot, *The English Constitution* (Fontana, London, 1963).
3. A Report of the Committee on Political Parties, *Toward A More Responsible Two-Party System* (Rinehart & Co. Inc., New York and Toronto, 1950).
4. S.H. Beer, *Modern British Politics* (Faber and Faber, London, 1965).
5. National Economic Development Office, *A Study of UK Nationalised Industries* (HMSO, London, 1976), p. 35.
6. Evidence of W.S. Ryrie to Committee on the Civil Service (*Fulton Report*), Vol. 5 (2) p. 1086 (HMSO, London, 1968), Cmnd 3638.
7. S. Brittan 'The economic contradictions of democracy', *British Journal of Political Science*, April 1975; for specific affinity with the thesis in this paper see 'Towards a new political settlement' (pp. 284–6) in his book *The Economic Consequences of Democracy* (Temple Smith, London, 1977). A. King, 'Overload: problems of governing in the 1970s', *Political Studies*, June 1975 (substantially reprinted in A. King [ed.]), *Why is Britain Becoming Harder to Govern?* (BBC, London, 1976). S.H. Beer, *Britain Against Itself* (Faber and Faber, London, 1982).
8. S.E. Finer, *Anonymous Empire* (Pall Mall Press, London, 1958) pp. 126–8.
9. *Ibid.*, p. 129.
10. E. Gibbon, *Decline and Fall of the Roman Empire*, Everyman edition (Dent, London, 1910), Vol. 3, p. 241.
11. *Britain Against Itself*, p. 13.
12. H. Macmillan, *Riding the Storm 1956–59* (Macmillan, London, 1971), p. 345, quoting diary for 14 March 1957.
13. S.H. Beer, 'Pressure groups and parties in Britain' in *American Political Science Review*, March 1956.
14. J. Barnett, *Inside the Treasury* (André Deutsch, London, 1982), p. 133.
15. A.L. Lowell, *The Government of England* (Macmillan, New York, 1908). Vol. 1, pp. 147–53.
16. B. Castle, *The Times*, 28 June 1982.

17. *Modern British Politics*, p. 349.
18. *Inside the Treasury*, pp. 180–1.
19. *Riding the Storm*, p. 345.
20. See S. Fay and H. Young, *The Fall of Heath* (reprinted by the Sunday Times, London, 1976) and D. Hurd, *An End to Promises* (Collins, London, 1979).
21. *Inside the Treasury*, p. 50.
22. R.H.S. Crossman (ed. by Janet Morgan), *The Diaries of A Cabinet Minister*, Vol. III (Hamish Hamilton and Jonathan Cape, London, 1977), p. 783.
23. This balance-sheet has some affinity with a schema developed by Irving Janis for analysing intra-personal conflict resolution. See I. Janis, 'Decisional conflicts: a theoretical analysis', *Journal of Conflict Resolution*, March 1959.
24. *Why is Britain Becoming Harder to Govern?*
25. Lord Hailsham, *The Dilemma of Democracy* (Collins, London, 1978), p. 125.
26. *Ibid.*, pp. 62–4.
27. P. Norton *Dissension in the House of Commons 1945–74* (Macmillan Press, London and Basingstoke, 1975) and *Dissension in the House of Commons 1974–79* (Oxford University Press, Oxford, 1980).
28. *Modern British Politics*, p. 351.
29. R. Jessop, 'Corporatism, parliamentarism and social democracy' in P.C. Schmitter and G. Lehmbruch, *Trends Towards Corporatist Intermediation* (Sage Publications, Beverly Hills and London, 1979).
30. *A Study of UK Nationalised Industries*, Appendix C, p. 84 and pp. 35–7.
31. P. Herring, *Public Administration and the Public Interest*, quoted in Beer, 1965.
32. R. Wilding, 'The civil servant as policy adviser and manager' in *Public Administration Bulletin*, April 1980, quoted in Beer, 1982, p. 14.
33. *The Diaries of a Cabinet Minister*, Vol. III, pp. 603–4.
34. Similarly, Joel Barnett, whose sensitivity to the problems of the cotton industry has already been mentioned, describes the building of a new aircraft, the HS146.

> The company, prenationalization Hawker-Siddeley, did not consider the prospects financially sound enough to put up the money. So the government kept providing sums like £½ million at a time to keep the design team going but which allowed the major decision on production to be deferred. *At the same time we created our own built-in pressure group.* (emphasis added).

The trade unions put pressure on the M.P.s for the constituencies where the Hawker factories were sited. . . . Most M.P.s in turn put pressure on Ministers to find the money. The pressure was even more intense if the Constituency was politically marginal.

35. *Britain Against Itself*, p. 23.
36. *Hansard*, 19 February 1981, Vol. 999, col. 457, and 26 January 1981, Vol. 997, cols. 639–46.
37. Gallup showed in early December 1973 that respondents by more than two to one thought the miners should not be treated as a special case. In January, the number thinking they should be so treated had risen from 28 per cent to 38 per cent; and in February, there was a further rise to 56 per cent. Moreover, in the same month 51 per cent denied that the three-day week imposed by the government was necessary, as against 29 per cent who thought it was (*Gallup Political Index* nos. 161, 162 and 163 for attitudes to miners' wage claim). For attitudes to dispute between British Rail and ASLEF over rostering see *Gallup Political Index* no. 264.
38. G. Dorfman, *Government Versus Trade Unionism in British Politics Since 1968* (Macmillan Press, London and Basingstoke, 1969) p. 60.
39. *A Study of UK Nationalised Industries*, pp. 46–51.
40. T. Hobbes (ed by M. Oakeshott), *Leviathan* (Basil Blackwell, Oxford, n.d.), p. 136.
41. J. Madison, Letter 10 in H. Cabot Lodge (ed.), *The Federalist Papers* (T. Fisher Unwin, London, 1886).

3 The Government Formation Process in the Constitutional Monarchies of North-West Europe[1]
Vernon Bogdanor

I

There is hardly any area of political science which Sammy Finer has not illuminated: comparative government, public administration, political history, sociological theory, Third World politics – all have benefited from the kiss of life which he has bestowed upon them. As open to new ideas today as when his career began nearly forty years ago, he makes most of his younger colleagues appear merely limited and parochial. Over-shadowed in his youth by his elder brother, Herman, he has been able to show that, in the fullness of maturity, his mastery of the subject is no less complete.

Sammy's achievement, like that of any great scholar, is as much one of character as of intellect. He has never lost that sense of excitement and wonder which the study of government and politics can engender, nor the enthusiasm to convey it to others. He is peculiarly receptive to the political developments of the age in which he lives, and his generosity in sharing his insights with colleagues and pupils is matched only by his discernment in isolating what is significant amidst the intellectual currents swirling around him. But perhaps, as one of his favourite authors has understood, the qualities of intellect and discernment are not quite as distinct as they may appear. For 'Discernment', as La Rochefoucauld tells us, 'is simply a great light of the intellect which shines into the roots of things, sees everything worth noticing, and perceives things thought to be imperceptible'. It is this quality which Sammy Finer possesses to such an abundant degree, and it has made him the dominant political scientist of his generation in Britain. This essay is offered as a token of admiration and affection.

II

Of the many subjects upon which Sammy Finer has cast fresh light, the most recent has been the comparative study of electoral and party systems. In the symposium which he edited, *Adversary Politics and Electoral Reform* (1975) and in his book, *The Changing British Party System, 1945–1979* (1980) he rescued from somnolence the debate on proportional representation and the merits of the British two-party system. One outgrowth of this debate has been a renewed interest in the formation and dissolution of government in multi-party systems, a topic to which both David Butler and the present author have made contributions.[2] The literature on this subject has, however, mainly been confined to the dilemmas that might arise in Britain were multi-party politics to complicate the government formation process. Examples from continental experience have been used solely for purposes of illustration. The present essay seeks therefore to analyse in rather more detail the government formation process in five continental countries in which democratic government and constitutional monarchy coexist together.

Democracy and monarchy – two elements which most nineteenth century radicals would have thought incompatible – find themselves happily combined in some of the most stable and long-lived of the democracies of Western Europe. During the years between the wars when the new democracies, based as they were on the abstract logic of republicanism, but containing within themselves no focus for popular sentiment, collapsed like a house of cards in the face of economic depression and political extremism, Britain and the Scandinavian monarchies remained entirely immune to fascism and communism, while Belgium and Holland were able to hold these forces at bay. Constitutional monarchy, far from being a threat to democracy has proved, in the twentieth century, to be a symbol of its stability.[3]

The synthesis between democracy and monarchy, however, is one in which the two elements are unequally combined, for, of course, the claims of monarchy have had to yield to the rights of the people. The basis of the democratic impulse – the demand for popular control over the choice of government – and of monarchy whose essence is the hereditary principle – clearly conflict, and the first is by far the stronger political force. So it is that the price of survival for monarchy has been a transformation of its role. Those monarchies that have endured have done so because they have surrendered most of their prerogatives. Where monarchs have insisted upon retaining wide prerogatives, they have generally not survived. But in constitutional monarchies, the Sovereign has been able to transcend that alienation from political institutions which is so marked a feature of popular attitudes in most modern democracies; and in such countries, the monarch often enjoys greater prestige and popularity than the political leaders, a paradox which would not have surprised Walter Bagehot, who in his classic work, *The English Constitution*, captured the essence of that elusive phenomenon, constitutional monarchy.

III

The story of the growth of constitutional monarchy remains, however, one of the great unwritten books of modern history. In Britain, the prototype of so many modern parliamentary democracies, constitutional monarchy developed in an evolutionary manner. Its origins lie in the seventeenth-century conflict between King and Parliament, but it took well over two centuries before the British monarchy assumed its modern form. Continental countries have been less fortunate in that they have not enjoyed so long a period of unbroken political continuity so that steady constitutional progress has often been impossible: and monarchy has not remained the predominant pattern amongst European states. In 1914, only France and Switzerland, of the twenty-three states in Europe, were republics. By the 1980s, however, only eight of the seventeen democracies of Western Europe – excluding such mini-statelets as Lichtenstein – were monarchies. They were, in addition to Britain, Belgium, Denmark, Luxembourg, the Netherlands, Norway, Spain and Sweden. Of these states, all but Spain lie in the north-west of Europe, and five of them – Britain, Denmark, the Netherlands, Norway and Sweden – are predominantly Protestant. Spain is the only state in southern Europe to have a monarch as head of state, but it was a republic between 1931 and 1975, and the monarchy was not restored until the death of General Franco.

In those countries in which monarchy survives, sovereigns have been willing to observe the limits imposed by the rules of parliamentary government. Instead of clinging to their prerogatives and their personal power, they have let themselves be guided by the advice of their ministers. For the principle of ministerial responsibility has as its corollary the notion that the acts of the sovereign are not his own acts, but those of his ministers. The sovereign therefore, is, in the constitutional sense, politically irresponsible. For at least the last thirty years, the monarchs of Belgium, Denmark, the Netherlands, Norway and Sweden have been quite scrupulous in the observation of their role. There has been no question of the sovereign attempting to exercise unconstitutional powers. The power of the constitutional monarch has, as Bagehot noticed, been replaced by influence: the extent of the influence open to a wise and sagacious monarch can, however, prove very great indeed, and in no sphere is this influence more likely to be exerted than in the government formation process.

This essay seeks to analyse the role of the constitutional monarchs of the continent in the government formation process. Spain, however, is excluded, precisely because the restoration of the monarchy in that country is so recent; and also Luxembourg, because it is perhaps too small for any very general lessons to be drawn from its political experience. The essay, therefore, confines itself to five constitutional monarchies – Belgium, Denmark, the Netherlands, Norway and Sweden.

IV

All of these countries have legislatures elected by one or other of the list systems of proportional representation, and all have multi-party systems. In such situations, the nomination of a prime minister and the formation of a government may not be so straightforward and innocent of difficulty as it generally is in two-party systems. For, if no single party enjoys an overall majority, then it is no longer obvious who should be called upon to form a government, nor what type of government should be formed – whether a majority or minority administration, a coalition or single-party government. This places the sovereign in a position of potential jeopardy, for in so far as he has to use his prerogative to decide such questions, his actions may be seen as having a political content. He loses the protection which comes from following uncontentious paths, and can find himself unwittingly thrown into the political arena, something which, in the long run, threatens his chances of survival.

It is not, however, the existence of a multi-party system *per se* which gives the monarch discretion, but rather a multi-party system in which political alignments are ill-defined. In some multi-party systems the affiliations of the various parties are easy to discern, and the parties signal their intentions with respect to coalition some time before the government formation process begins. In the German Federal Republic, for example, coalition government has been the norm since the foundation of the state in 1949, but there has been no need for the President to exercise his discretion in the government formation process, for the Free Democrats, the pivot party in the system, have generally declared during the election campaign which of the major parties – the Christian Democrats or the Social Democrats – they propose to support in government. Similarly, in Ireland, the Labour Party has in recent years been quite explicit that it will not support a government led by Fianna Fail, but it can be persuaded, provided that suitable terms can be agreed, to enter a coalition with Fine Gael.

In the five constitutional monarchies of north-west Europe, the task of the monarch is easiest where the coalition allegiances of the parties are well-defined. Such a situation occurs in Norway and Sweden where the parties are divided into two blocs – a socialist and a bourgeois bloc. In both countries, the electoral battle is between a Labour or Social Democrat Party, capable of forming a government either on its own, or with the support of a smaller party to its Left – the Socialist Peoples Party in Norway, the Communists in Sweden – and a bourgeois bloc compromising, in Norway, four parties – Conservatives (Høyre), Liberals (Venstre), Agrarians (Centre) and the Christian Peoples Party, and in Sweden, three – Conservatives (Moderates) Liberals (Peoples Party) and Agrarians (Centre). In both countries, it is generally quite easy to see who should be asked to form a government after a general election. The 1965 general election in Norway, for example, produced the result illustrated in the table.

Socialist parties		Bourgeois parties	
Labour	68	Høyre	31
Socialist Peoples Party	2	Venstre	18
		Centre	18
		Christian Peoples Party	13
	70		80

It will be seen that the bourgeois parties enjoyed an overall majority in the Norwegian Parliament, the Storting. There was no chance that any of the bourgeois parties would assist Labour, even though it was the largest single party, to form a government. The only question at issue, therefore, was which of the bourgeois parties would provide the prime minister. That, however, was a matter solely for inter-party negotiations, and did not require royal intervention. It took ten days for the bourgeois parties to agree upon Per Borten, the Centre Party leader, as Prime Minister. As soon as they had done so, the King accepted the resignation of Einar Gerhardsen, the incumbent Labour Prime Minister, and Borten was asked to form a government.

A similar pattern occurred in Sweden in 1976 and 1979, when the Social Democrats, who had been in power almost continuously for 44 years before 1976, found themselves defeated in two successive general elections by the bourgeois bloc. The three parties comprising this bloc had agreed before the elections that they would form an inter-party coalition if they won a majority, and so again there was no difficulty. In Sweden, for reasons that we shall later investigate, it is the speaker rather than the king who nominates the prime minister, but the Speaker's task in Sweden in 1976 and 1979 was as straightforward as that of the King in Norway in 1965.

In the other three countries that we are considering, however – Belgium, Denmark and the Netherlands – multi-party politics does not produce quite so convenient an outcome. For, in these countries, the formation of a government is decided not solely by the general election result, but by the process of negotiations which follows the election. The political parties are not divided into clearly defined blocs, and so general elections do not decide which parties should govern: instead they alter the power relations between the parties.

In Denmark, the Social Democrats have not been able to emulate the dominance of their Norwegian and Swedish counterparts and the Danish Social Democrats have never won an overall majority in the Folketing. Ever since 1905, Danish politics has been dominated by four major parties: the Social Democrats, Radical Liberals (Radikale Venstre), Agrarian Liberals (Venstre) and the Conservatives. But the division between the socialist and bourgeois bloc is not as clear-cut as it is in Norway and Sweden. Radikale Venstre attempts to play the part of a pivot like the German Free Democrats; but, unlike the FDP, Radikale Venstre does not usually declare its coalition intentions before the general election, preferring to hold open its options until the post-election bargaining situation is reached.

Since 1973, the Danish political situation has become more complicated as a result of the growth of new parties such as the Centre Democrats, a break-away from the Social Democrats, and Mogens Glistrup's Progress Party (Fremskridtspartiet), a populist anti-tax party. The increasing strength of the so-called 'anti-system' parties has made it more difficult to form viable governments from amongst the four 'old' parties. The government formation process has become more complex, and the Queen is frequently presented with a situation in which it is unclear who will be able to form a government.

In Belgium and the Netherlands, it is the confessional parties which are pivotal in the party system: in Belgium the Social Christians split (like their Socialist and Liberal rivals) into Fleming and Walloon wings, and in the Netherlands the Christian Democratic Appeal (CDA) is a federation of Catholic and Protestant parties. In both countries, the confessional parties can ally either with the Socialists or the Liberals, the other main parties in the political system, a situation which Hans Daalder has labelled 'semi-turnover – typically found in multipolar systems', in which 'one party or group of parties, is always represented in the government, but with alternating coalition partners'.[4] This situation arises because the confessional parties in Belgium and the Netherlands are a more powerful pivot than the German Free Democrats or the Radikale Venstre in Denmark. Indeed, only once have the confessional parties in Belgium or the Netherlands failed to secure at least 30 per cent of the vote in the period of mass suffrage. This means that they are almost always represented in government. Since 1884, the Social Christians in Belgium have been continuously in power except for two brief intervals after the Second World War. The Catholic component of the Dutch CDA – the KVP – is the only party in the world to have been continuously in government since 1918 with the exception of the Communist Party of the Soviet Union!

The confessional parties in Belgium and the Netherlands follow the practice of Radikale Venstre in Denmark in not declaring a preference for a particular coalition partner before or during the general election campaign. Instead, they wait until the result of the election is known, and begin to bargain. Their bargaining power is, of course, immensely strengthened by this method of operation since they have no prior commitments to any other party, but can, as it were, sell themselves to the highest bidder. The resulting complications before a government is formed can, however, be quite considerable, and the monarch has to exercise great care not to be caught up in them.

V

The situation is further complicated in that the constitutional monarchies of north western Europe, with the exception of Belgium, have adopted what has been called the principle of negative parliamentarism.[5] According to this constitutional principle, a government, instead of requiring a positive vote of confidence from the legislature, can maintain itself in power so long as there is no vote of censure passed against it. The effect of the principle is to facilitate the formation of minority governments, and it makes the task of the sovereign more difficult because, in addition to nominating a prime minister, he may also have to specify whether the government must command the support of a majority in the legislature or whether a minority government would be acceptable.

In Denmark (Article 16[2]), the Netherlands (Article 86), and Norway (Article 12), the government enjoys a juridical existence simply in virtue of its prime minister's nomination by the monarch, and no formal vote of investiture is needed, the government being presumed to enjoy the confidence of Parliament. In Sweden, there must, it is true, be a vote in the Riksdag on the speaker's nomination for prime minister, but the speaker's nominee is confirmed unless an absolute majority of the Riksdag votes against him. (Chapter 6, Article 2 of the 1974 Instrument of Government). This has a consequence similar to that of the provisions in the Danish, Dutch and Norwegian Constitutions in that it allows a minority government to continue for as long as there is not a positive majority against it in the legislature. For example, when in 1978 Ola Ullsten, the leader of the Swedish Liberals, was nominated by the Speaker as Prime Minister, he was confirmed in office even though he was supported only by the 39 members of the Liberal Party, but opposed by the 55 Conservatives and 17 Communists. To be defeated, there would have had to have been 175 votes – an overall majority of the 349 votes in the Riksdag – against Ullsten.

The purpose of such constitutional provisions exemplifying the principle of negative parliamentarism, then, is to allow minority governments to be constructed. This makes possible a solution to the problem of government formation in circumstances when a majority coalition cannot be formed and a general election, for one reason or another, is deemed undesirable. We may contrast such constitutions with the situation in Belgium, the German Federal Republic and Italy, where an incoming government requires a positive vote of confidence, a provision which makes majority coalition the norm and minority government very much the exception.

In the Federal Republic, the constitution requires the Federal Chancellor to be elected by the 'votes of the majority of the members of the Bundestag' (Article 63[2]). Further, and in even starker contrast to the Scandinavian countries,a chancellor can be removed through a vote of no confidence by the Bundestag 'only by electing a successor with the majority of its members'. (Article 67[1]). This provision was designed to ensure that, by contrast to Weimar, a government could not be defeated unless Parliament was agreed upon its successor.

In Belgium and Italy, the approval of both houses of the legislature is required. Article 94 of the Italian Constitution requires a newly formed government to present its programme to Parliament within ten days of its formation to secure a vote of confidence. In Belgium, the vote of confidence is not mentioned in the constitution, but, by convention, the prime minister of a newly formed government outlines its programme to each chamber, and he must obtain the approval of a majority in each chamber for it.

The encouragement which the provisions in the constitutions of the Scandinavian monarchies and the Netherlands give to the formation of minority government poses then an additional problem for the monarchs of Denmark, the Netherlands and Norway, and the Swedish Speaker. For they face not only the question of who to nominate as prime minister but also whether to specify a particular form of government. Should the sovereign insist, at least in the first instance, that a *majority* government be formed, or should he nominate a prime minister who can command the positive support of only a *minority* of the legislature.

The problem for the monarch (or in Sweden the speaker) arises because of the ambiguity of the basic principle of parliamentary government that a government must enjoy the support of parliament.[6] This principle can be interpreted to mean either that a government must receive the positive support of parliament through a vote of confidence or it can be interpreted negatively to mean that there is not a majority willing to bring the government down in a vote of censure. The principle can mean either that there is a majority *for* the government, or that there is no majority *against* it. These two interpretations may sometimes coincide and in the Netherlands they generally do, so that majority governments are invariably formed, but in Scandinavia they often do not coincide and, especially in Denmark, the notion of negative parliamentarism frequently permits a minority government to be formed where a majority administration would be impossible.

VI

The complexities to which multi-party politics give rise can easily serve to embroil a constitutional monarch and make the sovereign's role a matter of fierce political controversy. It is not enough for the sovereign to act with what he believes to be strict impartiality. For the problem is not that the sovereign would use his powers in the formation of a government in a deliberately discriminating manner, but rather that, acting in a manner which he genuinely believes to be consistent with the constitutional proprieties, one (or more) of the parties and the bulk of its supporters may come to feel that they have been unfairly treated. If constitutional monarchy is to be safeguarded, therefore, the sovereign must be protected from overt political involvement. There are, broadly, three ways of achieving this objective.

The first, which is almost certainly the method that would be adopted in Britain were hung parliaments to become the norm, is to develop a series of conventions which politicians would be prepared to observe and respect. Such an approach is characteristic of the government formation process in Denmark and Norway, and it would harmonise with the spirit of British constitutional development. The other two methods of protecting the sovereign, however, involve rather more formalised procedures.

In both Belgium and the Netherlands, it is customary for the sovereign to appoint informateurs to assist in the government formation process. The task of the informateur is to negotiate with party leaders to determine what political combinations are possible, and the development of this institution has enabled the sovereign to be shielded from the highly complex negotiations and manoeuvres which invariably take place. Informateurs have also been appointed on occasion in Denmark and Norway, but on an experimental basis rather than as a regular policy, and on the whole the experiments have not been a success.

The final method of protecting the sovereign from political involvement in the government formation process, the most drastic of all, is that adopted in Sweden, where the 1974 Instrument of Government denies the sovereign any role whatever in the process, and transfers his powers to the speaker. This is the method which Mr Benn has proposed for adoption in Britain in order to safeguard the monarchy if multi-party politics persists. Otherwise, the complexities which arise will, in his opinion, lead to the replacement of 'first-past-the-post' by 'first-past-the-Palace'.[7] It will be shown, however, that the Swedish solution, although it succeeds in protecting the sovereign, does so only at the cost of politicising the speakership, something which could in Britain seriously damage the working of parliamentary institutions.

VII

In considering how a system of conventions can serve to protect the sovereign from political involvement, we shall confine our attention to Denmark, where, as we have seen, the multiplicity of parties and the absence of clearly defined blocs makes the problem of government formation more complex than in Norway.

Article 14 of the Danish Constitution of 1953 declares that 'The King shall appoint and dismiss the Prime Minister and the other Ministers. He shall decide upon the number of Ministers and upon the distribution of the duties of government among them.' Apart from this purely formal statement, no guidelines are expressed as to the procedure or conditions for appointing the government except the general rule in Article 15 (1) that 'A Minister shall not remain in office after the Folketing has passed a vote of no confidence in him' and (2) 'Where the Folketing passes a vote of no confidence in the Prime Minister, he shall ask for the dismissal of the Ministry, unless writs are to be issued for a general election'. Article 15 gives explicit recognition to the principle of parliamentarism in its negative form. It is generally interpreted to mean that a government can be appointed only if it is assured of being able to survive a vote of no confidence in the single-chamber Folketing. But it does *not*, as we have seen, follow that a government needs a positive vote of confidence from the Folketing.

In the absence of specific provisions in the Constitution regulating the government formation process, a number of 'rules of the game' are generally observed. The first step after a prime minister (and with him his cabinet) delivers his resignation to the sovereign, is for her to seek the advice of the several party leaders who will be received by the sovereign, one at a time, in an order determined by their relative strength in the Folketing. The party leaders offer their recommendations as to which governmental combinations are feasible and desirable. Such recommendations do not, however, bind those who make them to offer positive support for all of the policies of the governmental combinations that they have recommended. The government could only be sure that it would not be met with a successful vote of no confidence when it presented itself to the Folketing. The principle of negative parliamentarism thus operates in Denmark to facilitate minority government, and indeed, majority government is very much the exception. Since 1945, Denmark has been governed by minority administrations – either single-party or coalition – for all but eleven-and-a-half years.

If party leaders representing a majority in the Folketing recommend that a particular person be asked to form a government then the Queen will ask that person to attempt the task, but if the first round does not result in such a majority, further consultations must be arranged until a majority of the parties can finally agree upon a particular candidate for the premiership. So far, the process has never led to total deadlock as it might perhaps in a country such as Italy or Spain, a tribute to the eagerness to reach agreement which is to be found at all levels of Danish government.

An alternative possibility in Denmark is for the monarch to appoint an informateur to conduct negotiations. By contrast with Belgium and the Netherlands, the informateur in Denmark (and in Norway) has always been a member of the legislature and in Denmark a party leader (except in 1975). The informateur can be the Prime Minister still in office, as with Anker Jørgensen in 1981. Exceptionally in 1975, the Speaker of the Folketing was asked to act. On this last occasion, it took no less than four rounds of negotiations to secure the formation of a government. Denmark had been governed from 1973 until the general election of 1975 by a single-party Venstre minority government led by Poul Hartling which commanded only 22 votes out of the 179 in the Folketing. As a result of the election, Venstre increased its representation from 22 to 42, but, when he met the Folketing, Hartling was defeated by a motion of no-confidence. The Queen then asked Karl Skytte, the President (Speaker) of the Folketing to act as informateur, giving him a mandate to set up a majority coalition, but Skytte had to tell the Queen that it was not possible to form a majority government. The Queen, undeterred, asked Jørgensen, the leader of the Social Democrats, to form a majority government, but he proved unable to do so. She then turned again to Hartling, asking him to form 'a broadly based government' and at first it seemed that Hartling would be successful in this task. He constructed a coalition comprising Venstre, the Conservatives, the Christian Peoples Party, and the Centre Democrats, which would have given him 65 votes in the Folketing, and he had an indication of support from Mogens Glistrup's Progress Party which had 24 votes, thus commanding almost one-half of the votes in the Folketing. At the last moment, however, Glistrup withdrew his support and Hartling failed. The Queen then called upon Jørgensen again, and he succeeded finally in forming a single party minority government.

The complexity of these negotiations would seem to provide ample scope for the Danish Queen to use her discretion so as to influence the outcome of the government formation process. In the absence of precise documentation, it is impossible to determine whether the Queen plays an active role in the process or not, but most Danish officials and academics are quite firm in their view that she confines herself to registering the recommendations which she receives, and giving effect to them as impartially as possible. There has been no major controversy about the role of the monarch in the government formation process since 1920, and at that time, the conventional 'rules of the game' had not yet been developed. These rules are accepted by all of the political groupings as laying down a fair procedure for settling what is bound to be a complex process. Nevertheless, there must be occasions when more than one course of action on the part of the sovereign is possible, and she will have no alternative to using her discretion.

To the outside observer, however, it is quite remarkable that the government formation process in Denmark arouses so little controversy, despite the multiplicity of parties and the seeming risk to the Crown of becoming involved in politically contentious decisions. It would, of course, be a mistake to imagine that the conventions developed in Denmark could be transposed, with equally happy results elsewhere. For the comparative ease with which the process of government formation takes place owes a good deal to the cooperative style of Danish political culture. Denmark is a small country without major territorial or regional conflicts, and with a powerful sense of national identity. It should not be assumed that the introduction of conventions similar to those adopted in Denmark would work equally well in countries where political differences are more intense and social conflicts less easy to resolve.

VIII

The procedure of government formation in Belgium and the Netherlands differs in a number of fundamental respects from that adopted in the Scandinavian countries. For, in the Low Countries, by contrast with Britain and Scandinavia, the monarch is allowed, and indeed expected, to play a more active role in the process. In both Belgium and the Netherlands the monarch is regarded as a very real guarantor of national unity – this is especially the case in Belgium where King Baudouin is sometimes called the only real Belgian, everyone else being either a Fleming or a Walloon. The King is seen as the only figure who is above the inter-communal conflict which threatens to tear the country apart. Both the Belgian and Dutch monarchs are thus accustomed to act in ways which would be thought unconstitutional in Britain and in Scandinavia.

Secondly, the government formation process in Belgium and the Netherlands is characterised by the highly active role which the informateur plays in both countries. By contrast with the Scandinavian countries, the informateur does not simply register the point of view of the parties, but also initiates an active search for agreement on the composition of a coalition government, the distribution of posts, and the government's programme. In the Netherlands, this last item is generally the most contentious of all, for coalition programmes tend to be long and detailed in an attempt to cover every possible contingency which might come to disrupt the coalition.

Finally, the government formation process in Belgium and the Netherlands is itself a vital part of the attempt to achieve consensus in those countries. In Belgium, the prime task of government is to satisfy the conflicting claims of the Fleming and Walloon communities. Indeed, the Belgian Constitution now requires there to be, with the possible exception of the prime minister, an equal number of French-speaking and Dutch-speaking ministers in the government (Article 86b). Moreover, a two-thirds majority of both houses voting together is required to secure constitutional change (Article 131), and this can act as a further constraint upon the government formation process. On occasion – as in 1972/3, for example – the king can press for a government comprising all three major political groupings in Belgium – Socialists, Social Christians and Liberals – so that the government will command a two-thirds majority in the legislature and enjoy the authority to make constitutional changes.

In the Netherlands, the government formation process is characterised by the length of time which it takes. During the inter-war period, the average time taken to form a government was 42 days; between 1946 and 1963 it was 68 days, and between 1965 and 1977, 95 days. In 1973, the process took 164 days and in 1977, 207 days – the longest so far. In the 39 years since the end of the Second World War, three-and-a-half years have been spent in forming governments. It is hardly surprising that such a lengthy process of government formation attracts public hostility in the Netherlands, and also derision abroad where it is sometimes erroneously regarded as the inevitable consequence of a system of proportional representation. But in the Netherlands, the resolution of conflicts between coalition partners occurs during the coalition negotiations, rather than after the government has been formed. For this reason, the Dutch political system cannot be regarded as basically unstable after the pattern of the French Fourth Republic. On the contrary, the long process of negotiation and the need to achieve a consensus before a government is formed make the Dutch political system highly stable if not stagnant.

In both Belgium and the Netherlands, the Constitution offers little guidance as to how the process of government formation is to be carried out. The only reference to the formation of a government in the Belgian Constitution is in Article 65, 'The King appoints and dismisses his Ministers', while in the Dutch Constitution, Article 86(2) states that 'The King appoints and dismisses his Ministers at will.' Neither constitution has anything to say about the principles that should be followed in nominating a prime minister or appointing ministers. In the absence of constitutional guidance in Belgium and the Netherlands, conventions regulating the government formation process have been developed; but, although these conventions are generally observed, no one is very clear how far precisely the conventions extend, nor the degree to which they bind.

In both countries, the sovereign begins the government formation process by consulting various national leaders. These consultations are of far wider scope than their Scandinavian counterparts. For they involve not only party leaders, but also prominent parliamentarians and, in Belgium, prominent individuals outside parliament. In the Netherlands, the Queen first calls spokesmen of the two chambers of Parliament, together with the Vice President of the Council of State, an advisory body with some judicial functions, and the leaders of the main party groups in the lower house. This has become an established practice and the Dutch Queen enjoys little discretion until this stage of the negotiations has been completed.

In Belgium, the King enjoys some discretion over whom he consults, and there are no clearly-defined rules regulating this part of the process. It is customary, however, for the King to consult the most prominent political leaders in the country – the outgoing prime minister, the speakers of both houses, and the leaders of the main party groups as well as ministers of state, former ministers and members of the legislature whom he regards as representative of public opinion. Unlike his Dutch counterpart, the Belgian King also consults the party chairmen, who can play a more important role in government formation than the parliamentary leaders. In addition, the Belgian King will consult the so-called 'interlocuteurs sociaux', the governor of the national bank, the Chairman of the Federation of Belgian Industries, and the leaders of the main trade unions. The number consulted can vary quite considerably. In 1961, for example, the King consulted only nine people before a government was formed; but in 1965, he consulted thirty-four, of whom twenty-eight were parliamentarians; in 1966, twenty-five, of whom twenty-one were parliamentarians, and in 1968, twenty-six, of whom twenty-three were parliamentarians. A further contrast with the Netherlands is that, in Belgium, government communiqués do not always proclaim the names of the persons summoned by the King, and when names are revealed, these do not necessarily denote those whose advice has been most influential. Nor, in Belgium, are details of the discussions disclosed, it being held that such secrecy 'is one of the basic conditions of the parliamentary monarchy'.[8]

In both Belgium and the Netherlands, the sovereign generally appoints an informateur, after the first round of consultations has been completed. Although the office of informateur is more highly formalised in the Netherlands than in Belgium, the first use of the informateur in fact occurred in Belgium in 1935 when M. Theunis was asked by Leopold III 'to make a rapid enquiry of the various parties concerning the broad lines of an economic programme which could meet the exigencies of the time'.[9] In the Netherlands, the office of informateur was not instituted until 1951, when the Minister for Foreign Affairs, Dirk Stikker, was appointed, for purely tactical reasons, as informateur: but the procedure did not become formalised until 1956 which was an extremely complex government formation process.

In both Belgium and the Netherlands, the sovereign has considerable discretion as to who the informateur should be; and it is, perhaps, at this stage of the process that a politically astute sovereign can do most to influence its eventual outcome.

The sovereign must, however, usually ensure that the informateur is someone without political ambitions so that he will be generally acceptable as a negotiator. Usually he is an elder statesman whose impartiality is respected, but, on occasion, the informateur can be an active politician as when in 1973 Andreas van Agt, leader of the Christian Democratic Appeal, was appointed to this office. In Belgium, but not the Netherlands, the informateur has always been a member of one of the two chambers. In five of the seven government formations between 1958 and 1975, the informateur was a member of the largest party in the lower house: on three occasions he was a minister in the outgoing government.

In the Netherlands, the informateur need not be, although he often is, a member of the legislature. On occasion, the vice president or another member of the State Council has been appointed informateur: provincial governors have also been used. But the informateur can also be an active politician. In 1958 and 1972/3, ministers in the outgoing government were informateurs: in 1959 and 1967, former prime ministers were asked to fulfil this role, while in 1965 the leader of the largest parliamentary group in the lower chamber was appointed.[10] In recent years, it has become customary to appoint more than one informateur. Indeed, in 1977 when the process of government formation took a record 207 days, no fewer than nine informateurs were appointed. In 1973, 1977 and 1981, moreover, two informateurs were appointed at a time – one for each of the two major parties involved in the negotiations.

When the informateur or informateurs report to the Sovereign, they may be forced to admit failure, and if this happens, they will either recommend that another informateur be appointed, or that elections be held. But if they have been successful in their task, the sovereign will then appoint a formateur, someone who can form a government. The formateur will generally consult with party leaders à deux, and at this stage the Sovereign plays no role at all in the process. He must not have parallel discussions with politicians while the formateur is at work. However, the formateur will call on the sovereign every two or three days to report on how the discussions are going.

In Belgium, the King gives the formateur a specific mandate whose task it will be to secure agreement between the parties under a given candidate for the premiership. In the Netherlands, the Queen does not specify any particular basis for the government, but contents herself with the use of a standard formula to the effect that a government must be found which can command the confidence of parliament. In practice, however, Dutch governments, except for caretaker administrations, are invariably majority coalitions, and there is no recent experience of any other form of government.

If the formateur succeeds in his task, he will normally become Prime Minister, but this is not always the case. In 1968, for example, in Belgium the formateur asked to remain outside the government, but presented to King Baudouin the agreement which he had secured between the parties naming M. Gaston Eyskens as Prime Minister, and Baudouin immediately asked Eyskens to form a government. Similarly, in Belgium, in 1950, M. Van Zeeland was formateur for a government, the Prime Minister of which was M. Pholien, while in 1979 M. Vanden Boeynants was formateur for a government headed by

M. Martens.[11] Occasionally, more than one formateur needs to be appointed before a government can be formed. In Belgium, for example, there were no fewer than four formateurs between September and December 1981 before M. Martens became Prime Minister, a consequence of Martens' strategy of allowing his political rivals to attempt to form a government in the expectation that they would not succeed and that he, Martens, would then be seen as the only possible Prime Minister

In both Belgium and the Netherlands, the Sovereign can always claim to be acting on advice in his or her appointment of a formateur, and to this extent, the sovereign's constitutional position is protected. But, as we have seen, it is at the earlier stages of the process that the sovereign can make his or her influence felt.

Queen Juliana of the Netherlands is said to have been particularly skilful in helping to ensure that negotiations proceeded in the direction which she desired. It has been suggested, although in the nature of things documentation must be impossible, that Juliana, both in 1973 and 1977, made a particular effort to ensure that the PvdA (Labour Party) gained office, since she intended to abdicate, and did not want the monarch to face republican opposition from the left. If this suggestion is correct, then the Queen succeeded in her aim in 1973, but not in 1977 when although, or perhaps because, it had made gains in the election, the PvdA was not included in the Government. For the Dutch government formation process is so complex and tortuous that the formation of cabinets often bears little relationship to the result of the election. Indeed, a party that wins seats in an election can, like the PvdA in 1977, impose such stiff conditions in its negotiations with the other parties, that it persuades its rivals to gang up against it. It is hardly surprising that there is a Dutch saying to the effect that one can win the election and afterwards lose the formation![12]

In Belgium, also, the sovereign enjoys considerable discretion in the government formation process. The King, it has been said, may 'at difficult moments – try to lead the negotiations into a certain direction and to advocate the solution that would coincide with his personal wish'; moreover, 'it is not altogether impossible that the monarch puts aside the personalities who do not enjoy his confidence'.[13] A recent occasion in which there could be little doubting the King's intervention was in 1965 when he appointed Pierre Harmel as formateur. At first, it appeared as if Harmel would not be able to form a government, but the King pressed him not to give up, and eventually he succeeded. Few could have been left unaware that it was Harmel who, on this occasion, enjoyed the King's favour.[14]

The complex institutional machinery developed in Belgium and the

Netherlands may appear outlandish, but it does illustrate how societies can generate constitutional expedients which may offer the only method of resolving their complex problems. But the intricate procedures presuppose for their success a high degree of secrecy, so that the party leaders can make bargains which their militants might reject, and also a political public which remains deferential towards elites, so that agreements, once made, are accepted by party activists. Neither of these two conditions, however, holds in the modern world, and, in both Belgium and the Netherlands, the machinery has come under increasing strain in recent years as a result of the breakdown of secrecy and the demand for the accountability of leaders to their rank and file. In the Netherlands, as a result of a Royal Commission report of the late 1960s, all relevant reports in the government formation process, including the advice of parliamentary leaders to the Queen, the reports of informateurs and formateurs, and the drafts of coalition agreements themselves, must be published. Such 'open diplomacy' constituted an attempt to legitimise a process which had come to appear increasingly unattractive to Dutch political opinion. But its main consequences have been to lengthen the time needed to complete the government formation process, and make it more difficult for politicians, compelled to look over their shoulders to ensure that they retain the support of their followers, to bargain successfully with those from other parties.

In both Belgium and the Netherlands, therefore, the conventions work less well than in the past, and it is perhaps doubtful whether they can, in either country, serve as an instrument for attaining consensus for much longer. But it is difficult to see what alternative procedures might be followed which would offer a greater prospect of success in achieving this aim.

IX

The final method of protecting the sovereign from involvement in the government formation process seeks to deprive him of any role whatever in it by transferring his powers to the speaker. That was the solution adopted in Sweden by the 1974 Instrument of Government – in effect the Swedish Constitution – which designated the Speaker of the single-chamber Riksdag as responsible for initiating the government formation process.

Although the Instrument serves to remove the Swedish king from any political involvement, the motive for its promulgation was less a desire on the part of monarchists to safeguard the sovereign, than a feeling on the part of some Social Democrats that a republic would be more in accordance with Sweden's egalitarian society. The 1974 Instrument was a compromise adopted by the Social Democrat leaders designed to satisfy the republicans without depriving the King of his throne.

The new procedure is clearly described in Chapter 6, Articles 2 and 3 of the Instrument:

Art. 2. When a Prime Minister is to be designated the Speaker shall convene representatives of each party group within the Riksdag for consultation. The Speaker shall confer with the Vice Speakers and shall then submit a proposal to the Riksdag. The Riksdag shall proceed to vote on the proposal, not later than on the fourth day thereafter, without preparation within any committee. If more than half of the members of the Riksdag vote against the proposal, it is thereby rejected. In any other case it is approved.

Art. 3. If the Riksdag rejects the proposal of the Speaker the procedure as prescribed in Article 2 shall be resumed. If the Riksdag has rejected the proposal of the Speaker four times the procedure for designating the Prime Minister shall be discontinued and resumed only after elections for the Riksdag have been held. Unless ordinary elections are in any case to be held within three months, extra elections shall be held within the same period of time.

Already in the short life of the new Instrument of Government, two new constitutional conventions have come to be accepted. The first is that when the speaker nominates a prime minister, he will at the same time specify the party composition of the government to be formed. The second is that when one party in a coalition leaves the government, the whole government is obliged to resign, and the speaker initiates the procedure for the formation of a new government. Thus, for example, in 1981 when the Moderates (Conservatives) left the three-party bourgeois government (Moderates, Peoples Party, Centre), because they could not agree to a proposed tax reform, the whole government was deemed to have resigned, and a new government had to be formed.

One of the aims of the 1974 Instrument of Government was to ensure that a left-wing government in Sweden would not suffer from the King's supposed prejudices. But the reformers did not seem to have asked themselves whether the speaker might not be more inclined than the King to manipulate the government formation process: nor did they appreciate the dangers which might follow if the speakership were to become politicised.

The Swedish speaker is elected anew in each parliament. Before the new Instrument, there was a tacit understanding that he should be a member of the majority bloc. But, after the first election following the promulgation of the Instrument, in 1976, the newly victorious bourgeois government agreed to support the existing Social Democrat Speaker, Henry Allard. The main reason for this was that Allard was widely respected by all parties, whereas the leading contender from the bourgeois bloc, the first Vice Speaker, Torsten Bengtson, was not. For this reason, Allard was re-elected as Speaker.

By the time of the next election, however, in 1979, Allard had resigned from Parliament, and the bourgeois bloc, which enjoyed a majority of only one in the Riksdag, decided to put forward its own candidate for the Speakership. This turned out to be not Torsten Bengtson, but instead Allan Hernelius, a leading Conservative parliamentarian. The Social Democrats refused to support a Moderate speaker and proposed as their own candidate, Ingemund Bengtsson. To some surprise, Bengtsson defeated Hernelius in the secret vote for the speakership. There had been one defector from the bourgeois bloc, so allowing Bengtsson to emerge victorious. This defector was assumed to have been Torsten Bengtson, indignant at not being the bourgeois bloc's candidate for the speakership.

These events show how easy it would be for the office of speaker in Sweden to become politicised. The danger would be that the parties choose for this office not a respected politician who can remain above the battle, but a skilful political operator who can be relied upon to offer advantage to his party in the battle for the nomination of a prime minister. The scope for manipulation is in fact quite considerable, since the Instrument regulates only the formal and less contentious part of the government formation process. It offers no other guidance.

It has been reported, although no precise documentation is possible, that, after the general election of 1979 when the Centre Party leader, Thorbjörn Fälldin was having difficulty in forming a three-party bourgeois coalition, Speaker Bengtsson, a Social Democrat, threatened to call on Olof Palme, the Social Democrat leader, if Fälldin did not proceed with speed. Were the Speaker to become publicly identified with partisanship in the government formation process, his position could become impossible since he would lose the respect of one of the blocs in the Riksdag and be unable to chair its proceedings effectively.

An occasion when the speaker could have attempted to manipulate the government formation process, but did not, was in 1981 when as we have seen, the Moderates resigned from the three-party bourgeois coalition, since they objected to the government's proposed tax reform, and the Speaker was required to initiate the government formation process. Since the bourgeois parties had a majority of only one vote over the Social Democrats and Communists, the Speaker might plausibly have defended a decision to call upon Olof Palme, the Social Democrat leader, to form a government, using the argument that the socialist bloc was now the largest in the Riksdag, since the Moderates and the two other bourgeois parties were at loggerheads. In fact, the Speaker asked Fälldin, the Centre Party leader, to remain in power at the head of a two-party government comprising the Centre and the People's Party. But the scope for dispute and controversy in such circumstances could clearly be very great.

The 1974 Instrument, therefore, although it ensures that the Sovereign cannot be involved in political decisions, gives rise to the danger of politicising the speaker. The speaker, indeed, is more likely than the sovereign to misuse his power since he will be a former party politician, whereas a constitutional monarch will not have been identified with any political party, and dare not display political partisanship. Moreover, the sovereign is likely to have enjoyed a longer and more continuous political experience, and he will have been able, from the time he became politically conscious, to keep in touch with the views of the parties through his personal advisers. The sovereign will have been trained from his early years for the responsibilities of government formation: the speaker will not. The sovereign alone has an interest in impartiality. For this reason, the 1974 Instrument of Government in Sweden does not offer a particularly happy solution to the problem of government formation in a constitutional monarchy. The remedy which it proposes is likely to cause more problems than the disease which it seeks to cure.

X

Although the methods used to protect the sovereign in the government formation process of the constitutional monarchies of north-western Europe vary considerably, there are some common themes. The first is that, in each of the countries, the written constitution offers very little guidance as to how the formation of a government should occur. The constitution plays a purely formal role. It may lay down certain general principles, such as the principle of parliamentarism, but, on the whole, constitutions possess, as far as the government formation process is concerned, a purely emblematic significance. They say nothing about the conventions that have arisen during the actual process itself. This is true even of Sweden, where the 1974 Instrument of Government purports to describe the procedure in some detail, but does not indicate how the speaker should be chosen, nor the conventions that should regulate his choice of Prime Minister.

In each of the countries, the early stages of the government formation process tend to be fairly formalised. Generally, the sovereign sees the leaders of all of the parties during the first stage of consultation, or, as in

Belgium, sometimes only the larger parties, in order of size. It is at the ensuing stages of the process that the sovereign's discretion is likely to become a factor in the nomination of a Prime Minister. Indeed, whenever there is the possibility of alternative nominees, it is hard to see how the exercise of discretion on the part of the sovereign can be excluded. In Sweden, the possibility of such discretion is thought intolerable and the sovereign's powers have been transferred to the speaker. In Belgium and the Netherlands, there is general acceptance of the monarch's active role, while in Denmark and Norway the sovereign is expected to act more passively after the British model.

As we have seen, the government formation process appears to operate more successfully in Denmark and Norway than in Belgium and the Netherlands. Although complex institutional arrangements have been devised in Belgium and the Netherlands to safeguard the sovereign from political involvement, there is in practice much more reliance upon the sovereign in those countries to secure the formation of a government which can preserve national unity. For the complexities of the process in Belgium and the Netherlands are a *reflection* and not a *cause* of the difficulties in those countries. The institutionalisation of the office of the informateur is a heroic attempt to create the conditions for consensus in societies which find themselves subject to centrifugal pressures and the continual fear of deadlock and immobilism.

It is a mistake therefore to regard the government formation process as a 'problem' to which there can be a 'solution' whether institutional or otherwise. The need for discretion on the part of the sovereign only gives rise to a 'problem' when there is disagreement on what the proper role of the sovereign should be. Such disagreement existed in Sweden, and was one of the main reasons for the promulgation of the new Instrument of Government in 1974. In Denmark and Norway, on the other hand, there is a wide consensus on the role of the head of state, and so the conventions governing the formation process are generally accepted, even though they do not – and cannot – eliminate the sovereign's discretion. For this discretion is an irreducible element in multi-party politics and it is not to be conjured away either by institutional reforms or by conventional rules of procedure.

In Britain, the whole question of the role of the sovereign has been re-opened by the formation and electoral success of the Liberal/SDP Alliance and the advent of multi-party politics. Constitutional experts are now being asked to pronounce upon how the Queen should act in various hypothetical situations of greater or lesser plausibility. But, if the central argument of this essay has any validity, such an exercise is bound to be a fruitless one. For it is not possible to lay down by fiat a set of conventions or code of conduct to which the sovereign should be expected to adhere. If, as a result of multi-party politics, hung parliaments come to be a regular occurrence in Britain, then, no doubt, conventions regulating the government formation process will arise. But the nature of these conventions cannot be predicted in advance. They will depend upon the extent of agreement between the party leaders and the degree of consensus in society. For constitutional rules, while they may help to create political stability or consensus, are also an expression of social reality. The best safeguard of constitutional monarchy, then, does not lie in any specific set of constitutional rules or conventions: it depends rather upon a general acceptance on the part of both politicians and people that monarchy and democracy are complementary rather than conflicting elements in the government of the modern state. For, as Walt Whitman has affirmed, it is only in logic that contradictions cannot exist.

Notes

1. The main work on the government formation process in multi-party systems is *Regeringsbildningen i flerpartisystem* by Henrik Hermén (Studentlitteratur, Lund, 1975). There is an English summary of Hermerén's ideas at the end of the book, and he has also written an article, 'Government formation in multi-party systems' to be found in *Scandinavian Political Studies* (1976). Future references to Hermerén, however, are to the book.

   Little has been written recently on this topic, and much of what is available is in languages other than English. There are, however, two good texts in English on government in Denmark: Kenneth E. Miller, *Government and Politics in Denmark* (Houghton Mifflin, Boston, 1968), and John Fitzmaurice, *Politics in Denmark* (C. Hurst and Co., London, 1981). Both of these books contain useful discussions of the government formation process in Denmark.

   On the Netherlands, the best work in English is by Jan Vis and is summarised in his essay, 'Coalition government in a constitutional monarchy: the Dutch experience' in *Coalition Government in Western Europe*, edited by Vernon Bogdanor (Heinemann, London, 1983). There is also a useful essay, 'Government formation in the Netherlands' by R.B. Andeweg, Th. van der Tak and K. Dittrich in Richard T. Griffiths (ed.), *The Economy and Politics of the Netherlands since 1945* (Martinus Nijhoff, the Hague, 1980).

   On Belgium, André Molitor, *La Fonction Royale en Belgique* (CRISP, Brussels, 1979) is very illuminating. M. Molitor was himself at one time Secretary to the Belgian king. See also Jan de

Meyer, 'Coalition government in Belgium' in Bogdanor, *op. cit.*, M. Boeynaems, 'Cabinet-formation' in *Res Publica*, 1967, Vol. IX, no. 3, and John Fitzmaurice, *Politics in Belgium: Crisis and Compromise in a Plural Society*, (C. Hurst and Co., London, 1983), pp. 78–84.

Little has so far been written on the working of the new Swedish Instrument of Government *Regeringsbildningen 1978* (Rabén and Sjögren, Lund, 1979). Chapters 8 and 9 deal with the problems raised by the Instrument.

Much of the information in this chapter is derived, however, not from books but from private conversations with officials in the various countries concerned.

2. David Butler, *Governing Without a Majority: Dilemmas for a Hung Parliament in Britain* (Collins, London, 1983); Vernon Bogdanor, *Multi-Party Politics and the Constitution* (Cambridge University Press, Cambridge, 1983).

3. Raymond Fusilier, *Les Monarchies Parlementaires* (Les Editions Ouvrières, Paris, 1960). See also Jan-François Lachaume, 'Le rôle du chef d'État dans les monarchies parlementaires d'aujourd'hui' in *Politique*, 1968.

4. Hans Daalder, 'Cabinets and party systems in ten European democracies', *Acta Politica*, 1971, p. 292.

5. Fusilier, *op. cit.*

6. Hermerén, *op. cit.*

7. Tony Benn, 'Power, parliament and people', *New Socialist*, September–October 1972.

8. Boeynaems, *op. cit.*, p. 477 (my translation).

9. *Le Soir*, 23 March 1935; quoted in Boeynaems, *op. cit.*, p. 493 (my translation).

10. Hermerén, *passim*.

11. de Meyer in Bogdanor, *op. cit.*, p. 199.

12. Vis in Bogdanor, *op. cit.*, p. 15but there is an excellent account of the 1978 government formation process in Sweden in Olof Petersson, 4.

13. Boeynaems, *op. cit.*, p. 488 (my translation).

14. Hermerén, *op. cit.*, pp. 141–3.

4 Dual Leadership in the Contemporary World: A Step towards Executive and Regime Stability?
Jean Blondel

To progress, comparative politics has to marry the general and the specific, cross-cultural analyses and in-depth country studies. It must do so, above all, on the basis of real political developments and not merely on *a priori* conceptualisations. Perhaps no one has been better able to achieve this result in recent years than S.E. Finer whose *Comparative Government* and *Man on Horseback* are in the tradition of the works of Aristotle, Montesquieu, Bryce, and Lowell, a tradition which, in the past, helped us to discover a number of basic trends while enabling us to pay attention to the characteristics of individual countries and situations. Thus the pathology – for example of military regimes – is becoming better known, and we are gradually coming closer to an understanding of the political and social conditions which are likely to make goverments less chaotic and more effective.

S.E. Finer's efforts teach us to look out for institutions, procedural arrangements, and behavioural patterns that cut across types of regimes and ideologies; we can then undertake better cross-country comparisons by identifying similarities that are not culture-bound. It is probably because the phenomenon of military intervention is so widespread that progress has been relatively rapid in this area; but progress can also be made in other fields despite the fact that, ostensibly at least, the political institutions of many Third World regimes are weak and formal. Rather than trying to imagine schemes that, like many of those that have been presented in the last decades, lose touch with the reality of the political system, we can achieve more by looking for characteristics that can be found in the political life of the countries themselves.

Much can indeed be gained if we examine closely the institutional arrangements that exist. For instance, there is still an immense ignorance about the life and organisation of political parties outside the Western world. Reliable information, indeed information *tout court*, may perhaps be difficult to obtain, but one is also sometimes over-inclined to exaggerate the difficulties, while at the same time dismissing some parties as having little influence on the political system. Similar comments can be made about other institutions. They are not described adequately; not enough effort is made to see whether comparable arrangements exist in other countries. A lack of knowledge of this kind relates to the structure of the executive, despite the fact that the arrangements and behavioural patterns through which leaders and ministers exercise their power are vastly different and can therefore be compared. It is possible to obtain information on the composition and duration of executives and thus have a clearer picture of the extent and type of experiences which are shared by the rulers of different countries.

Within the executive, the nature and characteristics of leadership deserve special attention. Yet so far this has been done in a rather superficial manner, largely because we seem to lack the means of examining concretely the extent and limits of the leaders' powers. Obviously, progress in this field will be slow, as so much depends on personalities and even on chance. But there are also some regularities which are more than occasionally translated into institutions and procedural arrangements. We usually know what these arrangements are in Western countries as well as in liberal countries elsewhere. We could try harder to delineate the arrangements which prevail in other countries. In the Communist case, for example, the basic division between party and state provides an important clue; elsewhere there are also some meaningful distinctions, two of which are relatively recent and deserve to be explored more fully.

One of these distinctions results from the setting-up, in many Third World countries, of military or revolutionary councils. Despite differences in importance, these councils seem to play an interesting part in the process by which new regimes and new leaders attempt to associate some men and some groups with decision-making. But another institutional development is even more widespread; this is the arrangement by which overall power is shared by two leaders. Dualism has so far been studied very little, except in the special cases of the French Fifth Republic, Finland and Portugal. Yet the development is far from confined to those countries; almost a third of the national executives are currently organised on a dual basis and they include traditional monarchical governments as well as communist systems, authoritarian semi-presidential systems as well as liberal regimes.

If the arrangement is so common and so widely adopted, does this not mean that it is viewed as a means of solving common problems faced by modern government? And does this not also mean that similar solutions are being sought irrespective of the ideological character and the level of socio-economic development of the country concerned?

Why has so little attention been paid to dual leadership as a form of government? To be sure, the phenomenon – as a world-wide development – is a recent one. But this is not the only reason for the lack of interest; it seems more probable that many believe that dualism is inherently a transitional arrangement, except perhaps in very special circumstances, as in the Lebanon. Dualism indeed tends to be viewed as part of the process by which, in eighteenth and nineteenth-century Europe, monarchies gradually lost power. Moreover, it is probably also believed that either dualism exists only on paper (for example, where the prime minister is deemed to be no more than an exalted '*chef de cabinet*') or, on the contrary, that it leads to serious clashes between the two leaders. One can indeed point to instances in the recent past where such clashes have occurred and have led to great instability. For example, in Zaire, at the time of independence, the opposition between President Kasavubu and Prime Minister Lumumba may have been fostered by dualism since both leaders had an independent power base. Similarly, the opposition between hereditary ruler and prime minister led to political upheavals in Uganda and Burundi. Such experiences suggest that dual leadership has little to recommend it.

Yet these are only a small proportion of the cases in which dual leadership currently obtains. The periods and countries in which severe clashes have occurred between king or president and prime minister are the exception, the rule being for the two leaders to conduct their relations in apparent and indeed effective harmony. These exceptions are probably no more numerous than the examples of malfunctioning of parliamentary systems, and they are indeed less numerous than the many cases of malfunctioning of constitutional presidential systems. Such occurrences need to be accounted for; but they should be accounted for in the context of the general influence of dual leadership on political life.

How then should a dual leadership be defined? A dual leadership system is one in which two, and only two, men or women share formally, effectively, and in a continuous manner in the general affairs of the government. Such persons would usually be a monarch or president. It excludes the cases in which the head of state has a symbolic role only, and it also excludes the cases in which a council or a junta of more than two persons constitutes the collective leadership. Such councils are exceptional; rarely do more than two persons become involved in a continuous manner in the conduct of governmental affairs.

Within the context of an arrangement in which two men share effectively the general running of the affairs of the state, however, there is ample scope for variations in the manner in which this sharing takes place. The leaders may be more or less equal in status and influence, or they may be unequal; they may decide to oversee jointly all the major policy decisions, or they may decide, formally or informally, to divide the burden according to fields or even degree of importance. The division of responsibility is also likely to vary over time. Thus the dual leadership system is most flexible; it is indeed this flexibility which constitutes one of the attractions of the arrangement, although a process of institutionalisation may nonetheless be taking place.

Where dual leadership occurs
The number of dual leadership systems has increased markedly in recent years, especially in the 1970s; but the geographical spread is not uniform. Western countries have rarely shown any desire, or felt any need to adopt it. Before 1958, Finland was the only example. Then came the French Fifth Republic and, in 1974, Portugal, but the last may be in the process of reverting to parliamentary rule, although the President is attempting to retain some influence. In Spain, dual leadership prevailed for a while at the end of the Franco regime and at the beginning of the new monarchy, but power had been transferred wholly to the prime minister; the period of dual leadership was there truly transitional and transitory – transitory in that it lasted less than a decade, transitional in that it enabled Spain to move from Franco's dictatorship to a fully-fledged parliamentary democracy in the smoothest of manners.

Nor has dual leadership been popular in Latin America, where Peru provides the only long-standing and not altogether felicitous example, although, as we shall see, the system might benefit the countries of the sub-continent. However, elsewhere in the world, dual leadership has truly flourished. It has been widely adopted in the communist countries; it has existed for substantial periods in some monarchies and it has been maintained or reintroduced occasionally when these monarchies were replaced by republics; and it has been adopted in a substantial number of African and Asian countries that had previously been presidential (and occasionally parliamentary): this is where the arrangement has proved to be truly popular (see Appendix I to this chapter).

Dual monarchies
The most traditional form of dual leadership is the one which now is the least common – the dual monarchy. The king and prime minister system, which has existed in Britain, Sweden, and some other Western European countries since the eighteenth or nineteenth centuries, has been adopted, in the course of the twentieth century, by a number of

non-European monarchies, such as Egypt, Iraq, Jordan, Ethiopia, Nepal, and Morocco. But most of these states became Republics in the course of the post-war period; Jordan, Nepal, and Morocco are the principal cases of dual monarchies in the 1980s. Although a similar system has begun slowly to be introduced in the monarchies of the Arabian Peninsula (Kuwait, United Arab Emirates), most of the countries in the area are ruled by a king or emir who also holds the position of prime minister.

Clearly, the importance of dualism with respect to monarchical systems has become limited. Clearly, too, the system has been transitional in most cases, but it has provided a transition which has lasted many decades in a number of countries, such as Jordan or Morocco, but also Iran or Ethiopia. Where, as in Spain, the transition was rapid, it has undoubtedly helped the country to move in a stable manner from one type of political system to another. Moreover, if the dualist system has not prevented many monarchies from being replaced by republics, it has delayed the process in some cases and it may even have made the evolution towards a parliamentary system occasionally possible. Indeed, some of the republics that were established after the fall of the monarchies have kept the dual system as one of the traditions inherited from the previous regime (for example, Egypt, Iran).

Communist systems

If dualism has been transitional in monarchies, it does not have this character any longer in communist systems. In European and north Asian communist countries at least, it has become a near-universal rule for the positions of party secretary and of prime minister to be held by two different men. This has reversed a trend which seemed at one point to prevail in the Soviet Union and in some other communist states and which suggested that dual or collective leadership corresponded only to the scramble for power in the aftermath of a change of leader. In fact, there were already in the early post-war years several exceptions to the single leadership of the party secretary, for example China, North Vietnam or Albania; since the 1950s and 1960s, however, dual leadership has become the norm. While Khruschev eventually displaced Bulganin and took over the chairmanship of the Council of Ministers, his successor, Brezhnev, seemed content to rule in collaboration with Kosygin. So far, in eastern Europe and north Asia, the trend has been reversed in only one case, that of Poland, where, in the middle of the 'Solidarity' crisis, the party secretary, Jaruzelski, assumed the position of prime minister as well. Moreover, the distinction has been reinforced by the increasingly common practice in the 1970s in some communist countries of the party secretary becoming not prime minister, but head of state; this took place in the Soviet Union, Bulgaria, Czechoslovakia, East Germany and Romania (but not in Poland and Hungary). Thus the top structure of many communist states resembles the top structure of the third type of dual leadership systems to which we are coming, the semi-presidential republics.

This evolution may have coincided with a change in the relative position of the two leaders, however. In the early post-war period, when dual leadership was the exception and several party secretaries were also prime ministers, the sharing of power tended to correspond, where it existed, to situations of relative equality between two 'comrades-in-arms'; this was the case in China, North Vietnam, and Albania, although, admittedly, even in these countries, the top leader was clearly the party secretary. Since the 1960s the institutionalisation of dual leadership appears to have corresponded to the generalisation of a hierarchical arrangement, the prime minister being markedly 'below' the party secretary. For instance, although communist prime ministers stay in office for long periods (from eight to ten years), they are nonetheless replaced more frequently than, and apparently at the instigation of, the party secretary, whether or not he is also president. Perhaps this hierarchical relationship has prevented conflicts between the two leaders and has contributed to the maintenance of the arrangement, for, in the present state of development of communist countries, dual leadership has been fully adopted and is part of the institutional structure.

Semi-presidential republics

While there was always a potential for dual leadership in communist countries in view of the division between party and state and while the evolution of monarchies seems to lead naturally to at least a period of dual leadership, only recently has such an arrangement been widely adopted in republican regimes; traditionally, republics were presidential in the strict constitutional sense, occasionally parliamentary and, if they were not liberal, purely and simply absolutist. In the late 1940s, there were only six cases of semi-presidential dualist systems – in Finland, Peru, the Lebanon, Syria, South Korea, and Indonesia; a quarter of a century later, over two dozen republics were of this type. Although the number of independent countries markedly increased during the period, the expansion of dual leadership was more than proportional.

Black Africa is the area where the change from single presidential rule to a dual leadership system occurred most frequently. In the early 1960s, only Zaire and Somalia had a dual system; elsewhere, a form of parliamentary or prime ministerial system was often adopted at first, soon to be transformed into strong presidential rule. From the early 1970s, in many countries, this presidential rule became somewhat modified by the appointment of prime ministers, both in civilian and in military regimes. Sometimes the appointment was short-lived and the post of prime minister quickly abolished, but the arrangement survived in about a dozen Black African countries. Meanwhile, similar developments, though not quite on the same scale, occurred in North Africa, the Middle East, and South Asia; thus Tunisia, Algeria, Burma, and Sri Lanka, for instance, acquired a dual system. In Sri Lanka, the change occurred after decades during which a parliamentary system had functioned relatively smoothly and in a pluralistic context; thus dualism is making inroads in liberal Commonwealth countries as well as in more authoritarian or 'charismatic' presidential polities.

Dual leadership has thus ceased to be primarily a transitional arrangement by which monarchs gradually lose power to the people's representatives; it has become a mechanism used by many presidents of new states – both civilian and military – to devolve some of their powers to someone of their choice who continues to depend on them, but who nonetheless may exercise considerable influence. By doing so, these presidents begin to institutionalise the national executive, even if it is only to a limited extent and, in the early period in particular, even if the institutionalisation remains weak. This cannot but have some effects on the president's power and freedom of manoeuvre; one can see why the experiment is sometimes abandoned, indeed at times very quickly, while the return to single-man rule may also occur after many years, as in Senegal. But, in the majority of cases, the new institutional arrangement is maintained. The repeated occurrence of this phenomenon in such diverse countries and regimes surely suggests that leaders are conscious of a need and that some problems can be solved by the appointment of a prime minister. What is the nature of this need and does dual leadership appear able to meet it?

The raison d'être for dual leadership

It is of course difficult to know why, in each case, a dual arrangement is set up. In the French example, the best documented of all, there was little consciousness of the change which was taking place. De Gaulle did not state categorically in 1958 what the relationship between president and prime minister was to be; French politicians seemed content to leave the matter in a state of some obscurity, as there was fear that the post of prime minister might be abolished and a fully-fledged presidential system instituted. There was probably much relief in many quarters that de Gaulle did not go further and settled for a half-way system. In other countries the specific motivations of leaders are even less well-known. But, if these cannot be fully assessed, one can at least discover from the way the political system developed since the introduction of dualism a number of reasons that singly or in combination provide a case for a dual system.

Five such reasons stand out as most important. The first results from the existence of a variety of political constituencies which no leader alone can control and which have to be represented jointly at the top. The second, which may over time lead to the first, stems from the need to manage groups of politicians outside the government (for instance in an assembly). The third reason relates to the desire to administer the country more efficiently, while the fourth comes from the need felt by the head of state to allow his probable successor to familiarise himself with the decision-making process. Finally, dual leadership may also result, in a more diffuse manner, from the desire of the head of state to keep some distance apart from 'ordinary' politics.

Existence of two political constituencies

The first two reasons relate generally to the characteristics of the broader political system. In one case, however, there are groups, ethnic, religious, or political, which have to be represented at the top, while, in the other, the head of state needs an 'agent' who will manage for him the wider political world. In the first case, the two leaders are equal or near-equal; the prime minister is indispensable. His removal might lead to such difficulties that it becomes in practice unthinkable. Indeed, the arrangement may become wholly institutionalised; in the Lebanon, which is, however, the only example of a clear-cut division of this type, the prime minister represents the Moslems and the president represents the Christians. Such a division has been or was relatively harmonious in that country until the Palestinian issue arose, but, elsewhere, arrangements of this kind have tended to be unstable, as they have corresponded to moments in the fights of various tribal or ethnic groups to exercise predominance: Zaire, Uganda, or Burundi at the time of independence are good examples of such situations.

A division among political constituencies can also be said to exist, at least after a period, in dual monarchies. Originally, prime ministers are appointed in these countries as agents of the monarch and with a view to ensuring the loyalty of politically-relevant groups; the increased role of parliaments and of the representative process, however, tends to lead to a cleavage between the political support for the monarch and the political support for the prime minister. In western Europe, the opposition between the two leaders led to the gradual withdrawal of the monarch, who normally agreed to play just a symbolic part; when he did not, or when he re-asserted his position after having accepted to be a parliamentary head of state, serious conflicts occurred. These sometimes led to the end of the monarchy. This was to be the case in Burundi and Uganda, for instance, though divisions in these countries were, as we saw, tribal and ethnic as well. It is because they are based on a division between two political constituencies that dual monarchies have tended to be transitional, although, in many cases, the transition lasted for several decades.

Political management
While the prime minister may ultimately acquire a constituency of his own in a dual monarchy, the political *raison d'être* for the creation of his office is typically different; it is to manage the political elite. This was clearly the case in Britain in the eighteenth century; this is also the case in several semi-presidential republics of the contemporary world, in particular France. The role of the prime minister is to help the king or president to ensure that some political groups which either might be hostile or, more often, might show sings of declining loyalty are kept within the fold. The prime minister can only fulfil this role, of course, if he is close to these groups and is an influential number of a party or of the legislature: but this is not to say that he has a 'constituency' of his own, especially one which is distinct from that of the head of state. This may well tend to occur over the years, but, so long as the prime minister is only, so to speak, a 'technician' who applies his skills to control the groups that are necessary for the government's political survival, there need not be a conflict with the head of state. To some extent at least, this is still the position in Morocco; such was also the situation in Iraq before the fall of the monarchy. But there are dangers, especially in a monarchical system where the head of state cannot claim a democratic legitimacy and has to rely on traditional loyalty.

These dangers are much less marked in semi-presidential republics where there is not – or there need not be – a different legitimacy base for the two leaders. Presidents have popular support – or they might claim that they have. Either they have been directly elected or they came to power with the aim of 'cleaning' a political system which in their opinion was detrimental to the well-being of the people. They therefore can assert that they have overall authority and normally the prime minister is in no position to challenge this ascendancy.

Administrative management
Dual leadership also exists for reasons of administrative management. Indeed, prime ministers were appointed by monarchs in the past in part in order to achieve better coordination between the ministries: in England and Sweden this administrative role was at least as prominent

as the political role. With the modern expansion of government services, heads of state are likely to feel that they neither have the time nor the technical competence to supervise and give impetus to ministers and civil servants.

Thus, almost certainly, the requirements of administrative management are at the root of most, if not all, the dual leadership arrangements which exist in the contemporary world. This is particularly true in communist states where the division of the whole decision-making structure into a party and a state hierarchy makes the existence of the office of prime minister logical, if not necessary. The demands for coordination are obviously particularly pressing in a governmental system in which the public sector compromises a large number of activities, especially industrial. It would therefore be unrealistic to expect the party leader, whether or not he is also head of state, to be effectively in charge of coordination; this is indeed the main function of the prime minister, although he will collaborate, in these matters as in others, with the party secretary.

Administrative management is also the *raison d'être* for the existence of the office of prime minister in semi-presidential republics. In the early years of the French Fifth Republic, de Gaulle did point out that this was indeed the main role of the prime minister, thereby also reminding the head of the government that he was not to be too deeply involved in what might be called 'high politics'. This situation changed somewhat after de Gaulle left power; the division between two levels – 'high politics' and administration – has consequently become more blurred, in part because French presidents have been markedly involved in matters of administrative management, but in part also because French prime ministers have been seen to be deeply interested in questions both of defence and of foreign policy (especially with respect to Europe). Nonetheless the function of administrative management does remain one of the main aspects of the activities of the prime minister.

Similar considerations obtain in much of the developing world, in part because the need for technical development makes administrative management increasingly complex and in part because presidents wish to see their load lightened by someone who can supervise more closely the activities of the bureaucracy. Prime ministers can also be replaced if and when their ability to coodinate the administration becomes less impressive.

The succession process
The fourth *raison d'être* for dual leadership is to help smooth the succession process. Leaders have long attempted, with more or less

success, to play a part in the selection of those who follow them. The hereditary mechanism was obviously the best means of achieving that goal. But, with the virtual ending of the hereditary principle as a means of appointing rulers, a more circuitous route has to be discovered. Thus leaders who wish to have an influence on their country's policies after they leave office try and prepare the ground by placing someone whom they trust in a key position which comes to be recognised as a natural stepping-stone to the office that they hold. They can meanwhile train this potential successor in the problems they will face when they become rulers. The office of prime minister tends naturally to fit this type of strategy; it seems more flexible than that of vice president, which is sometimes used, however, to select future presidents, as occurred for instance in Kenya. Prime ministers can be appointed and dismissed without ceremony, while vice presidents, who are normally elected for a specific term, cannot be easily changed if they appear unsuited to become successors. Moreover, prime ministers are naturally more involved in governmental affairs than are vice presidents; there is a supernumerary and at most a purely political character to a vice-presidential office which the position of prime minister does not display.

Although the office of prime minister has sometimes been instituted in order to prepare the succession of the head of state, this is probably rarely the only consideration, despite the fact that President Diouf of Senegal stated that the reason for the abolition of the post in 1983 was that the succession had taken place from President Senghor and that there was therefore no longer a need for a prime minister. Naturally enough, new and perhaps less 'charismatic' presidents may be wary of prime ministers who might be too readily viewed as potential successors; this was indeed why the office had already been abolished once before in Senegal by President Senghor himself in the early years of his presidency. But the succession aspect is usually only one factor; it even appears to be of little or no significance in the European dual leadership systems, in the Communist States and, indeed, in many semi-presidential systems of the Third World.

Standing aloof
Finally, the head of state might wish to appoint a prime minister in order to be relieved from the burden of daily politics. This may be particularly the case with older leaders whose interest in political life has declined and who may wish to concentrate on a limited range of matters – foreign affairs, for example. But even newer and younger leaders may like to be able to keep some distance from current problems; they may especially wish to avoid having to adjudicate

between ministers on secondary issues which are likely to undermine their authority. Admittedly, even in single leadership presidential systems, there are 'filters' which stop many matters from coming to the chief executive. But, if the persons involved in the dispute are influential, if, for example, they are ministers, the presidential aides who act as 'filters' may not be able to prevent the matter from reaching the leader. A prime minister is better able to act because he holds a formal position.

The case for dual leadership is thus strong. Although the result must be a reduction in the ability of monarchs and presidents to exercise full discretion, some substantial advantages accrue to them. Indeed, the appointment of a prime minister may seem inevitable in the context of the growth and increased complexity of government services. It may therefore not be surprising that the arrangement should have currently become popular and should appear to serve the interests of many rulers. How far, however, do these advantages also contribute to a genuine improvement of the political process? Does dual leadership have a measurable and positive impact on the characteristics of political life?

The value of dual leadership

Dual leadership and political stability
Even a rapid survey of the *raison d'être* for dual leadership suggests that this arrangement can help to solve some of the difficulties which contemporary leaders can face. But, beyond these technical advantages, it is not immediately clear, either from past or from present evidence, that dual leadership improves significantly the overall character of the political process. It is difficult to measure degrees of administrative efficiency or achievements in political management, but levels of regime stability are not apparently noticeably improved under a dual leadership system. In some cases, as in France, Portugal, or Spain, dual leadership had a significant effect on the system, but there have been also many failures.

The countries of the contemporary world that have been ruled jointly by two leaders have not been distinctly better run that those in which there has been a single executive. In Black Africa, *coups* have taken place in about the same proportion in countries in which the dual leadership system has been introduced and in countries in which more classical forms of 'charismatic' presidential rule have prevailed. Even a detailed analysis does not reveal any systematic difference between countries that have experienced dual leadership and those that have not in terms of the longevity or resistance to succession crises of these regimes. If Senegal, Cameroon, Gabon, or Zambia have been stable under dual leadership, others, such as Upper Volta, have not. Elsewhere in the world, while Tunisia or Burma have been stable since the experiment of dual leadership has been introduced, Korea, Syria, or Peru have had *coups* or other forms of political upheaval. And a number of countries have had stable systems of government without having experienced dual leadership.

But it would be wrong to halt the examination at this point and conclude that dual leadership has no effect on the behaviour of the political system as a whole. First, it is clearly premature to draw conclusions from current evidence, as dual leadership has been introduced recently in many countries. Second, and more importantly, the analysis of the characteristics of dual leadership suggests that there is a need to distinguish between cases in which the system is based on two leaders who have a different power base and those in which there is a common source to the authority of these leaders or indeed where the authority of one leader buttresses that of the other. Only if the two leaders operate in harmony will the arrangement be viable, let alone, likely to increase the stability of the regime. However, as there *are* two leaders, there is no guarantee that there shall be harmony; there has to be something more than the institution of dual leadership, namely the existence of a power configuration in which the two leaders are made to work together and are prevented from believing that things would be better for themselves and for the country if each of them were to decide to take overall control.

It is because dual leadership systems can create frequent sources of conflict that they have often been, and will continue to be in some cases, rather unsuccessful. What happened after independence in countries such as Zaire, Burundi, or Somalia, where the two leaders were antagonistic, weak, or both, is an indication of the way in which dual systems may go: *coups* then occur and the dual leadership system may be abolished in the process.

Harmony between the leaders can be achieved in a number of ways. There can be real comradeship, resulting for instance from a long common struggle during a war of independence; there can be the recognition, as in the communist states, that both leaders are part of an institutional structure which they have to manage, but cannot change or replace; there can be a hierarchy, by which one of the leaders recognises the authority of the other leader, his greater legitimacy base, although there is genuine sharing in the decision-making process. This last type of arrangement is perhaps the easiest to achieve in a situation in which political structures are relatively weak and where the dual leadership system is part of nation and institution-building. In general, the dual leadership system can be really successful in the long term only if head of state and prime minister have broadly the same constituency, although there may be exceptions as, for example, when there is a high dose of 'consociationalism' (as there is, or was, in the Lebanon). Such cases are exceptional, precisely because they require the pre-existence of a political culture which has successfully solved problems of legitimacy and of nation-building.

But it is not sufficient to have a 'top leader' who has greater authority than the 'second' leader. To be effective, a dual leadership system also needs to be based on a genuine devolution of power to the prime minister. The prime minister has to be, and seen to be, influential, albeit within the context of the policies of the head of state. The arrangement gives the 'top leader' a breathing space, because he can remain at some distance from daily political life. It is as if the prime minister operated as a 'shock-absorber'; if he appears to be unsuccessful, he can be replaced by another who might have greater appeal. But skill has to be displayed by the head of state if the prime minister is indeed to fulfil this role of 'shock-absorber'. Although the head of state must in this type of arrangement retain the ultimate power to dismiss and replace, he should not do so too often (this might be the case in Jordan) because the prime minister may then have little influence, or too infrequently (this was the case in the years before the Iranian revolution) because the policies of the prime minister may then appear undistinguishable from those of the head of state. The head of state must show that he is a leader, and not merely a spectator; but he must not intervene so much that the prime minister's role becomes unclear, both to himself and to others. The dual system thus provides an opportunity, but only if a middle course is adopted between interference and passivity.

A dual leadership system thus needs two leaders who respect each other, who can count on each other, and who can work in harmony. The 'top' leader must have genuine authority, but the prime minister must be able to influence and indeed direct the administration while also having some effect on the political elite. This is a tall order – not one which any country can automatically stumble on, but one which requires, on the part of the leaders, a clear understanding of goals and a subtle sense of the extent and limits of the exercise of power. Such a system takes time to establish itself. Premature abolition, as in a number of African states (Benin, Gambia, Mali, Upper Volta, for example), may simply mean that the arrangement has not been tried out. The equilibrium point will be found only gradually. Almost certainly, the role of the head of state is too large in many current cases; perhaps it was too small in some of the early post-independence situations. The dual leadership system offers a challenge; if the opportunity is missed, the arrangement may prove as unable as any other to provide countries with regime stability.

Dual leadership and stable liberal systems

Dual leadership may not merely be examined from the angle of the stability of political systems in general; it can also be assessed as a mechanism designed to help countries to achieve stability within a pluralistic context. Clearly, dual leadership systems have, to a greater or lesser degree, helped some Western countries to achieve better results. France is the outstanding example; dual leadership brought about, somewhat unexpectedly, a major improvement in the political stability and indeed responsiveness of the government. But similar conclusions can be drawn, though in a less clear-cut manner, about Portugal; the President's intervention has probably prevented party divisions from leading to a crisis of regime – indeed parties have occasionally come closer together in order to avoid leaving the president with an open field for intervention. In neighbouring Spain, the authority of the king has given strength to the early governments of the new democracy and helped the development of a responsible party system.

In general, however, dual leadership systems have not been used so far consciously to promote a stable liberal system. This is almost certainly because the arrangement is not normally viewed as a 'system' in its own right, to be compared to the parliamentary – or prime ministerial – systems and to the presidential system, which are the only two types of arrangements commonly regarded as able to insure a working liberal regime. Yet it is worth examining the potential of dual leadership in view of the clear inability of both parliamentary and 'constitutional' presidential systems to make substantial inroads in the Third World.

While the parliamentary system has worked satisfactorily in most of Western Europe, in the Old Commonwealth and, indeed, in parts of the New Commonwealth, it has clearly not been successful elsewhere; even in the Commonwealth, especially in Africa, it has been abandoned for varieties of 'charismatic' presidential regimes. Outside the Commonwealth, except in Japan and Israel, the parliamentary system has usually not been adopted at all or it has quickly been replaced, often by a *coup*, by authoritarian presidential regimes as well.

For genuine motives or not, the parliamentary system has been blamed by those who have abolished it for being unable to provide strong leadership and for fostering divisions among irresponsible legislators. This, of course, is not true of all parliamentary systems, but an effective and streamlined party system is needed if these consequences are to be avoided. The French pre-1958 experience, as well as that of other southern European states, shows that, without such a party system, parliamentarism does give rise to semi-anarchic 'assembly rule' and to ineffective government. *Coups* are therefore possible or even likely. This has been the usual scenario in Third World countries where parliamentary government was at first established. It has been avoided in some Commonwealth countries not merely because of luck but because of the establishment of strong party systems in the British tradition (India, Malaysia, Jamaica, Mauritius).

As it is not possible suddenly to engineer a pluralistic party system which has no roots in the society, the only liberal alternative appears to be the setting up of a constitutional presidential system. This seems to have advantages, as presidentialism does not rely so directly on a party system since the president is elected directly and for a fixed term. But the experience of Latin America and of the few other countries in which constitutional presidentialism was introduced (Philippines) shows that there are other defects which may even be more dangerous to the maintenance of liberal government. Presidentialism extols the prestige of the chief executive. He can exercise leadership, but as there are limits to presidential power (such as the right to stand for a second or third term, the power of the legislature which he cannot control), the temptation is great to use his 'leadership' to by-pass the system. If it embodies the principle of separation of powers with no provision for a constitutional mechanism to bring about a solution (such as the right of dissolution or the censure motion), the presidential system will tend to lead to an escalation in the struggle between the 'powers' and, ultimately, to 'caesarism' because of the elevated position in which the chief executive is placed by the constitution itself.

Thus neither parliamentarism nor constitutional presidentialism can be expected to bring about a solution to the problems of a country in which efforts are made to set up a pluralist system but where the party configuration is weak or insufficiently streamlined. A dual leadership system, on the other hand, may be able to provide a combination of authority and flexibility which can create the necessary conditions for a more stable liberal regime. In a parliamentary system, the president needs the support of the majority of the chamber to keep his government in office; this may be difficult to achieve if the party system is inchoate. But, as the president is elected for a substantial period by universal suffrage, he has authority and can be expected to rally at least some of the political waverers to himself and to his government. The party system may then become better organised. The system is not foolproof, but it gives the executive a breathing-space as well as some means of exercising pressure on the chamber, for instance through dissolution and a share in the government.

This is, indeed, how the party system gradually became streamlined in France under the Fifth Republic and, to a more limited extent, how it came to have a degree of cohesion in Portugal. This has not happened in Peru, admittedly, probably because the president has tended, by and large, to appoint technicians as prime ministers and has exercised power in ways which have been little different from those of chief executives in strict presidential systems. A greater stress on the relationship between prime minister, government, and the congress might have had, and might have in the future, some positive effect.

Dual leadership is no panacea for the success of liberal democracy. Its achievements in France and a small number of other Western countries do at least signify, however, that there are interesting potentialities in the mechanism. The system creates links between president, government, and the rest of the political forces which may sometimes produce tensions but which may also bring about the necessary combination of authority and pluralism on which liberal government has to be based if it is to be stable. In this chain, the prime minister constitutes a vital element because his own somewhat more accessible position enables the president to remain more distant and therefore to keep some of the authority which, in turn, the prime minister requires in his relations with the chamber. But such a result can be brought about only if the various actors, and the president and the prime minister in the first place, recognise the importance of their respective roles while consciously endeavouring not to overstep these roles. The temptation is always great for presidents to order about prime ministers or to act in their place; and the prime minister, who may occasionally not have enough real political power of his own, may even concur in the reduction of his own influence. In such a case, dual leadership cannot provide the links or the 'shock-absorbers'; the system may then go the same way as many constitutional presidential systems have gone in the past.

Whatever its relative success and failures in different types of political systems, the dual leadership arrangement provides an interesting departure from the more established and better studied institutional structures of government. Successes have been balanced by failures in dual leadership systems, but no more and indeed probably less than in other forms of government. It seems that dual leadership can provide modern states with a framework which can, slowly perhaps, lead them towards less arbitrary forms of government and might even bring about stability in liberal political systems which had not known it before. Thus, at the least dual leadership systems need to be studied and assessed, both in general and in the specific context of various experiments; it is also worthwhile pressing for its introduction in countries where the political arrangements have not, so far, given much cause for comfort.

Appendix I

Dual leadership in the contemporary world
(countries that became independent before 1975 only)

Atlantic countries

Finland	1945–present
France	1958–present
Portugal	1974–present?
Spain	1981

Eastern Europe and north Asia

Albania	1945–present
Bulgaria	1954–present
China	1952–76/1981–present
Czechoslovakia	1948–present
East Germany	1949–present
Hungary	1953–present
North Korea	1973–present
Mongolia	1974–present
Poland	1947–1981
Rumania	1955–present
USSR	1953–57/1964–present
North Vietnam	1954–present
Yugoslavia	1965–present

Middle East and north Africa

Algeria	1980–present
Bahrein	?1963–present
Iran	1945–present
Iraq	1945–1958/1963–1968
Jordan	1945–present
Kuwait	1963–present
Lebanon	1945–present
Libya	?1952–present
Morocco	1956–9/1964–5/1968–present
Saudi Arabia	1962–1964
Syria	1945–51/1954–present
Tunisia	1970–present
Turkey	?1962–65/1981–present
Egypt (UAR)	1945–52/1954–5/1962–6/1971–2/ 1975–80/1982–present
Yemen Arab Republic	1964–66/1968–present
United Arab Emirates	1972–present

South and South-east Asia

Burma	1974–present
Cambodia	1954–60/1963–78
Sri Lanka	1978–present
Taiwan	1945–present
Indonesia	1949–58
South Korea	1949–50/1952–3/1954–8/1961–present
Laos	?1954–present
Maldive Republic	?1960–69/1973–74
Nepal	1951–54/1956–60/1963–present
Philippines	1982–present
South Vietnam	1964–75
Bangla Desh	1975/1980–present

Africa south of Sahara

Benin	1967
Botswana	1966–74
Burundi	1962–66/1977
Cameroon	1976–present
Central African Republic	1975–present
Chad	1979
Congo	1964–8/1976–present
Ethiopia	1945–74
Gabon	1976–present
Gambia	1975–76
Guinea	1973–present
Lesotho	?1966–present
Madagascar	1976–present
Mali	1968–69
Mauretania	1979/1981–present
Senegal	1960–62/1970–83
Sierra Leone	1971–75
Somalia	1960–69
Swaziland	?1968–present
Tanzania	1977–present
Uganda	1981–present
Upper Volta	1971–73/1979–80
Zaire	1960–66/1978–present
Zambia	1974–present

Latin America

Brazil	1961–62
Cuba	1945–51/?1958–76
Guyana	1981–present
Peru	1945–present

5 Pressure Groups and Pressured Groups in Franco-British Perspective
Jack Hayward

Preliminary clarifications

There is some dispute about what Goethe meant by his expiring phrase: 'Light! More light', the evocative words with which S.E. Finer concludes his *Anonymous Empire*. However, there is no scintilla of doubt about what Finer intended to commend by this invocation of the embodiment of the Enlightenment. Having asserted that 'For better or for worse, such self-government as we [in Britain] now enjoy is one that operates by and through the Lobby', he sought to make this major adaptation of the liberal democratic process more open and transparent.[1] In the process, he fired an early salvo in the continuing battle over the coercively-enforced official secrecy which shrouds the processes of British government. However, in his laudable desire to prescribe arrangements that were in closer conformity with the liberal democratic ideal, Finer omitted to follow to its conclusion the logic of the new style of government-group relations on which his pioneering study directed a searing shaft of light. For, if the pluralistic conception of groups as intermediaries between the public and the government is to be effectively fulfilled by a permanent, participatory dialogue, their transactions need to be shielded from the light of publicity, *at least while the negotiations are proceeding*. If the mutual concessions being proffered are revealed prematurely, both the governmental and group elites may be compelled to withdraw them because of ensuing tumult. The controversy may be aroused either by the inquisitive press as self-designated defenders of the public interest or by dissentient or rank-and-file members of groups who consider themselves about to be betrayed by their leaders' failure to hold out for the maximum group demands.

Such official secrecy may of course be carried to a ridiculous extreme or simply be a device to protect elected or appointed state officials from individual accountability for their actions or inactions.[2] However, the need to preserve confidentiality – for a period of years – of the proceedings of the cabinet, enshrined in the principle of collective responsibility, may be extended to bargains struck between private and public actors. This process may stop well short of the incorporation of the groups into government or the colonisation or corporatisation of government by groups, as it does notably in Britain and in France. Nevertheless, if the interdependent agents of the state and of society are to conduct their conflicts in a collaborative context, with a view to attaining mutually acceptable compromises, a large measure of confidentiality is required, secluding the negotiators from the curiosity of the public, of the mass media and even of Parliament. In these circumstances, there is an unavoidable 'anonymity' about many stages in the policy process because the objectives would not be attained except at that price. Mass participation and policy efficacy are often antithetical. Should Finer have instead concluded his book with a less ringing phrase: 'Darkness! More Darkness'? This paper explores the problem in a comparative context, Finer having been a champion of the virtue of comparison both for pedagogical and research purposes in the social sciences generally and politics in particular.[3]

Given his breadth of comparative vision, both temporally and spatially, it is surprising that Finer should have adopted the term 'lobby' which, at first sight, appears to be inspired by a parochial Anglo-American institution. It is particularly inappropriate for Franco-British comparisons because it has additionally acquired in France precisely the pejorative connotations that led him to prefer it to the more popular term 'pressure group'. Clearly, to the extent that groups generally come into existence and serve purposes other than the unilateral exercise of pressure upon some part of the apparatus of government, the term is most misleading. As Salisbury has argued, interest group theory dubiously 'assumes that group members have public policy-related interests, values and preferences which (i) antedate the existence of the organized association; (ii) are the rational basis for joining and remaining members of the association; (iii) are articulated and heightened by virtue of the associational interactions; and (iv) are represented through the association to the policy-making arenas by virtue of lobbying activities.'[4] Building upon Mancur Olson's by-product or selective incentive theory, which undermines the standard arguments explaining why people join and remain members of any group and shows that exerting pressure on government is not its primary function, Salisbury pushes Olson's economic type of argumentation further by suggesting that groups come into existence because a leader-political entrepreneur identifies a potential market of consumer-followers to whom benefits can be offered at the price of a membership fee.[5] Despite the insights that such economistic reasoning affords into the *raison d'être* of groups, it has severe limitations. The wholly subjective conception of group interests by the pluralists generally not only leads to normative bias but narrows the subject matter to the randomly generated data of individual consciousness. Thus Bentham not only reduced all group interests to a sum of individual interests,[6] but he got around the problem of the ethical and psychological foundations of this theory by assuming that 'everyone knows his own best interest'. However, as Balbus had argued, 'If preferences or wants are taken as the starting point of theoretical analysis, then the origin of preferences or wants is not amenable to empirical investigation.'[7] One does not need to share his Marxist standpoint to believe that there are powerful social determinants of individual behaviour or that the collective interests are not simply reducible to a sum of subjective interests. After all, Bentham's own concern with sinister, sectional interests might suggest this sociological corrective to his psychologistic perspective.

Terminological problems have already led us far afield but it is important to be aware, in these preliminary remarks, that the term 'pressure group – when abstracted from the working of the politico-administrative system generally – is not merely too narrow, as we have briefly indicated, but too one-sided and too all-embracing as well. For a start, the word 'group' is misleading because many of the major actors in the policy process – notably large public and private enterprises – are sufficiently powerful to act in their own right, without seeking collective strength through combination. However, the companion word 'pressure' presents more complex difficulties. Pressure groups work within a multilateral and reciprocal system of influence in which groups are pressured as well as exercising pressure. The study of pressure groups was pioneered by scholars in the USA and UK and unconsciously incorporated a value-laden liberal and unilaterally pluralist emphasis upon societal influences upon the state rather than vice versa, characteristic features of their own 'Anglo-Saxon' political systems. This bias was uncritically adopted by the pioneer in the field of French pressure group studies, Jean Meynaud, in his initial, overall description of the subject. His later work was more speculative and divorced from detailed empirical verification, the necessary work having simply not been done. For the most part it still remains to be done.[8]

Sensing, perhaps that there was a missing dimension to his work, notably in the field of economic policy, this former economist went on to become a pioneer investigator of the phenomenon of technocracy but he did not live to bring the two sides of his work together.[9] The techno-bureaucratic preoccupation came naturally to a fellow countryman of Saint-Simon but it was Henry Ehrmann, whose superb pioneering study of the French peak business organization, the CNPF, had brought him into direct contact with the interface between the most conspicuously capitalist pressure group in French society and the major techno-bureaucratic agencies of the French state, who focused on group-government links.[10] In a remarkable 1961 article on 'French bureaucracy and organized interests' (which has never been followed up by the large-scale systematic investigation for which it cries out) he suggested that the relationship between big business and government was not just reciprocal rather than unilateral; it was frequently collusive.[11] This insight was exploited by others, notably by Andrew Shonfield in the contrast he made between France and Britain in his magisterial investigation of Modern Capitalism.[12] So, the term 'pressure' is misleading in yet another way. Through the notion of institutionalised 'concertation' between selected 'insider' groups and government agencies, leading perhaps to a consensus that avoided zero-sum confrontations and conflicts, the way was open for a re-emergence of the notion of corporatism, the linkage in the French case being indicated by Ehrmann in his 1957 study of French big business.[13] However, in the 1960s, the analysis remained essentially a pluralist one, with clear indications that it should be slanted in a neo-corporatist direction, characterised by concerted capitalism-cum-statism.

The pluralist character of Ehrmann's analysis was emphasised by the way in which he argued that, despite the monolithic structure attributed to the French state by legalistic studies, both sides of the state-society equation were highly fragmented. It was not just French society which was the prey of endemic and profound cleavages; the French state was itself fractured by numerous fissures. While 'horizontal' ministries, notably the Finance ministry, sought to assert an overall public or general interest, the bulk of the state machine consisted of 'vertical' ministries which worked primarily with a single interest, exercising powerful, joint, fissiparous, disintegrative pressures in the making of public policy. While Ehrmann's analysis was understandably oversimplified (for example playing down the splits within the Finance ministry) nevertheless the broad picture is accurate. Detailed studies of French administration have subsequently shown that such fragmentation is a feature not merely of relations between ministries but between *directions* (divisions) in the same ministry and between bureaux in the same *direction*.[14] While in Britain the permanent secretary at the head of each ministry, much more than the passing ministers, provides the capacity for effective unitary bureaucratic coordination, the more collective and transitory French style of coordination by a *directeur de cabinet* and the minister's personal staff, not only offers greater scope for pressure group penetration, it leads to more intra-ministerial conflict between line and staff and accentuates the inherent tendencies towards administrative pluralism. However, counterbalancing this propensity to dissensus is the historically and culturally dominant status of the French state and its agents, with their claim to represent the general interest in a way few political leaders have surpassed. The salient twentieth-century example was General de Gaulle, for whom the general interest simply equated the General's interest.

However, as Ehrmann had already indicated, while the interpenetration of certain groups with particular parts of the government apparatus might and sometimes did lead to the group leaders absorbing something of the senior officials' general interest values, the senior officials might and sometimes did identify the public interest with one or more specific private interests. Although officials in the Budget and Treasury divisions of the Finance ministry or in the Planning commissariat, 'who have to assign priorities to what are frequently contradictory demands, believe themselves to be free of the corporatist* leanings for which they criticize their colleagues in the vertical branches', in practice this is far from the truth. 'What is obviously intended is to eliminate the top political organs from the determination of important community purposes and to place the full responsibility for the manipulation of interests in the hands of the administrator and his like-minded counterparts representing those very interests . . . . They are also frankly selective about the interests to be admitted to the process of common decision-making, inasmuch as they share the preferences of many of their colleagues for large-scale interests deemed to be less rapacious and less narrow-minded than organizations of "little men".'[15] Ehrmann circumspectly concluded on the basis of early post-war experiences (the Fourth Republic and the start of the Fifth Republic) and in the light of the notions of 'concerted economy' developed by Bloch-Laîné from the planning practice of Jean Monnet,[16] that the main impetus for economic policy had come from a bureaucratic-big business alliance. 'The best-organized forces in the nation, the bureaucracy and the large economic interests, leaned on each other and drew increasing strength from mutual support until, at least in some cases, authoritative decision-making became the result of a near-amalgamation between them.'[17] In his turn, Shonfield and others analysed and explained the failure of Britain to achieve a

---

* Ehrmann is using the word in the French sense of the narrow pursuit of sectional interest.

comparably rapid and sustained rate of economic growth after the Second World War in terms of the failure to establish such a beneficent alliance between selected big businessmen (normally former senior civil servants who had moved to the semi-public or private sector) and senior state officials.[18]

Before leaving the subject of terminology, one could certainly substitute the term 'interest group' for pressure group, given the latter's misleading implications. However, interest group is a term not without its own problems. Finer – while conceding that it is more neutral – reduced it to a sub-category, contrasted with disinterested groups promoting a cause. While this type of distinction had its vogue, it has a major weakness, reflecting an introspective pluralism, *almost exclusively preoccupied with the groups themselves*, their motivations and capacity to attract members, *rather then their extrovert relationships with government and other groups*. If we were to focus upon this latter distinction, which reflects current concerns more closely, one would instead contrast the 'insider' groups, which have acquired a more or less formally institutionalized relationship with one or (usually) more agencies of the state and 'outsider' groups. The latter are denied official recognition – and the legitimacy which goes with it, especially in countries like France, with a long statist tradition – as well as the routine, regular access to public decision-makers which the 'insider groups' enjoy as a matter of course. The clientele-conferred 'legitimacy from below', which is particularly characteristic of the USA or Britain is not wholly absent from countries such as France and the Federal German Republic, which normatively rely to a great extent upon a state-sponsored 'legitimacy from above'. The crucial notion of 'social partnership' – which attains its full development in neo-corporatist systems such as Austria – is confined to the representative, responsible, respectable, cooperative, useful and trustworthy 'insider' groups. Regular contact with them would not taint the official paragons of the public interest with the pitch of particularist demagoguery.

In France, the distinction made by senior civil servants is between the reliable *organisations professionnels* and the unrepresentative, irresponsible, disreputable, potentially disruptive, pressure groups or lobbies, the use of the foreign term being intended to suggest that they are outlandish, untrustworthy and undesirable imports that disturb domestic state-society harmony.[19] In Britain, the absence of a dominant public law tradition of the hierarchial superimposition of state authority over society and the strength of liberal and pluralist norms inclines group-government relations to be conducted – in principle – between equals. The opposite is true in France. Those groups that are accepted by government bodies as 'social partners' – a more select category than those formally recognized as 'representative' – acquire this status on the understanding that they are junior partners. Public recognition constitutes a privilege, selectively according a measure of public legitimacy to private organizations. In return, the government's social partners strengthen the position of their official patrons by lending them support from outside the public decision-making system. In France, the juridical chasm between public and private actors is bridged in part thanks to the collaborative activities of these intermediaries or mediators. So, a preliminary step in studying any public policy sector must be to identify which, if any, groups have acquired the privileged status of social partner, when they attain it, who the actors on both sides are, what form their transactions assume and with what frequency they occur; before investigating their role within the policy process from problem identification through to the implementation of practical solutions, whose defects prompt the re-emergence of problems.

Why some groups are selected for privileged 'insider' status depends, as we have seen, in part upon their willingness to act as (junior) partners. However, the transigent or intransigent behaviour of any group is usually derivative from other, more fundemantal factors; in particular the structural and functional indispensability of some groups, which confers upon them what Finer has called 'socio-economic leverage', defined as the 'power to disrupt society'.[20] A similar notion was adumbrated earlier (without Finer's gift for garbing a concept in an arresting formula) by Grant McConnell: 'Through the private associations, it has time and again been possible to discover authoritative spokesmen for segments of the population which have the capacity to disrupt common life. Through these leaders, it has been possible to strike bargains permitting a reasonable degree of social peace.'[21] Thus, while Finer – preoccupied with the disruptive capacity of British trade unions which was such a feature of the 1970s – dwelt upon the negative, dissentient aspect of socio-economic leverage, it may also take the positive, acquiescent form of a capacity to help society work more smoothly. More generally, thanks to their strategic location in the socio-economic system, some groups acquire a major capacity materially to help or hinder decisions by offering or withholding their cooperation or engaging in various forms of covert or overt opposition to defend old privileges enshrined in the status quo or to extract new ones.

In discussing this indispensability – traditionally attributed to business and more recently to trade unions – Finer argued that 'It is the power to withhold a function that constitutes their strength; not their power to coerce.'[22] Ultimately, when it becomes a trial of strength, the coercive power at a group's disposal is decisive, particularly in the case of outsider groups such as trade unions to some extent still are in Britain and France.[23] The strike has been historically and still is in these countries at least as important an instrument of popular participation in the political process as the vote. This may not fit comfortably into the traditional constitutional rules of liberal democracy but as against would-be totalitarian political systems, pluralist democracies or polyarchies are conspicuous for the existence of groups that operate independently from government. While the coming of universal suffrage has reduced somewhat recourse to more or less violent direct action in Britain and France, public demonstrations which may degenerate into riots continue to provide a medium for mass pressure when public opinion fails to influence the governing elites. Extra-parliamentary and extra-partnership action continue to be available for use by exasperated dissentient groups that are outside the organized and authorized channels of communication between the mass of the powerless and the powerful elites provided by the major political parties and insider groups. Any theory of the relationship of groups and governments needs to take account of the groups that remain, as it were, outside the normal political processes, particularly because almost all groups are willing, on occasion, to cross the legitimacy boundary. However, the insider groups are conscious that they will pay a high price if they become outlaws for more than the briefest crisis episodes.

A number of alternative models of interest group-government relations have been proposed to account for the complexities of the French case. Vincent Wright suggested a fourfold classification: 'domination-crisis', 'concerted politics', 'endemic conflict' and 'pluralist'. These models are based on attempts by others to offer an overall explanation which only partially accounts for some of the phenomena observed.[24] I have attempted to reformulate this characterization – with a major amendment – into two pairs, each having a heroic or crisis style decision making variant and a humdrum or routine style variant along one dimension and a consensus/imposition variant along the other dimension.[25] However, as I regard all four situations as types of general pluralist relationship, I replace pluralism with 'institutional collapse' as the fourth variant in the matrix (see figure 5.1). Thus 'concerted politics' combines the day-to-day, normal, routine relationship of social partnership between insider groups and government capable of habitually achieving and jointly enforcing comprehensive consensus. 'Domination' corresponds to crisis situations, when a breakdown of the customary capacity to secure consensus leads to either the government or one or more groups seeking

Figure 5.1   Alternative group-government relations in a pluralist context

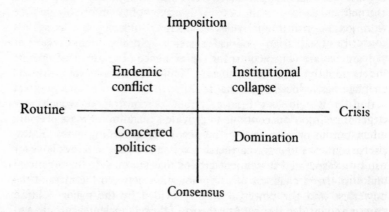

to coerce the other, without threatening the survival of the political regime. Shifting to the imposition dimension, 'endemic conflict' describes a stable, routine situation in which group activists see their function as that of wresting piecemeal concessions from an unresponsive, arbitrary or oppressive government. For its part, the government's officials and ministers regard the groups as prone, at worst, to indulge in violent confrontation and to have recourse to illegal, direct action tactics or at best to mass demonstrations and rabble-rousing campaigns calculated to discredit public policies. Finally and catastrophically, there is the situation of 'institutional collapse' in which one or more groups push conflict – intentionally or unintentionally – beyond the attainment of piecemeal concessions to the extent of bringing about a comprehensive paralysis or collapse of the regime. This situation, while more common in the military *coups*-prone countries of Africa, Latin America and Asia, is not unknown in France (eg. 1940, 1958) when war has put the political system under intolerable pressure. The fantasy that trade unions in Britain might paralyse the economy and polity does not survive more than a moment's reflection but the Polish free trade union movement 'Solidarity' did threaten to bring about institutional collapse, leading to the Jaruzelski *coup* of 1981.

In France and Britain, group-government relations are best analysed – depending upon the type of actor and policy issue involved – in the context of the typology of endemic conflict, concerted politics and domination, with the possibility that any particular predicament can be tackled at different phases by methods appropriate to more than one of these models. General characterizations of group-government relations in Britain and France should be treated circumspectly. While the cultural norms and historical tradition may make domination more 'normal' in France than in Britain, where endemic conflict is tolerated with greater equanimity, there are numerous examples in both countries of state domination and non-insurrectionary group exertion of socio-economic leverage. What is less common is the attainment of the stable state of social partnership, which in its most advanced form is characterized as neo-corporatism.

A different typology has been used by Frank Wilson, involving either three or four theoretical models specifically to explain French interest group-government relations. In a 1982 study, he proposed four alternatives: the pluralist, marxist, neo-corporatist and protest models, while in 1983 he dropped the marxist model and confined his analysis to the other three.[26] Having distinguished eight characteristic features of interest group activity concerning the boundary between state and groups, consensus on procedures and goals of government, group autonomy, group access to decision-making, perceived equality of access, expectations about involvement in decision-making, attitude towards participation and motives for participation, Wilson specified how interest groups (his preferred term) could be assumed to behave. Despite the interesting nature of his findings, based upon an opinion survey of 99 interest group leaders, one should stress that it is conceived in an Anglo-American perspective, with the focus on the groups themselves. This unilateral rather than reciprocal emphasis – as well as the subjective character of the data and the size of the sample – means that his general conclusion: that the French group-government relationship is one of 'limited pluralism' does not take us very far. While Wilson's evidence helps to undermine any claims that France – outside the farm and educational sectors – has moved appreciably in a corporatist direction, he admits that the approach adopted was not likely to confirm the 'protest' model. Finally, the neglect of the state side of group-government relations in the survey means that it has to be introduced *in extremis*. He sums up: 'The absence of political consensus in the ruling elite decisively explains the absence of corporatism in France. . . . Our final conclusion is that the French government is above the interest groups. The executive is so powerful that it is better to talk of a situation of limited pluralism rather than just pluralism.'[27]

Having on occasion myself engaged in such sweeping generalizations, it ill becomes me to do more than state that unless the analysis is broadened to subject the government side of the equation to equally rigorous scrutiny and unless the actual behaviour of group and government actors in policy contexts is investigated, we will have done little more than scratch the surface of part of the problem. This ambitious task will require the work of many scholars, who may be stimulated by Wilson's courageous return to a fascinating yet neglected area of the subject. Meanwhile, it may be useful to indicate who the major 'insider' actors are in the public policy area, at what stage they tend to intervene in the policy process and how they differ in their behaviour in the two countries concerned, preparing the way for the formulation of hypotheses which will be qualified or refuted after detailed empirical enquiry.

The domestic hexagon of pluralist power

How can we give concepts such as 'limited pluralism' a less elusive and more operational embodiment for purposes of cross-national comparison, while going beyond concepts such as 'tripartism'? This notion had a 1960s and 1970s vogue in Britain at and after the time when the National Economic Development Council and economic planning looked as though they might occupy the central place in public economic policy that the Planning commissariat and the national plans were already beginning to lose in France. Some observers have suggested that this 'toothless tripartism' was a staging post or even the actual embodiment of neo-corporatism, based upon the peak collaboration of government, business and the trade unions, while others more presciently perceived that neither trade unions nor business were able or willing to accept incorporation.[28] In any case, the model referred primarily to economic policy-making and important though this is, it is neither all-embracing or even all-determining. It would be most convenient for political analysts if all matters of major significance could be traced to one set of decision-makers. Intractable complexity precludes such simple solutions and, depending upon the type of policy decision and policy area one is investigating, the policy actors either will be different or will exercise different degrees of political influence on the eventual outcome.

However, the political system is not an ultra-pluralist free market in which no pattern of control can be discerned, with decisions emerging in wholly unpredictable fashion from the confused mêlée of a mass of individual or group wills. Between these extremes, it may be helpful to offer a less drastically over-simplified middle-range model of a hexagon of pluralist power, provisionally and artificially excluding here both the influences external to the particular state investigated and the local levels of power. Moreover, this model focuses its attention upon the 'insider' actors, who engage simultaneously, successively or alternatively in tactics which conform to the typology of endemic conflict, domination or concerted politics. Finally, the model gives pride of place to those actors that impinge most directly upon the economic policy process, which we have already conceded is only part of reality. For example, the role of the church or cultural institutions other than the media of elite and mass communication do not find a place in this hexagon of pluralist power. It should also be made explicit that this is a static model, focusing upon intra-systemic change and that it would be necessary to add a temporal dimension at a later stage. With all these limitations, let us see how far we can proceed.

Figure 5.2   The hexagon of limited pluralist power

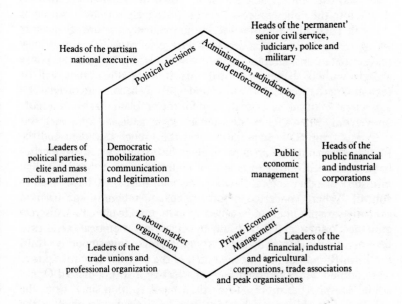

In Figure 5.2 (and proceeding in a clockwise direction) the heads of the partisan national executive in Britain and France – which together with the heads of the 'permanent' senior civil service, judiciary, police, military, public financial and industrial corporations constitute the public sector – are formally assumed to be at the summit of a pyramid of state power, with which 'private' groups have to deal, either directly or through the intermediation of political parties, parliament and the elite and mass media of communication. Familiar conceptions such as 'presidential government', 'prime ministerial government' or even 'cabinet government' personalize the partisan executive. In France, the president of the republic contrives to be both the partisan head of the efficient executive and the non-partisan head of state and this is significant not only at the meta-political level. Given the need to transcend or compromise conflict within and between each of the clusters of decision-makers who participate in the hexagonal process of persuasion, 'bribery', cajolery, and outright coercion, this capacity to utilize the headship of state more directly than is possible in Britain, where the two functions are separated, strengthens the hand of the French president. However, the existence of a prime minister in France leads to another kind of duality which presents its own advantages and difficulties. The extent to which the partisan executive is drawn into the policy process – either collectively, through its head or through particular ministers acting individually or through cabinet committees – varies a great deal with the type of issue. Sometimes, they may initiate consideration of the matter, placing it upon the policy agenda without being prompted. Much more often, they will be responding to external 'pressures' and will only become involved when a practical solution has to be devised for the problem that has emerged, or even only when a formal decision has to be made and implemented.

One is tempted to hypothesise that the French president and the British prime minister are most likely to be involved when major crises have developed out of situations of endemic conflict that individual ministers or other actors, to whom we shall turn later, have failed to control. Where concerted politics reigns, members of the partisan executive are not likely to be called upon to provide more than discreet guidance, punctuated periodically by celebratory rhetorical exercises to reassure all concerned that everything is proceeding smoothly. Until the Fifth Republic, the fragmentation of the partisan executive power was coupled with the absence of an effective institutionalized Opposition. Despite the process of partisan bipolarization since 1958, the ephemeral establishment by Mitterand of a shadow cabinet in the mid-1960s and attempts when out of office to unite the left in the 1970s and the right in the 1980s, there is no clear alternative partisan executive which can play a really significant part in the policy process, which is usually the case in Britain. The groups that wish to exert pressure in France are therefore much less inclined to rely upon a non-existent 'Opposition', though they can play the alternative left and right-wing party leaders off against each other to secure incorporation of their demands into party programmes. They take competitive advantage of political fragmentation.

The epitome of the public sector side of group-government relations is constituted by the heads of the permanent administration, adjudication and enforcement machinery of the state, using the value-laden liberal language which presupposes a separation of the public and private 'sides' as a prerequisite of a free society and an uncontaminated state. The meritocratic, bureaucratic and technocratic traditions are much more firmly and operationally institutionalized and normatively accepted in France than in Britain, the public *grandes écoles*, school-made men being regarded as entitled to influence public policy decisions because they embody a disinterested and elevated conception of the public interest. When pushed to extremes, this statism can amount to a desire to dominate all private, group-manifestations of a potentially disorderly society, prone to the seductions of sinister sectional interests. Such a view is not unknown in Britain and Finer's classic biography of the Benthamite Edwin Chadwick is a reminder that this minority tradition has had vigorous if ultimately ineffective exponents of bureaucratic centralism.[29]

The contrast between the relatively independent role of the judiciary in Britain and the French tradition of judges working in conjunction with the police to enforce the law should not be overdone, notably because the French administrative courts have restrained the abuse of power by developing a remarkable measure of state self-restraint.[30] However, both in France and Britain, most groups are either reluctant or unable to use the courts to further their cause *vis-à-vis* government or each other, cost and delay being decisive factors for those who cannot afford to pay or to wait. Unlike Third World countries, or even those advanced societies that have come under the influence of a 'military-industrial complex', outside the specific sphere of defence policy the irruption of the military into the centre of the French political stage, coupled with claims that it is the guardian of the national interest, only occurs on the rare occasions when crises need to be dominated by recourse to armed force.

Normally, the spending ministries, which have close clientelistic ties with 'their' groups, seek to develop 'concerted politics' practices, though the relationship usually stops well short at the consultative level, when not actually embroiled in 'endemic conflict'. While the senior civil servants sometimes play an important role in identifying problems – in the case of British membership of the European Community with the help of leading private businessmen, whereas in France private business was reticent, to put it mildly, about the creation of the Coal and Steel Community and the EEC[31] – they come into their own in the preparation of detailed projects and in the final stage of implementation, though cost may play a major role in preventing proposals proceeding to the legislative or regulatory stage. The sponsor ministries' freedom to strike bargains is constrained in numerous ways, more especially by the general financial constraints enforced by the Treasury and Bank of England in Britain and by the Budget and Treasury divisions of the French Economy and Finance Ministry and the Bank of France. This leads us to the next cluster of actors, those responsible for public economic management.

While the policy role of the permanent civil service is not devoid of ideological controversy in France, it has under Mrs Thatcher's leadership taken on a harsh and acrimonious tone in Britain. Senior officials are being accused of an intrinsically unbusinesslike incapacity to manage, as well as an inertia-inclined unwillingness to innovate, especially in ways that reduce the role of state intervention. How much more highly charged is the issue of the role of heads of public financial and industrial corporations, as well as the size and composition of the publically owned sector, particularly in Britain where maximum privatization has been proclaimed as a salient objective of Conservative public policy in the 1980s. Since 1981, the massive extension of the public sector in French banking and industry, with the consequent change in heads of the enterprises concerned, has represented a dramatic move in the opposite direction (accounting since 1982 for a sixth of gross domestic product and over a third of investment), even though it is different members of the same school-made elite that continue to run large business in France, whether public or private. Although the public-private split in personnel and ideology is such a live issue in Britain, nationalized firms were admitted first as associate and then in 1969 as full members of the Confederation of British Industry. In France, while public utilities do not belong to the *Conseil National du Patronat Français*, the industrial enterprises in the competitive sector belong to their relevant trade associations as well as to the CNPF.

The major contrast between the two countries – accentuated by the extension in 1982 of public ownership in France from the three major deposit banks to cover over 90 per cent of bank deposits – is the traditional, autonomous, world-wide financial power of the City of London's merchant banks, whereas in France state agencies have nearly always managed to keep a firm control over credit. Banking has remained primarily national in the scope of its activity as well as its management. While the nationalization of the Bank of England did bring about greater concertation between public and private financial actors, there is still a state of endemic conflict between the financial and industrial worlds in Britain which is regarded in France as fratricidal. In some areas of public policy, notably nuclear energy, French public enterprise has played a crucial role in the closed politics initiation of an exceptionally ambitious policy that was driven through to implementation, albeit at the cost of an astronomical level of indebtedness. State financial control has been minimized because *Electricité de France* had political and techno-bureaucratic backing at the highest levels.[32] While avoiding the journalistic extravagance of the polemical epithet 'EDF-State', it is significant that in a much more pluralistic type of policy context, that concerning the Rhine-Rhône canal, a key factor in the recurring cycle of indecision has been the opposition of EDF.[33] Without generalizing from the case of EDF (which is far from isolated, if one considers the ELF petroleum corporation or Renault) French public corporations are much more uninhibited actors in the policy process than doctrinaire political and cultural constraints usually allow them to be in Britain.

In both his 1955 study of 'The political power of private capital' and his 1973 companion article on 'The political power of organised labour', Finer provocatively described private business, 'so-called *free enterprise*' in identical terms, as '*a very highly decentralized form of public administration*'.[34] Had this been intended as a description of the statist, paternalistic and *dirigiste* French relationship of business and government, it would not have given as much cause for surprise at its controversial application to liberal Britain, where the market traditionally ruled the wealth-creating sector, with minimal interference from governments that prudently remained at arm's length. In practice, with ups – especially in wartime – and downs – notably during the premiership of Mrs Thatcher – business and government have remained much further apart in Britain than in France. As I put it elsewhere, the 'trickle of senior officials at the end of their career into posts that utilize their Whitehall knowledge and contacts in the service of their firm rather than the occupancy of key managerial positions' cannot compare with the reverse 'process of *pantouflage*, which peoples the top managerial posts in the French public and private corporations and creates an interlocking economic directorate trained in the *grandes écoles* and apprenticed in the public service . . .'[35] While small-scale business organizations tend to be pushed into a peripheral position both in Britain and France, farm organizations in the two countries have been the most inclined to accept co-optation as the acquiscent clientele of the ministry of agriculture. Being little concerned to influence public policy outside the farm sector, although in many respects they have developed corporatist-style structures, attitudes and behaviour, the farm leaders are parochially pluralist in their lack of concern with non-agricultural matters.[36] In France, I have argued, 'the farm organizations, usually controlled by the farmers who would prosperously survive the transmutation to a market-oriented agriculture (long since completed in Britain) have made a show of resistance to public policy. They have usually been resigned to slowing the process down and extracting the maximum financial concessions in return for controlling the more desperate of their condemned members.'[37] In industry the major firms are seldom allowed to collapse completely because of the politically and socially intolerable consequences, governments being concerned primarily to organize a retreat with a semblance of good order.

Business groups exercise a substantial measure of *indirect* influence through friendly political leaders and parties, with financial contributions moving from firms and actual or former politicians moving into firms as directors, particularly in Britain. However, businessmen are above all interested in profits and inclined to sacrifice the medium-term survival of a Conservative government to their short-term viability. The CBI's attempt to help the Heath government's anti-inflationary policy by a voluntary price restraint initiative in 1971–2 was in this respect an exemplary failure, while French governments' periodic resort to price freezes and restraint agreements reflect a complex combination of state domination and concerted politics, mainly in the industrial sectors and endemic conflict, mainly in the service and distribution sectors. The most interesting development since the 1960s in France has been the proliferation of contractual agreements between firms and government, reflecting a partial move beyond concerted politics to contractual politics.

Both in Britain and France, peak business organizations have a complex about their public role, partly because of their poor image in France and their apparent lack of influence in Britain. For example, the initiative in preparing Conservative industrial relations legislation to curb trade union action, both in the early 1970s and early 1980s, owed little to the CBI, although in both countries the employers' associations have resisted attempts to increase worker participation through their trade union representatives in decision-making within the firm. The unions have themselves been ambivalent about direct involvement in decision-making, either within government or within the firm. Both the British and French labour movements have not wholly abandoned the 'outlaw' mentality they acquired during the nineteenth century, when they were regarded as illegal conspiracies. While in Britain the nominally united but in practice decentralized trade union movement has been 'labourist' in ideology and practice, primarily concerned to use its power to improve the material conditions of union members rather than to displace the existing elites, much less to abolish the capitalist system, in France the two largest trade union confederations are committed to do just that. However, in reality these French unions have had to confine their inordinate ambitions to acting rather negatively, resisting policies that they disliked rather than promoting policies which they desire. They have been less effective in this 'veto group' role than the British trade unions, partly because their political friends were out of office for most of the Fifth Republic.

The Mitterrand presidency has presented them with similar problems to those faced by the Trades Union Congress during periods of Labour government, notably the acceptance of sacrifices in their members' standard of living in return for policies of which they approve, without anything like a formal 'social contract' being proposed. The Socialist-led unions (the CFDT, Force Ouvrière and the teachers union FEN) remain jealous of their autonomy, while the Communist-led CGT is capable of greater control over its rank and file but is less inclined to use it. This is because the policies pursued owe little to the views of the French Communist Party, which is a dispensable minority in a Socialist-dominated coalition. So, while state domination over the unions – currently being experimented with by the Thatcher government in Britain – is less appropriate than it was in the de Gaulle, Pompidou and Giscard presidencies, and neo-corporatist social partnership is unacceptable, the government-trade union relationship in France has settled down to a more or less amicable form of endemic conflict. The unions – and more especially their members – find it difficult to accept that the international economic constraints mean that, far from 'everything being possible', what they regard as essentials – job security and rising incomes – have become luxuries.[38] In the case of middle-class liberal professions, the conflict has taken a much more acrimonious form, with the use of weapons like strikes and direct action by French doctors in 1983 against the policies of a left-wing government. In an economic context in which the government has to improvise solutions to immediate domestic and foreign pressures, hopes that a decentralized and democratic planning process would give the major organized interests an important place within the priority-setting and decision-making process, generally and not merely in relation to their own sectional concerns, have had to be played down in France. The British trade union leaders, having sacrificed the interests of the Labour party when they came into collision with the interests of their members as the activists conceive them, not merely in the late 1970s but in the late 1940s and the late 1960s, are faced with a labour market and a political balance of forces that is unfavourable to them.

So, full employment – a major trade union gain in the post-1945 period – important for its indirect leverage effects as well as for itself, is no longer an agreed objective of public policy to whose attainment all are committed.

The sixth cluster of decision-makers within the hexagon of pluralist power is made up of the liberal democratic agencies of partisan mobilization, the media of elite and mass communication and the institutions of legitimation. The leaders of the major political parties, inside and outside Parliament, are supposed to play an important part in processing, selecting, modifying and transmitting the pressures from society – whether or not they have originated from the major organized groups like trade unions or trade associations – to the executive in both countries. Because the heads of the partisan national executives acquire office thanks to electoral victory, they have to ensure that they act in such a way as to win the necessary popular support, if not at all times at least in the medium term. So, while the political party does not play the monopoly role that it enjoys in the one party state and parties pursue less divergent policies when in power than would be expected from their ideologies or programmes in opposition, it continues to have an important place among the plurality of political actors in the liberal democratic polity.

In France, the complex, confusing and constantly shifting party system has in recent years stabilized into a bipolarized double duality, so that although coalition government continues to be the order of the day, both the left and right-wing coalitions at least end up with a leader when in office. In Britain, although there has been some retreat from the two-party system, governments can usually rely upon a parliamentary majority, so that the proposals that have figured in the successful party's electoral programme move to the top of the formal legislative and regulatory agenda. In France, where party government has never been fully accepted, it is the successful presidential candidate's electoral programme, not a party programme as such that sets the formal policy agenda. However, all the other hexagonal actors come into play in both countries to reinforce the partisan commitments they welcome and may have contributed to formulating in the first place or to block or amend those to which they are opposed. In this process, the role of the media of communication, the daily and weekly press, the radio and television, often play a crucial role, particularly when they are independent actors in their own right, i.e. not propagandists for one of the other actors: government, public or private corporation, trade union, political party.[39] Because of the secrecy that these other actors seek to preserve while they consult, negotiate and exchange concessions, the power of publicity that the communication media exercise can play an especially decisive part in the most delicate, 'closed', confidential stages of the policy process. The greater openness of the French political process has ensured a higher capacity to learn from errors if only because there is a more widely diffused awareness of them.

Conclusion

While the study of group pressures played an important part in the emergence of politics as a social science in the early twentieth century, it came to be associated with a sub-species of the pluralist approach and the investigation of group pressures waned as the limitations of this approach became manifest. Yet, as alternative research strategies have been tried and found wanting, there has been a revival of interest in the activities of pressure groups, although among some of Finer's former Keele students and colleagues interest was sustained during the years when the subject went out of fashion.[40] However, this work has tended to be confined to Britain, rather than developed in a comparative perspective. The problems of comparison in this context would be hard to overstate, particularly if – as has been argued here – the group pressures must be studied as part of a system of multilateral and reciprocal influence. The sheer volume of empirical work required on the groups themselves, as well as on the context in which they are operating, focused on the origins, making and implementation of particular policies, is so intimidating as to discourage all but the most intrepid of scholars from undertaking more than isolated, single-country case studies or general speculative essays. Clearly, teamwork will be required to tackle tasks of the scale and complexity involved. There will, however, always be a role for isolated and innovative craftsmen who, like SEF, have the breadth and acuteness of vision, as well as the boldness and incisiveness of execution to lead their colleagues towards the attainment of breath-takingly ambitious objectives.

Notes

1. S.E. Finer, *Anonymous Empire. A Study of the Lobby in Great Britain*, 1958, revised edn., Pall Mall Press, London, 1966, p. 112 and chapter 9 *passim*.
2. S.E. Finer, 'The individual responsibility of ministers', *Public Administration*, Winter 1956, pp. 377–96.
3. S.E. Finer, *Comparative Government*, Penguin, Harmondsworth, 1970, pp. 39–40.
4. R.H. Salisbury, 'An exchange theory of interest groups', *Midwest Journal of Political Science* **XIII/I**, February 1969, p. 23. On

Finer's choice of the term 'lobby', see *Anonymous Empire*, pp. 3–5.

5. Salisbury, p. 23; cf. pp. 24–9. More generally, see Mancur Olson's classic *The Logic of Collective Action*, Harvard University Press, Cambridge, Mass., 1965.

6. Jeremy Bentham, *A Fragment on Government and Principles of Morals and Legislation*, 1948 edn., Blackwell, Oxford, p. 126 (from chapter 1 of the *Principles*, 1st edn., 1789).

7. Isaac D. Balbus, 'The concept of interest in pluralist and Marxist Analysis', *Politics and Society* I, February 1971, p. 165; cf. pp. 151–77.

8. Jean Meynaud, *Les groupes de pression en France*, Presses Universitaires de France, Paris, 1960 and *Nouvelles études sur les groupes de pression*, Colin, Paris, 1962.

9. Jean Meynaud, *Technocracy*, Faber, London, 1965.

10. Henry W. Ehrmann, *Organized Business in France*, Princeton University Press, Princeton, 1957.

11. Henry W. Ehrmann, 'French bureaucracy and organized interests', *Administrative Sciences Quarterly*, March 1961, pp. 534–55.

12. Andrew Shonfield, *Modern Capitalism*, Oxford University Press, London, chapter 8, 1965.

13. Ehrmann, *Organized Business in France*, p. 487, cf. pp. 91–4, 262–3, 274–5, 303. Note Ehrmann's remark that 'generally, pluralist doctrines and practices have travelled on the continent in corporatist clothes' (p. 478). See also Wyn Grant, *Insider groups, outsider groups and interest group strategies in Britain*, University of Warwick Department of Politics Working Paper no. 19, May 1978.

14. See particularly Ezra N. Suleiman, *Politics, Power and Bureaucracy in France*, Princeton University Press, Princeton, chapter 6, 1974.

15. Ehrmann, 'French bureaucracy', pp. 540, 554–5.

16. François Bloch-Laîné, *A la Recherche d'une 'Economie Concertée'*, Editions de l'Epargne, Paris, 1964. Monnet attributed parenthood of the concept to his collaborator and successor as planning commissioner, Etienne Hirsch. See Jean Monnet, *Mémoires*, Fayard, Paris, 1976, p. 306.

17. Ehrmann, 'French bureaucracy', p. 555 (emphasis added).

18. Shonfield, *Modern Capitalism*, pp. 71–2, 86, 99, 160, 164. See also Jack Hayward's Introduction to Jack Hayward and Michael Watson (eds.), *Planning, Politics and Public Policy*, Cambridge University Press, London, 1975, pp. 9, 16.

19. Suleiman, *Politics, Power and Bureaucracy in France*, pp. 337–59.

20. S.E. Finer, 'The political power of organized labour', *Government*

and Opposition **VIII**, no. 4, Autumn 1973, p. 393. In an earlier article on the 'The political power of private capital', *The Sociological Review* **III**, no. 2, p. 285, he discussed the capacity to thwart government policy as constituting 'surrogate-ship'.

21. G. McConnell, 'The public values of the private association', in J.R. Pennock and J.W. Chapman (eds.), *Voluntary Associations*, Nomos XI, 1969, p. 157.

22. Finer, 'The political power of organized labour', p. 394.

23. Andrew Cox and Jack Hayward, 'The inapplicability of the corporatist model in Britain and France. The case of labor', *International Political Science Review* **IV**, no. 2, 1983, pp. 217–40.

24. Vincent Wright, *The Government and Politics of France*, Hutchinson, London, 1st edn. 1978, pp. 174–85.

25. Jack Hayward, 'Mobilising private interests in the service of public ambitions: the salient element in the dual French policy style', in Jeremy J. Richardson (ed.), *Policy Styles in Western Europe*, Allen & Unwin, London, 1982, pp. 119–20.

26. Frank L. Wilson, 'Alternative models of interest intermediation: the case of France', *British Journal of Political Science* **XII**/2, April 1982, pp. 173–200 and 'Les groupes d'intérêt sous la Cinquième République: test de trois modèles théoriques de l'interaction entre groupes et gouvernement', *Revue Française de Science Politique* **XXXIII**/2, April 1983, pp. 220–54.

27. 'Les groupes d'intérêt', p. 253; cf. pp. 252–4.

28. On the epithet 'toothless tripartism' see Jack Hayward in *Planning, Politics and Public Policy*, p. 12. More generally, see Wyn Grant and David Marsh, 'Tripartism: Reality or Myth', *Government and Opposition* **XII**/2, 1977, pp. 194–211 and J.J. Richardson and A.G. Jordan, *Governing Under Pressure*, Martin Robertson, Oxford, 1979, pp. 48–53.

29. S.E. Finer, *The Life and Times of Sir Edwin Chadwick*, Methuen, London, 1952.

30. Jack Hayward, *Governing France. The One and Indivisible Republic*, Weidenfeld and Nicolson, London, chapter 5 1973, 2nd edn., 1983, *passim*.

31. On the French case, see Ehrmann, *Organized Business in France*, pp. 403–19 and Henry W. Ehrmann, 'The French trade associations and the ratification of the Schuman Plan', *World Politics* **VI**/4, July 1954, pp. 453–81.

32. J.E.S. Hayward, *Governing France. The One and Indivisible Republic*, pp. 226–8; cf. pp. 222–40. See also N.J.D. Lucas, *Energy in France. Planning, Politics and Policy*, Europa Publi-

cations, London, 1979, and Duncan Burn, *Nuclear Power and the Energy Crisis*, Macmillan, London, 1978.

33. Jack Hayward, 'Mobilising Private Interests' in J.J. Richardson (ed.), *Policy Styles in Western Europe*, p. 136; cf. pp. 128–37.
34. S.E. Finer in *The Sociological Review* III, no. 2, December 1955, p. 285 and in *Government and Opposition* VIII, no. 3, Autumn 1973, p. 395. It is in the latter article that the key phrases are italicized.
35. Jack Hayward, 'Employer associations and the state in France and Britain' in Steven J. Warnecke and Ezra N. Suleiman (eds.), *Industrial Policies in Western Europe*, p. 120 and chapter 5 *passim*. See also Ezra N. Suleiman, 'Industrial policy formulation in France', ibid., chapter 1, pp. 31ff. In Britain, S.E. Finer's article on 'The Federation of British Industries', *Political Studies* IV, no. 1, 1956, was followed up by Stephen Blank, *Government and Industry in Britain. The Federation of British Industries in Politics, 1945–65*, Saxon House, Westmeads, 1973, and Wyn Grant and David Marsh, *The Confederation of British Industry*, Hodder and Stoughton, London, 1977. More generally, see Philippe Schmitter and Wolfgang Streeck, *The Organization of Business Interests*, October 1981, Berlin International Institute of Management discussion paper, the prelude to an ambitious comparative project including Britain but not France.
36. On Britain, Peter Self and Herbert J. Storing, *The State and the Farmer*, Allen & Unwin, London, 1962, remains the classic study, while on France see J.T.S. Keeler, 'The corporatist dynamic of agricultural modernization in the Fifth Republic' in W.G. Andrews and S. Hoffmann (eds.), *The Fifth Republic at Twenty*, State University of New York Press, Albany, 1981, chapter 16. See also, Frank L. Wilson, 'Alternative models', p. 199 and the data reported in Tables 4, 5 and 6 in Frank L. Wilson, 'Les groupes d'intérêt', as well as Jack Hayward, 'Dissentient France: the Counter Political Culture' in Vincent Wright (ed.), *Conflict and Consensus in France*, Cass, London, pp. 56–7.
37. Jack Hayward, 'Interest groups and the demand for state action' in J.E.S. Hayward and R.N. Berki (eds.), *State and Society in Contemporary Europe*, Martin Robertson, Oxford, 1979, pp. 26–7. See also Hayward, *Governing France*, pp. 68–9.
38. See Andrew Cox and Jack Hayward, 'The inapplicability of the corporatist model', pp. 217–40. More generally, see Klaus von Beyme, *Challenge to Power. Trade Unions and Industrial Relations in Capitalist Countries*, Sage, London, 1980.
39. In France, it is not only political parties who receive time for

broadcasts but six trade unions, the CNPF, two farm organizations (FNSEA and MODEF), one craftmen's organization and the Chambers of Commerce, of Agriculture and of Craftsmen. The trade unions and CNPF have four slots of ten minutes on the TV and five minutes on radio, while the others are only allowed one of each, annually.

40. A number of books (as well as numerous articles) in which Jeremy Richardson has played a leading role illustrate this admirably: *Pressure Groups in Britain* (edited with Richard Kimber), Dent, London, 1974 and *Campaigning for the Environment* (also edited with Richard Kimber), Routledge, London, 1974, but especially, written in conjunction with Grant Jordan, *Governing under Pressure*, Martin Robertson, Oxford, 1979. A rare example of comparative analysis which is tantalizingly brief is by the author of several studies of British pressure groups: Graham Wootton, *Interest-Groups*, Prentice-Hall, Englewood Cliffs, 1970.

6 The Soldier as Politician: Military Authoritarianism in Latin America
Alan Angell

Military intervention in the political life of Latin America nations has a long history, and almost certainly a long future. However, the late 1960s and early 1970s saw an apparently qualitative change in the type of regime that followed a successful *coup*. Moreover, the *coups* took place in the most developed Latin American countries, societies marked by complex social organisations and institutionalised political systems. On most indicators of modernity, Chile, Brazil, Uruguay and Argentina would score high, though Argentina had a poor record of political stability, and Peru has many of the features of backwardness associated with developing countries. The military no longer intervened to correct the political system; it intervened to govern. Explanations for this new development stressed a number of factors, including internal changes in the military itself, the need to press on with a particularly difficult stage of economic development, the need to suppress the agitated politics of the praetorian state, and the need to adjust national development to changes in the international economic and political system.

Yet the most striking feature to the outside observer was the brutality of the *coups* and the subsequent development of formidable agencies of repression and social control – and this in societies whose political life had been relatively tranquil, at least in comparison with many European countries in this century. The *coup* in Chile in 1973 shattered a long tradition of constitutional government; Uruguay in the same year saw the disappearance of a long history of rather indulgent political tolerance; in Argentina violence moved from the shadows of the political system into the limelight; Brazil after 1968 also found that repression was crucial to the maintenance of military rule; and even in Peru a reformist, though never liberal, military government was forced to abandon reform and adopt tough measures of censorship and suppression.

Was this state violence necessary for something other than dealing with opponents? Were military governments responding to new demands from the ruling class, from international capital, from the USA? Was this the Bonapartist 'state of exception', fascism revived, the last stand of the free world, corporatism renewed – or whatever other convenient theory lay to hand? The theories all had in common the feeling that a decisive break with the past had been made. And there was evidence at least for that feeling, if not always for the underlying theories. There were in these countries decisive changes in the economy, in the role of the state as an agent of economic and social control, in the exclusion of popular sectors from political influence, and in the way that political life was regulated. But how much further can we go with the comparison?[1] How similar were these Latin American regimes in their objectives, structure and behaviour? Before discussing these questions it is necessary to examine the theories offered to account for the new departure.

The rise of the bureaucratic authoritarian state?
The term 'bureaucratic authoritarian state' was developed by the Argentine sociologist Guillermo O'Donnell. He argued that the new state was more

> comprehensive in the range of activities it controls or directly manages; dynamic in its rates of growth compared to those of society as a whole; penetrating, through its subordination of the various "private" areas of civil society; repressive in the extension and efficacy of the coercion it applies; bureaucratic in the formalization and differentiation of its own structures; technocratic in the growing weight of teams of *técnicos* . . .; and furthermore closely linked to international capital.[2]

Many of these features were not new, and they have been well described by earlier writers on the military in politics.[3] But there were differences. Not only was the working class and peasantry excluded from politics, but elite groups that had formerly continued to exert substantial influence under military governments – intellectuals, the church, politicians as a class, national entrepreneurs, agrarian interests – were now pushed to the margins of political influence.[4] It was difficult to interpret the military as representatives of any particular class or sectional interest. Nor was there any attempt at political mobilisation: the new regimes preferred political apathy.[5] Nationalistic rhetoric of an earlier generation of military leaders was also muted.

Moreover, these coups were made by the armed forces acting as a corporate institution. Apart from the rather special case of Pinochet in Chile, personalism or *caudillismo* was discouraged. Indeed one reason for the Argentine military's insistence on collective leadership and a restricted executive is precisely to curb the ambition of any would-be imitator of Perón.[6] Even in Chile, Pinochet's power lies in the close identification of his own fortunes with those of the army as a whole. Brazil has gone furthest in institutionalising the principle of corporate rule and limited terms of office for the president, and unlike their Argentine equivalents, the Brazilian officer corps respects the rules of the game. This agreement surely helps to explain why the regime has enjoyed considerable stability.

Armies can and do act in unison to defend their corporate privileges.[7] This can often explain the timing of a *coup*. But a military regime that subsequently attempts a dramatic restructuring of the social and political order and not just a restoration of the status quo, obviously has some other motive than sheer self-preservation.

One influential school of explanation located the rise of the new military regimes in the ideology developed by the military to deal with a threat that was seen as internal and subversive rather than external and belligerent. The 'new professionalism' led to armies defining their duties largely in terms of combating internal subversion (widely defined) by a combination of repression and development. In Brazil, Stepan writes, 'almost all military officers agreed that since agrarian, fiscal and educational problems were intrinsic to the security of the nation, it was legitimate and necessary for military men to concern themselves with these areas'.[8] And elsewhere, 'the scope of military concern for and study of politics became unrestricted, so that the "new professional" military man was highly politicised'.[9] Officer training schools came to resemble universities. Lectures on economic development complemented more orthodox military training. Peruvian generals, in particular began to talk like sociologists.

These new concerns however did not mean any greater tolerance or liberalism on the part of the armed forces. On the contrary, since this new training gave greater confidence to would be military politicians it made more, rather than less, likely military intervention, and it did not break down the caste like nature of many Latin armies. The new professionalism was a technique to be used, not a way of modifying authoritarian structures. But what exactly did it amount to, in terms of the political vision of the military? The problem here is that of penetrating the military mind, of reconstructing the political thinking of the officer corps, of which we know very little. According to Jacobo Timerman, a journalist whose experiences of torture at the hands of the Argentine military gave him special authority in this murky area, 'The world of the Argentine armed forces is a closed, hermetic structure. Most of the officers' wives are the sisters or daughters of men in the military. Nearly all are related and whenever there's a military regime, the civilians who participate are mostly relatives of the military or individuals who have frequented military circles . . . This pattern has separated the military from the most elemental currents of modern life. . . .'¹⁰

One must not exaggerate the extent or importance of this 'new professionalism'. It may have improved the military's understanding of economic planning, but it did nothing towards increasing their political sophistication. Many of the issues treated in the Higher War Academies can be traced back to much earlier times.¹¹ And some armies, like the Chilean, showed little evidence of interest in the issues debated in Brazil, before, or indeed after, 1973.

A more plausible explanation for the wave of *coups* that established military regimes lies in the crisis that was undoubtedly affecting civilian governments and the military's interpretation of the causes of that crisis. Countries in which military regimes replaced civilian ones were experiencing long-run problems of economic growth, and short-term fiscal crises. Superimposed on these, were problems of extensive and intensive political mobilisation and polarisation. Attempts to combine social reform and populist politics had gone disastrously wrong. Balance of payments deficits showed the failure to develop the export sector, and the failure to control the level of imports (too often of basic consumer goods to meet popular demands). High and accelerating rates of inflation demonstrated the inability of the executive power to control a multiplicity of social groups demanding satisfaction from the state. Low levels of investment reflected the anxieties of the entrepreneurial sector. Low agricultural productivity pointed to long-term neglect. Chile in 1973 was the most dramatic example of the breakdown of a democratic regime, but the other countries exhibited the same symptoms if in lesser degree (or, in the case of urban violence, greater degree).

The military saw this crisis as the failure of civilian politicans to live up to their national responsibilities and even more drastically, as the failure of the civil state to represent the national interest. It was not only politicians who had to be replaced, the whole state had to be restructured. The immediate post-*coup* tasks were the stabilisation of the economy and the demobilisation of an over-politicised society. This would create the conditions for the development of an alternative growth model that would avoid the excesses of the past.

Such a project could not, by its very nature be other than long-term and drastic.¹² In the Southern cone countries, Argentina, Chile and Uruguay, monetarist economics provided the perfect blend of a reversal of economic policy, with the political need for authoritarian controls to eliminate the distortions brought about by populism and to create the right conditions in which market forces could operate. Reducing the size of the public sector would remove the basis for popular or sectional pressures for concessions from the government; redirecting the surplus to the private capital market would strengthen those forces supportive of the military's policies and penalise those who were likely to be against; opening the economy to free trade would provide the means for growth without having to give state support for uncompetitive sectors; allowing market forces to regulate wage rates would undermine the political bargaining strength of the labour movement.[13] All of these would combine to eliminate the greatest propagator of social unrest – inflation. And the beauty of the solution was that the regulatory mechanism would be that most liberal of concepts, the operation of free market forces.[14] At the same time the old forms of political allegiance would be eroded, and new forms, classless and national, would develop.

Monetarism offered a new panacea in contrast to the failures of the past, one which might 'justify' the brutal suppression that followed military *coups*. According to Whitehead the new economic orthodoxy was attractive to the military because it offered coherence (an overall battle plan for the conquest of civil society), discipline, and the redistribution of resources from vanquished to victor.[15] Once under way, the process was to be irreversible, and as necessary means for national salvation its premises were not to be questioned.

Many sectors, hitherto protected by populist governments, would find the new measures unpleasant. Interest rates, often negative to help the numerous small business sector, would rise. Devaluation, necessary for the exchange rate to find its market level, could lead to inflation unless there was strict control over wage rises and unless public sector expenditure was held back. Tariffs would come down, in spite of the opposition of industry. Nationalist opposition to foreign firms would be ignored; foreign capital had to be guaranteed the right economic incentives and political stability. In great need of foreign loans, aid and investment, these countries had to present themselves as models of economic orthodoxy, as more IMF than the IMF itself. Even the Peruvian military, which embarked on a social reform programme distinct from the other military regimes, still relied upon export-led economic growth, with all the restraints that that came to imply with the change in the international terms of trade in the 1970s.[16]

The necessary political conditions for the experiment in monetarist economics were social stability, political tranquility and above all a powerful executive. These conditions could only be achieved in the first instance by repression and control, although in the long term it was assumed that the population would come to appreciate the benefits of the new order. This control was achieved in two stages. The first was massive repression. For obvious reasons estimates in this field are unreliable, but there is little doubt of the scale of repression. In Chile, estimates of those killed by the armed forces in the immediate aftermath of the 1973 *coup* range from five to thirty thousand; in the first six months there were an estimated eighty thousand political prisoners. Three years after the Argentine *coup* of 1976 an estimated five to fifteen thousand people had 'disappeared'. In Uruguay between 1973 and 1977 about seventy thousand people were arrested for alleged political offences, but though many were tortured, the number of deaths was far fewer than in Argentina or Chile.[17]

The second stage was the development of massive counter intelligence and security agencies, often with US help and training. These agencies, in addition to those in the armed forces, also called for highly trained police and paramilitary forces 'dispersed throughout the population to identify and neutralise dissidents without creating major disturbances'.[18]

Before we examine how well the military regimes performed according to the targets they set themselves, it is interesting to locate this 'new' authoritarianism in the context of comparative discussion on the nature of authoritarianism.

Authoritarianism: does the model fit Latin America?
Linz' definition is the best known.

> Authoritarian regimes are political systems with limited, not responsible, political pluralism: without elaborate and guiding ideology (but with distinctive mentalities): without intensive nor extensive political mobilisation (except some points in their development): and which a leader (or occasionally a small group) exercises power within formally ill-defined limits but actually quite precise ones.[19]

How well does this definition fit the initial stages of military authoritarian regimes in Latin America? In the first place, power is not particularly restrained or precise in its limits. The essence of its operation is arbitrariness; no one is safe, no one knows the rules. These surely are characteristics of police power in totalitarian societies. Secondly, it is not clear what limited pluralism is in operation. Some groups do influence policy-making, but the policy-making process as such remains arbitrary and unpredictable (outside the general framework of free market economics, in theory at least). There are no generally accepted rules as to the extent of influence of certain groups, or the procedures of attempting to exercise influence. The system has been described as 'centralisation without integration'.[20] Sectors that exercise great influence in one era – the private banking sector in Chile for example – become enemies of the state in another. The policy-making process is not institutionalised. Finally, it is by no means obvious that the 'mentality' of such regimes is as hazy as all that. Linz defines mentalities as 'ways of thinking and feeling that are more emotional than rational, that provide non-codified ways of reacting to different situations'.[21] Adherents of monetarist economics, or even of doctrines of national security of the 'new professionalism' variety, would no doubt believe that their ideas were indeed rational and codified.

Linz's model is derived mostly from Western European experience. If authoritarians in Latin America were looking towards a regime that they would wish to emulate, it would be Mexico rather than Franco's Spain or Salazar's Portugal. If the model is Mexico we would have to look for the following elements: (i) a popular revolution which destroyed the old order; (ii) a political system which for all its faults is responsive to social demands; (iii) a record of sustained and stable growth; (iv) a political system which although it certainly employs repression relies more on cooptation and mobilisation and which enjoys considerable support from labour and domestic capital; (v) a good working relationship with the Church which is important because the Church is both popular and a source of legitimacy; and (vi) control over the army and police.

One immediate contrast between this rather idealised portrait of the Mexican political system and that of military regimes is over the question of legitimacy. How can a military government legitimise itself? Charismatic legitimacy is hardly possible for the grey men who rule in military dictatorships, especially if their economic policies impose considerable austerity. A corporatist state structure would invoke too many unflattering comparisons with fascism, would be opposed by the Church, and is hardly congruent with an economic model based on modern capitalism. An embracing one-party system cannot be manufactured to order, and anyhow a one-party or two-party system would dent the monopoly of political power held by the military; and parties have a habit of running out of control. So the military faces a paradox. The only long-term legitmacy it can claim employs the language of those whom it has overthrown and those who oppose it. The basic political discourse of Latin America, for all the times it has been violated, is still that of constitutional and representative government. And this is the tradition that the military claims it has come in to protect, perfect and eventually transfer to civilians. As Linz points out for Brazil, 'the constant restatement of the intention to restore competitive liberal democracy was and still is a drawback for the legitimation of permanent authoritarian elitist rule'.[22]

The fact that such countries form, or would like to form part of the Western political bloc adds international pressure to adhere, nominally at least, to the democratic tradition.

A military government has therefore to present itself as transitory. As Rouquié writes, 'A permanent system of military rule is almost a contradiction in terms. The army cannot govern directly and durably without ceasing to be an army. And it is precisely the subsequent government, the successor regime that legitimates the prior military usurpation.'[23] When President Bordaberry of Uruguay proposed, in 1976, to introduce *de jure* as well as *de facto* a new authoritarian state in which the armed forces alone would have legitimacy, he was dismissed by the army high command. The form of the civilian state, a non-military president and executive, are traditions the Uruguayan military feels called upon to uphold in theory, in spite of the massive violations in practice.[24]

Another problem that arises in the analysis of military regimes is the question of state power. Is there a ruling elite behind the military? In whose interest is the military governing? Most recent explantions have revolved around the concept of the relative autonomy of the state from civil society. The *coup* has destroyed most of the institutions that regulated political life. Civil society is disorganised to such an extent that the new government has relative freedom from social pressures. The military can choose its own allies and dictate the terms of alliance. The idea of course is not a new one. As Trotsky wrote,

> As soon as the struggle of two social strata – the haves and the have nots, the exploiters and the exploited – reaches its highest tension, the conditions are established for the domination of bureaucracy, police, soldiery. The government becomes 'independent' of society. Let us once more recall: if two forks are struck symmetrically into a cork, the latter can stand even on the head of a pin. That is precisely the scheme of Bonapartism.[25]

The idea of the Bonapartist state has been developed by marxists to explain how the military rules in the interests (even if against the wishes of some members) of the higher bourgeoisie. As Parkin has argued however, 'this vision of the state as a bureaucratic monster that has wrenched itself free of class control to become parasitic upon the rest of society cannot easily be squared with the unshakeable Marxist assumption that the only natural habitat of power is in social classes'.[26] He points out how the notion of relative autonomy can be deduced from the ideas of writers as varied as Weber, Durkheim and even the economists of the Chicago school.

It is undoubtedly true that at least initially the military is relatively free from social pressures, though this isolation becomes a source of weakness when the government discovers that it needs a social base. It should be pointed out very strongly that one thing the government is not autonomous from, not even relatively, is the international economy.

One attempt to transfer this rather abstract theory to the level of specific political alliances has been proposed in analysing the power structure in Brazil. The argument is that the essential function of the military is to orchestrate the alliance between the state bureaucracy, the transnational companies and local capital.[27] It is obviously unsatisfactory to reduce the role of the military to the representation of national capital, given the relative weakness of that sector in most Latin American countries. But one comparative difficulty with this argument is that it could equally well be argued that the function of the civilian administration in Mexico, or in Colombia or Venezuela, is to perform the same role with the same partners. Military power therefore does not seem to be a necessary condition of such an alliance. Moreover, the concept of relative autonomy is a very static one. Even in the case of Brazil there have been some remarkable shifts in the relative power of the three major agents of the alliance, with the local capitalists by the late 1970s acting as an important force urging the return to constitutional government. To claim that military governments in Latin America constitute a new kind of authoritarian system based on the relative autonomy of the state confers a higher purpose on the military than it has in practice been able to sustain; the authority that the military possess is based on force, and not on serving the higher interests of the state.

The idea that the authoritarian state strengthens itself by allowing a limited degree of pluralism does not seem applicable to the recent military regimes of Latin America. The striking characteristics of the way military governments deal with non-military organisations are their clumsiness of approach, their ambiguities and their indecisiveness. After the initial repression important questions arise. Should trade unions continue to be coerced, or can they be incorporated into the government machine? Should associations of entrepreneurs be integrated into the policy-making process? Should popular demands be ignored or should there be some attempt to meet them? How should the government act to counter increasingly hostile criticism from the Catholic church? To all these questions military governments have given half-answers, and more often than not changed their minds several times. But most pressing of all is the question of how the government should deal with political parties, especially those of the centre and right, which cannot be accused of forming part of the marxist conspiracy. Every military government has had its own particular solution, none of which have worked very well.

The Brazilian military decided upon a two-party system, a party of government and a party of opposition (very loyal opposition of course). The Chileans banned some and put others in recess. The Peruvians ignored their parties and elaborated an unconvincing 'theory of no party' (it does not sound more convincing in Spanish). But previous political allegiances remained stubbornly immobile in spite of the appeal to a higher nationalism free from sectarianism that the military offered.

Latin American military governments do not fit particularly well the model developed from Western European experience to differentiate authoritarian from totalitarian regimes. Perhaps the reason lies in the extent to which Western European regimes were able to distance themselves from the military, in the way that both Franco and Salazar were able to do. This has not happened in Latin America, at least not in the modern states which which we are concerned. This inability to transcend the *military* character of the government is insufficiently emphasised in discussions of the new authoritarianism. The next section will underline this point by examining the record of military governments in the countries under discussion.

Military governments in practice: a new departure, or variations on an old theme?

There is nothing modest about the claims of the military governments when they take power. They promise to restore order, deal firmly with subversives, eliminate corruption and rule in the national interest. Their rule will be technocratic and just. Harmful political conflict will be eliminated. These conditions will allow for economic growth. When all this has been achieved and the nation re-educated, power can gradually be transferred to responsible politicians. These claims might have some plausibility if at the time of the *coup* the military were united not just in opposition to the civilian politicians, but also around a clear programme of government for the next few years. This claim assumes also that the military acted in the national interest and not out of any specific interest of its own. Neither of these claims can be sustained.

(a) The intentions of the military

It is certainly true that military *coups* enjoy considerable popular support. Indeed this support can persist over a long period of time even in the face of economic difficulty. The evidence, however, does not indicate that the military assumes power with any clear plan of government: it reacts to events rather than pursues objectives.[28] The initial rhetoric of the Brazilian military, for example, was conservative-liberal: no one in 1964 would have foreseen the extent to which the state sector of the economy developed (nor the extent to which the security apparatus developed).[29] To rebut accusations of lack of a coherent programme, the Peruvian military published its *Plan Inca*. But it was not published until 1974, six years after the military took over, and almost certainly was written in the year of its publication. The Chilean military adopted a whole range of political ideas in the initial period of power, mostly from the Catholic right. It was some time before the Chicago economists won over the ruling junta, and one can assume that many of their ideas were very new to the politically inexperienced men ruling after 1973. The Uruguayan military command had no real political experience. The background of the officer corps was mostly rural, lower middle class, with very basic levels of education.[30]

Most military officers are faced at the time of the *coup* with a new experience, for which they have had little preparation. Even those who had participated in previous *coups* were not expecting to assume the tasks of long-term government of the military regimes of recent years. It is an error to attribute to the armed forces either great knowledge of, or even particular interest in, the details of politics. Potash has consistently pointed out that even in the Argentine military the proportion of officers with clear and stable political opinions was very small: most officers were politically neutral, though of course they shared the general viewpoint of men of their position and class.[31] They were certainly united in their opposition to Perón, but one suspects that this had more to do with the threat that Perón represented to the independence of the armed forces than to any rooted dislike of the economic and social programme of Peronism.

The organisation of the military is hierarchical; its behaviour emphasises discipline and obedience. These values obviously colour the general social outlook of the military, but do not transfer easily into the world of political choices. 'The barracks becomes the world', wrote S.E. Finer,[32] and he could equally well have added that the world becomes the barracks. Timerman commented that 'the incapacity of the Argentine military to formulate a structured ideology leads to their general acceptance of the phobias of reactionary groups with whom they feel more closely aligned than the democratic sectors'.[33] The Peruvian military was more open to a wide spectrum of ideas and doctrines than other armies in Latin America, but the problem was that it was too open, and the contradictory positions assumed by members of the officer corps reduced important areas of government policy to incoherence.

A certain degree of self-interest is present at the time of most military *coups*. The Brazilian military in 1964 was very concerned that President Goulart's interference in internal military matters would lead to increasing executive control over the armed forces. The Peruvian military in 1968 avoided some unpleasant charges involving contraband. Bolivia is unusual in the degree to which its military is disunited, factionalised and corrupt, but the statement made by Whitehead is not without application elsewhere. A recent *coup* was due 'not so much to fear for the survival of the institution (which if anything is more threatened by the proliferation of para-military forces than by the left) nor to any deep ideological commitment. Rather it was the prospect of large-scale illicit enrichment for the officer corps through a more unfettered development of the narcotics trade.'[34]

No military *coup* ever takes place without some, even substantial, civilian support. There are always civilian groups hoping to manipulate the military to its own ends. In every one of the six successful *coups* in Argentina between 1930 and 1976 substantial sectors of public opinion – political parties, trade unions, industrialists, landowners – have urged the military to intervene.[35] 'Nothing is stranger in Argentina than anti-militarism' said Rouquié.[36] Opposition forces often prefer a military *coup* rather than allow an elected government to serve out its term of office. The 'propensity to intervene' seems stronger amongst civilians than it does amongst officers. Civilian groups are rarely satisfied with the military in power, but they lack the means to change its policies. The alternative is to conspire to bring about another *coup*, either to return power to civilians or to a more sympathetic group inside the military. This constant see-saw of public opinion helps to explain why Argentina has so many military governments, and why those governments are themselves unstable and prone to internal division. Military executives last no longer than civilian.

(b) Rule by technocrats?
Who, then, makes policy in military regimes? What is the role of the technocrat? Military officers in countries such as Brazil and Argentina do at least have some experience in the administration of public enterprises. In the other countries not only was this background rare, but as in Argentina and Brazil, it was felt that overall competence in managing the economy was the preserve of the civilian technocrats. But was this really rule by technocracy? In practice the military would not leave well alone. In the first place there is always an area of state expenditure that even the most daring technocrat must not touch – defence. Considerations of national security can lead to the military overruling the wishes of the technocrats; the Chilean military, for example, has always resisted plans to sell off the state copper mines. In Uruguay, residual populist ideas in the military led to the vetoing by the military of plans to dismiss large numbers of government employees.[37]

In Peru the military, perhaps more than elsewhere, sought to define itself as the government of the armed forces and kept civilian advisers at arm's length.[38] Cabinet changes take place quite as regularly under military governments as under civilian. Long-term planning is rarely implemented and technocrats are hired and fired with regularity as much vaunted plans for economic growth fail. Beliefs that policy-making under military rule becomes more technical, is removed from distorting pressures, and is made with a longer perspective are thus not borne out in reality. Some distortions are removed; but others are introduced.

Another claim which is equally ill-founded is the boast that political conflict and sectarian infighting has no place under the austere neutrality of military government. On the contrary, political conflict is as intense as before, but now it takes place inside the armed forces. One of the ironies of Brazilian politics, it has been argued by McDonough, is that 'there may be more *de facto* pluralism within any one of the elite sectors, including the military, than there is in the relations among the groups themselves – a tendency that helps explain the air of simultaneous disorganisation and despotism'.[39] In Uruguay in 1977, more than twenty officers were arrested for issuing a document criticising the regime and advocating a return to civilian rule.[40] The Argentine military divided in 1962 over the question of how to deal with Peronism, and so bitter were the divisions that a pitched battle was fought. The instability of military presidents in Argentina is an indicator of continuous internal differences over personalities and policies. The one country where internal differences have not surfaced, or been allowed to surface, is Chile. The reasons for this may well have to do with the political inexperience of the armed forces in that country, and with the need for a strong executive to implement ruthless measures of repression and far-ranging plans of economic transformation.[41]

The different branches of the armed forces have to be accommodated inside the governing coalition, even at the expense of weakening political unity. Military unity comes first. Different tendencies inside the armed forces have to be given their share of power. Inexperienced military officers can easily fall prey to the sectional interests they are supposed to control, especially where that interest is in collusion with the bureaucracy. Military hierarchy is a poor guide to policy-making, especially to dealing with political crises which can develop in any regime. Each ministry in Peru became a personal empire of the military man in charge, used to build up the political base of that officer, and military ministers behaved as selfishly when asked to accept reductions in budget or responsibilities, as any previous civilian minister.

(c) The military and civil society

The military are unsure about the generation and maintenance of support for the new regime. Initially the need was to demobilise, but that is a short-term solution. To establish their claim to rule they need to demonstrate some evidence of popular consent, if not enthusiasm. They cannot follow the easy path of populism because it was precisely to end that style of politics that they took over.

This uncertainty is reflected in the attitude of military governments towards political parties. The Peruvian military went furthest in its rejection of the idea of a party system (even the Chileans envisaged parties operating in the rather distant future). The Peruvian military argued that to introduce a party or parties to try to mobilise support for the regime would undermine the technocratic bureaucracy that they were trying to establish. It would be divisive because some officers would join the party and use it as a lever for power; or nobody would join it and it would be redundant; or everyone would join it and it would weaken military command structures by allowing civilians into policy-making circles.[42] The military experimented with 'national mobilisation' agencies but these produced as little success, and as much confusion, as a party system would have done. The Brazilian military found equal difficulty in creating a managed two-party system. For the first few years the parties were allowed little autonomy and were useful neither in supporting the regime nor in providing more than a façade of democracy; given some autonomy and increasingly free elections the opposition party became a genuine expression of majority disapproval of the military, and undermined its authority. The Uruguayan military left a purged two-party system, and held a referendum in 1980 on a new constitution, confident that they would win. Unfortunately for the military the middle-level leaders of the parties mobilised opinion sufficiently to inflict a humiliating defeat on the military by 57% votes against the proposal to 43% in favour.[43]

Perhaps more surprising than the failures to control the party system has been the inability to tame the labour movement. Trade unions had reached such levels of organisation and support in many Latin American countries that permanent repression would be a mammoth undertaking. Moreover, as open economies depending upon trade with the West, they had to tread carefully: more than once North American unions had provided important defence of trade union rights in Chile. The very pattern of Brazilian growth led to the conditions for the development of a modern industrial proletariat, above all in the automobile plants, that weakened the Government by strikes from 1978 to 1980. Monetarist economists wanted the market to regulate wages, and they were prepared to allow for a minimal union organisation to engage in limited bargaining. The Peruvian military created its own federation to rival the existing ones, but as real wages declined and the government began to repress labour organisations, even the government's own creation deserted it and joined the ranks of the opposition.[44] Successive attempts by the Uruguayan military to win over workers from their previous allegiances have been dismal failures.

It is difficult to understand the reasons why the military thought they might gain support from the unions. The military assumed that workers would be prepared to accept short-term sacrifices for long-term promises; that unionists' attitudes were manipulated by corrupt and anti-national subversives; and that class consciousness was a meaningless invention of the left. All these assumptions were false. Perhaps the attempt to incorporate labour might have worked in a genuinely corporative system. But though there was some flirtation with corporatist ideas, it never went any further. Individuals were coopted, but not social groups or organisations.[45] The military wanted subordinates, not partners. A genuine corporate state would have weakened the military's monopoly of power.

The military used to be able to count on the support of the Catholic church in the past, but no longer. Although the recent wave of military *coups* received support from most sectors of the Catholic church (the extent and influence of radical currents inside the church has often been exaggerated), that support has gradually turned to opposition. The reasons for opposition are to be found in the increasing repression of priests and active Catholic laity by the government, the desperation of oppressed groups turning to the church for help, active international encouragement, and a realisation that the military governments regarded repression and control not as temporary expedients but as permanent features of political life. The reaction of the church has not been uniform, either inside the national church, or between countries. Although the Chilean church is very progressive, it has a number of bishops who support the military. Although the Uruguayan church has been relatively indifferent to the repression of the regime, there are some outspoken priests in that country. What is most interesting, however, is that opposition has evolved from defence of basic human rights to rejection of government policies *per se*. The Chilean church hierarchy reserve for the Chicago school of free market economics the kind of criticism they used to direct at communism. Moreover, the church plays a vital role in the protection of groups such as trade unions. By these criticisms and activities, the church refuses to legitimise military governments, in spite of the claims such governments make to be defending christian values against the marxist conspiracy.

(d) Control through terror: the development of the intelligence agencies

One undeniable common feature among the various military governments of Latin America has been the development of sophisticated agencies of control and repression. If opposition is defined as subversion, if politics is seen as war, if the army is convinced that the nation is under threat from the enemy, if there exists a powerful guerrilla movement (which there was in Argentina and Uruguay) then it follows that all measures to defend the nation and the military are justified. If opposition grows, then it proves the point that the challenge is there and needs tough measures to counter it; if the opposition declines, then it shows that the tough measures were justified.

Yet there is an obvious contradiction between the stated political goals of the military – the eventual return to constitutional government, respect for law and order – and the activities of these intelligence agencies. Properly conducted legal trials are unacceptable to the military because they might not lead to convictions; trials based on the 'revolutionary legality' of the communist systems are inappropriate given the lip service paid to liberalism; and so the adopted method is that of private violence, the development of paramilitary forces, assassinations and 'disappearances'.[46]

This is the structure in which extreme beliefs and practices can flourish. The political isolation of many military officers produces a siege mentality in which they are prepared to accept excesses committed in the name of the state. Timerman reported that his Argentine military interrogators believed that in fact the Third World War had already broken out, but not as a confrontation between democracies and communism but rather between the entire world and left-wing terrorism (synonymous for some with Zionism).[47] Argentina, they believed, had been chosen as the initial battleground of the first phase of the war. Ludicrous as this is, one can understand why military officers would prefer a sinister plot to explain why they had been unable to erase the memory of Peronism from the working class, and why a powerful urban guerrilla movement had for a time run rings around them, rather than the more obvious explanation (in terms of the unpopularity of the military and the genuine popularity of Perón).

Such intelligence agencies become a state within the state, a method of surveillance over the military itself, with methods and structures which make it difficult for the executive to control. In Brazil the security forces began to conduct vendettas against senior members of the government. But following the death of a prominent Jewish journalist in 1975 (the Jewish marxist conspiracy fear existed in Brazil as well) President Geisel was able to carry out a purge in 1975, only to have to do so again in 1976 after another death under torture.[48]

These agencies become involved in the economy, and establish dealings, often clandestine, with powerful economic groups. They are, after all, large establishments. At the height of DINA power in Chile, the head of the agency, General Contreras, commanded a small army of 9300 agents and a network of paid and volunteer informants several times larger, honeycombing all walks of life inside Chile and abroad.[49] Several important firms taken over by the state under the Allende government were passed secretly to the control of the DINA. Extortion and blackmail of victims is commonplace. In Brazil there is strong evidence of deals between members of the São Paulo business community, the intelligence agencies, and hardline civilian and military politicians, against the interests of the official government in Brasilia.[50]

Important though these agencies are in consolidating the power of military governments, it is by no means certain that they continue to be an asset. Continued reliance upon such agencies undermines the already weak claims of the government to legitimacy. It underlines the fact that the basis of the government remains that of arbitrary power. In so far as these agencies seek to establish control over the armed forces themselves, they are seen as weakening the overall unity of the military and the authority of the executive. They arouse considerable international hostility towards the government, especially when they engage in activities abroad, as the Chilean DINA has with two assassinations, one in Buenos Aires of a former Commander-in-Chief of the Army unsympathetic to the government, and another, in Washington of a leading opposition politician. International criticism weakens the attractiveness of these regimes to potential foreign investors who fear that such criticisms could point to future political instability. The more important the role of these agencies, the more difficult is the return to the barracks. Victims will seek redress, the prestige of the armed forces will be further undermined, and the independence of the army may be called into question. In such circumstances it is not uncommon for hardliners to try to provoke artificial crises, and thus the continuance of military rule. These security agencies (and each important branch of the armed forces has its own) have a strong interest in the perpetuation of military rule, and with their links with the world of crime and with unscrupulous businesses, constitute a strong impediment to the return to constitutional rule.

(e) Uniformities in economic policies?
Most of the search for comparisons among the so-called bureaucratic regimes has concentrated on their economic policies. While it is true that the new economic orthodoxy is monetarism, the only country that made a really systematic effort to apply it was Chile; Argentina and

Uruguay deviated in some unorthordox ways; it influenced economic policy-making in Brazil only in the 1964 to 1967 period, and has influence during the present crisis; and assumed importance in Peru after 1975 when the first reformist phase of the military government was over. Rather than monetarism the characteristic of Peruvian and Brazilian development was an enormous development of the state sector.[51] In both those countries the level of repression at the time of the *coup* was relatively slight, so the need to combine fierce measures of economic stabilisation with political control was less intense than in the cases of Chile, Argentina or Uruguay. The Brazilian military in particular played an important role not simply in the formation but also in the control and administration of a number of important state enterprises. The air force for example controls Embraer, the state aviation industry which has an impressive export performance. The navy dominates nuclear research, and a part of the nuclear power industry. And the central role is occupied by the army which runs a whole series of industries from shipyards to communications, and electrical power to the arms industry. The financial sector is also an area of military activity: Brazil's biggest pension fund began as the army's own institution Capemi.[52]

Even amongst the southern cone countries that proclaimed their loyalties to monetarism there were substantial differences.[53] Argentine monetarists lacked the influence of their Chilean counterparts. Army officers controlled one of the biggest industrial complexes in the country, *Fabricaciones Militares*. The military-industrial complex interfered with many of the proposals of the economic team and contributed to the incoherence and failures of policy in that country. Similarly the Uruguayan military veered sharply away from monetarist orthodoxy. There were fairly strict controls over wages and even over prices; large fiscal deficits accumulated; exports were subsidised; and the real level of public investment increased.[54]

In Chile the monetarist experiment went furthest, in part because those groups that might have opposed such measures had their powers eroded, because the tradition of military involvement with basic industry and public services was much less developed, and because a relatively inexperienced military was more inclined to place its trust in the plausible sounding remedies of the 'Chicago boys'. But even here the state retained an impressive presence in the economy. The top eight firms in Chile in 1970 were state firms and they remained in state hands in 1980, even though they were being forced to operate as private firms and lost many of their traditional advantages.[55] Further extensions of the monetarist experiment into areas hitherto safeguarded by the state were brought to an abrupt halt by the severe recession which hit Chile from 1981 onwards, discredited the monetarists, and forced the state to take into public ownership most of the private banking sector.

In two respects, however, one could point to considerable uniformities among the regimes: the way in which real wages declined, and the transfer of resources from the industrial to the financial sector. The reasons for the first are fairly obvious, both as a political and economic measure. The second was less consciously planned but resulted from opening relatively weak economies to international forces at a time of high levels of international liquidity, abolition or reduction of exchange controls and the general deregulation of banking activities. These factors, combined with high domestic interest rates aimed at reducing inflation, created the conditions for speculation.

Yet the military gained no long-term benefit from either of these measures. Lower living standards eventually led to an intensification of popular protest. A general strike in Peru in 1977 was of great importance in influencing the military to return to the barracks; strikes in Brazil in 1978 accelerated the programme of liberalisation; and demonstrations against even the seemingly impregnable Pinochet forced the Government into panic measures in 1983. The banking sector, riding high in Chile in the boom of 1977 to 1980, crashed in spectacular fashion with the recession from 1981 onwards; and there were similar disturbances though on a lesser scale in the other countries. A great deal of the huge international debt accumulated by Latin American countries in recent years consists of short and medium-term loans from private overseas banks to national private banks.[56] The problem of severe indebtedness has made governments more concerned with state regulation of these activities and less with the free operation of market forces.

(f) The failure to gain legitimacy through economic success

It is possible that if the military regimes of Latin America had achieved economic success on the Mexican scale then they might have established some vestige of legitimacy. In fact it was crucial for them to achieve stability, if not prosperity, because that was one of the main justifications they gave for the *coup*. It is no coincidence that Brazil, the longest established military regime in Latin America, also has the most impressive economic performance.

The record of military governments in economic management is rarely bright, and that of the military regimes in Latin America is no exception. Argentina has not seen inflation fall below 100% for some years; real incomes fell by 20% in 1982, and unemployment rose from 3% in 1978 to 13% in 1982. The Chilean economy suffered from two massive reductions in GDP of about 15% in 1975 and again in 1982;

unemployment in 1983 was over 30%; and industrial production has fallen to levels current about twenty years ago. The Peruvian military left a legacy of high inflation, high unemployment and dismal growth rates. Even though Brazil has managed to grow at respectable rates since 1974, the turn to reliance upon the old style of import-substituting industrialisation meant a return to balance of payments deficits. All these countries face huge external debts in the 1980s and in all income distribution has become increasingly unequal.[57]

Why was there such a failure? Even if the economy had been managed with technical efficiency, Diaz Alejandro has pointed to the caution that entrepreneurs show when faced with the possible uncertainties that attend dictatorial governments.[58] But the economies, apart to some extent from Brazil's, were not managed efficiently and flexibly. The most dogmatic team has produced, in Chile, the worst of the recessions. The monetarist gamble did not come off. Insensitivity to non-military opinion helped to produce badly planned decisions, badly executed. Targets were set without sufficient regard to real world factors. Continual interference by sectors of the armed forces for particular ends, disrupted the coherence of policy-making. Industrialists and landowners were alienated from governments that failed to consult them.

There were factors outside the control of national governments. The oil price rises, high international interest rates and the world-wide recession were bound to undermine the basis of export-led growth economies. Not only military governments found the new international climate harsh and damaging. But governments that concentrate all power in their own hands, and do not in theory have to bow to sectional demands, should be able to respond more rapidly to the down turn in the economy. In practice their response was uncertain.

One factor that could have been controlled quite easily in theory to lessen the pressure on the balance of payments is defence expenditure. Apart from the special factor of the conflict in the South Atlantic, defence expenditure rose constantly, though accurate figures are difficult to establish as much defence-related expenditure is disguised. In Uruguay the armed forces' share of the national budget rose from 13.9% in 1968 to 26.2% in 1973 and in the mid-1970s to an estimated 40–50%.[59] In 1979 Chile was spending an estimated 9.4% of its GDP on arms, and Peru 4%. Much of this expenditure is for imports, which consumes scarce foreign exchange. In mid-1980 Brazil was running an annual balance of payments deficit of US $6 billion while at the same time US $2 billion was being spent on arms imports.[60] In the ten-year period after 1970 the armed forces in Argentina grew by 35% while military spending rose by 51%. Chile doubled its military spending between 1977 and 1980.[61] The days of easy US military aid to Latin America are now over. Arms are bought on the international market and paid for in scarce foreign exchange, even by Argentina and Brazil which are by now considerable producers and exporters of arms. The effect of such conspicuous expenditure is to distort economic policy, and to lay the military open to the charge of feathering their own nests to the detriment of everyone else (and the fact that a great deal of secrecy surrounds these transactions only fuels the unpopularity of the military).

The retreat to the barracks

Bureaucratic authoritarianism which once seemed so secure in Latin America was gradually eroded in the late 1970s and early 1980s. The promise of rule in the national interest with technocratic efficiency had not been fulfilled. The Peruvian military returned power to the civilians in 1980 and, as if to demonstrate its disdain for military rule, the electorate chose the president who had been ousted in the *coup* of 1968. Brazil has held increasingly free elections, culminating in the opposition triumph of 1982 when nearly all the major states elected opposition governors. Argentina is to hold presidential elections in late 1983 and Uruguay shortly after. Even Chile in 1983 was shaken by a wave of protest, and the military promised to bring forward the electoral timetable.

The reasons for this retreat are not substantially different from those that obtained in earlier instances of the military returning to the barracks. The officier corp felt that to hold on to power would undermine the unity of the armed forces and deepen the ever-widening divisions in its ranks. Support for the government had dwindled, while the forces of the opposition had grown stronger. The economic failures of the military taunted them with the memories of earlier promises and led to a withdrawal of support among the dominant economic sectors.

But what kind of political system is left when military governments resign from office? Such a long period in power, and so many transformations, are bound to have deep and lasting effects on the nature of the political system. The military may leave office, but it does not surrender all its political power.

The techniques of extrication are a field of study all of their own. There must be an instititional framework not necessarily democratic but at least impersonal and accepted, within which the transition can be managed. The civilians who will occupy office must be acceptable to the military. There must be no reprisals against officers for excesses committed during the period of military rule – an enormously tricky problem given the strength of popular feeling on the subject. The accumulated privileges of the military must be respected. This can mean anything from maintaining the level of arms expenditures to ignoring military involvement in the drug trade in Bolivia and Peru.

The management of the transition demands political skill from the politicians as well. If the experience of Argentina is typical the most important lesson is not so much military respect for civilian authority as civilian respect for constitutional forms. But an outbreak of guerrilla violence, as took place in Peru in the early 1980s, can recreate the conditions in which the military is likely to intervene and in which civilian groups. anxious to restore law and order, and of short political memory, are likely to urge such intervention. The example of Spain is much quoted in Latin America, but even apart from the obvious difference of the absence of a unifying monarchy, the relative lack of large moderate political parties will make the Spanish experience, itself precarious at certain moments, difficult to imitate.

Military intervention in politics becomes a habit and one which is difficult to cure. Writing in the late 1960s Samuel Huntington sounded an optimistic note. 'Intermittent military intervention to stop politics or to suspend politics is the essence of praetorianism. Sustained military participation in politics may lead a society away from praetorianism.'[62] Writing earlier, the pessimistic note sounded by S.E. Finer is surely more appropriate. 'If ever we are asked to endorse a military regime . . . we must surely ask ourselves whether any immediate gain in stability and prosperity it brings is not outweighed by the very great likelihood that, for an indefinite time to come, public life and all the personal expectations that hang upon it will continue to be upset wilfully and unpredictably by further military threats, blackmail or revolt.'[63]

Notes

1. Some influential Latin America writers argued that one could not go very far at all. See, for example, Fernando Henrique Cardoso, *The Authoritarian Regime at the Crossroads: The Brazilian Case*, Working Papers no. 93, 1981, Latin American Program, The Wilson Center, Washington, D.C.

2. Guillermo O'Donnell, 'Corporatism and the question of the state' in James Malloy (ed.), *Authoritarianism and Corporatism in Latin America* (University of Pittsburgh Press, Pittsburgh, 1977), p. 37.

   The Weberian heritage of this formulation is striking. See the discussion in Frank Parkin, *Marxism and Class Theory* (Tavistock Publications, London, 1979), p. 127.

3. Not least of all, of course, is the first, highly influential contemporary account in S.E. Finer, *The Man on Horseback: the Role of the Military in Politics* (Pall Mall Press, London, 1962).

4. Peter McDonough, *Power and Ideology in Brazil* (Princeton University Press, Princeton, 1981), p. xxviii.

5. Fernando Henrique Cardoso, 'The characteristics of authoritarian regimes' in D. Collier (ed.), *The New Authoritarianism* (Princeton University Press, Princeton, 1979), p. 37.

6. George Philip, *Military-Authoritarianism in South America: Brazil, Chile, Uruguay and Argentina*, unpublished MS 1983, (forthcoming, *Political Studies*), p. 20.

7. As Finer pointed out, 'Anxiety to preserve its autonomy provides one of the most widespread and powerful of the motives for intervention.' *The Man on Horseback*, p. 47.

8. Alfred Stepan, in Luigi Einaudi and Alfred Stepan, *Latin American Institutional Development: Changing Military Perspectives in Peru and Brazil* (Rand Corporation, Santa Monica, 1971), pp. 84–5.

9. Alfred Stepan, 'The new professionalism of internal warfare' in Abraham Lowenthal (ed.), *Armies and Politics in Latin America* (Holmes and Meier, New York, 1976), p. 247.

10. Jacobo Timerman, *Prisoner Without a Name, Cell Without a Number* (Penguin Books, London, 1981), p. 94.

    Writing about the Chilean military one journalist commented that 'military dislike of publicity about their internal affairs has turned them into a near complete mystery to civilian politicians. . . . What little does emerge is a narrow view of the world, complete ignorance of the North-South dimension of international relations, scant and equivocal knowledge of Chile's own history and a verticalist attitude that renders them impermeable to the arguments of any group whose aims go beyond the defence of national sovereignty and national security (understood as the struggle against Marxism).' *Latin America Weekly Report* (London), 11 August 1983, p. 9.

    Stepan also refers to the ways in which the Brazilian military in the 1950s and 1960s was moving towards becoming a professional caste. *The New Professionalism* p. 256.

11. See, for example, José Murilo de Carvalho 'Armed forces and politics in Brazil' in *The Hispanic American Historical Review*, May 1982, pp. 221–2.

12. Though this did not involve 'deepening' of the industrialisation process to include the development of a capital goods industry in the way that O'Donnell had argued. Unfortunately for this

attractive theory there was little empirical verification and a great deal of refutation.

13. This is a central argument of the excellent work of Alejandro Foxley, *Experimentos Neo-Liberales en América Latina* (Colección Estudios, CIEPLAN, no. 7, Santiago, 1982). For an account of the Argentine experience see Adolfo Canitrot, 'Discipline as the central objective of economic policy: an essay on the economic programme of the Argentine Government since 1976' in *World Development*, Vol. 8, no. 11, November 1980.

14. Two stimulating explorations of the relationship between economic liberalism and political authoritarianism are Albert Hirschman, 'The turn to authoritarianism in Latin America and the search for its economic determinants', in Collier, *op. cit.*; and John Sheahan, 'Market-oriented economic policies and political repression in Latin America' in *Economic Development and Cultural Change*, Vol. 28, no. 2, January 1980. Sheahan makes the important point that several civil governments in Latin America have managed successful programmes of economic orthodoxy *without* recourse to repression.

15. Laurence Whitehead, *Whatever Became of the Southern Cone Model?*, Institute of Latin American Studies, La Trobe University, Melbourne, Occasional Papers Series, no. 5, 1982, p. 6. E. Fitzgerald points out that 'the species of monetarism pursued in Latin America is of the "structuralist" type associated with the Stanford School where much stress is placed on the active construction of capital markets, adjustment of interest rates, management of reserves and control of real wages'. 'The new international division of labour and the relative autonomy of the state', *Bulletin of Latin American Research*, Vol. 1, no. 1, October 1981, p. 11.

16. Rosemary Thorp has explored these problems in illuminating detail; see for example her chapter on Peru in R. Thorp and L. Whitehead (eds.), *Inflation and Stabilisation in Latin America* (Macmillan, London, 1979).

17. Karen Renmer and Gilbert Merkx, 'Bureaucratic-authoritarianism revisited', *Latin American Research Review*, Vol. xvii, no. 2, 1982, p. 13.

18. Michael Klare and Cynthia Arnson, 'Exporting repression: U.S support for authoritarianism in Latin America' in Richard Fagen (ed.), *Capitalism and the State in U.S. – Latin American Relations* (Stanford University Press, Stanford, 1979), p. 156.

19. Juan Linz, 'An authoritarian regime: Spain' in E. Allardt and Y. Littunen, *Cleavages, Ideologies, and Party Systems* (Helsinki,

Westermarck Society, 1964), p. 297. In a later article Linz refers, rather cautiously, to Brazil as an 'authoritarian *situation* rather than an authoritarian regime'. In A. Stepan (ed.), *Authoritarian Brazil* (Yale University Press, New Haven, 1973), p. 235.

20. McDonough, *op. cit.*, p. 125.
21. Juan Linz, 'Totalitarian and authoritarian regimes' in Fred Greenstein and Nelson Polsby (eds.), *Handbook of Political Science*, Vol. 3 (Addison-Wesley Press, Massachusetts, 1975), p. 267.
22. Linz, *Authoritarian Brazil*, p. 239. See also the comment of McDonough, 'Military rule in Brazil was never justified as a final solution. Instead it was seen as a temporary, exceptional phenomenon to be abandoned to the degree that it succeeded. Ideologically it was fugitive.' *Power and Ideology in Brazil*, p. xxviii.
23. Alain Rouquié, *Demilitarization and the Institutionalization of Military-Dominated Politics in Latin America*, Working Paper 110, 1982. Latin American Program, The Wilson Center, Washington, D.C., p. 3.
24. *Ibid.*, p. 4.
25. Quoted in Parkin, *op. cit.*, p. 123.
26. *Ibid.*, p. 123.
27. This is one argument of Peter Evans, *Dependent Development: the Alliance of Multinational, State and Local Capital in Brazil* (Princeton University Press, Princeton, 1979).
28. Alain Rouquié, *Poder Militar y Sociedad Política en la Argentina: vol. 11 1943–1973* (Buenos Aires, Emece, 1982), p. 347.
29. Cardoso, *The Authoritarian Regime*, p. 5. Also see Paul Cammack, 'The electoral legitimation of military role in Brazil', *Politics*, Vol. 2, no. 1, April 1982, pp. 10–11.
30. Howard Handelman and Thomas Saunders (eds.), *Military Government and the Movement towards Democracy* (Indiana University Press, Bloomington, 1981), pp. 224–5.
31. Robert Potash, *The Army and Politics in Argentina, 1928–1945* and *The Army and Politics in Argentina 1945–1962* (Stanford University Press, Stanford, 1969 and 1980).
32. Finer, *op. cit.*, p. 9.
33. Timerman, *op. cit.*, p. 99.
34. Laurence Whitehead, *Bolivia's Failed Democratization*, Working Papers no. 100, 1981, Latin American Program, The Wilson Center, Washington D.C., p. 19.
35. Potash, *The Army and Politics in Argentina 1945–1962*, p. 381.
36. Rouquié, *Poder Militar*, p. 342.

37. Handelman and Saunders, *op. cit.*, pp. 228–9.
38. Peter Cleaves and Henry Pease Garcia, 'State autonomy and military policy making' in Cynthia McClintock and Abraham Lowenthal (eds.), *The Peruvian Experiment Reconsidered* (Princeton University Press, Princeton, 1983), p. 223.
39. McDonough, *op. cit.*, p. xxvi.
40. Handelman and Saunders, *op. cit.*, p. 234–5.
41. One dissenting member of the military junta, Air Force General Gustavo Leigh, was removed from office; several high-ranking offiicers were killed by the government after the *coup*; and Pinochet has paid special attention to forcing the retirement of officers considered to be unsympathetic.
42. Luis Pásara, 'When the military dreams', in McClintock and Lowenthal, *op. cit.*, p. 330.
43. *Latin America Regional Reports: Southern Cone* (London), 10 September 1982, p. 9.
44. For a discussion of the Peruvian military's ambivalent record see the author's, *Peruvian Labour and the Military Government since 1968*, Working Paper no. 3, 1980, Institute of Latin America Studies, University of London.
45. Cardoso, in Collier, *op. cit.*, p. 37.
46. Linz, in Greenstein and Polsby, *op. cit.*, p. 287.
47. Timerman, *op. cit.*, p. 102, reports the following exchange with an interrogator:

Questioner Israel secure in three centres of power has nothing to fear. One is the USA where Jewish power is evident. This means money and political control of capitalist countries. The second is the Kremlin where Israel also has important influence. . . .

Timerman I believe the exact opposite in fact.

Questioner The opposition is totally fake. The Kremlin is still dominated by the same sectors that staged the Bolshevik Revolution in which Jews played the major role. This means political control of Communist countries. And the third centre of power is Argentina especially in the south which, if it were well developed by Jewish immigrants from various Latin American countries, could become an economic emporium, a food and oil basket, the road to Antartica.

48. Philip, *op. cit.*, p. 19.
49. John Dinges and Saul Landau, *Assassination on Embassy Row* (Pantheon Books, New York, 1980), p. 132.
50. Philip, *op. cit.*, p. 19.
51. In Peru, the proportion of the Gross Domestic Product of the

corporate sector, produced by the public sector, was 16% in 1968; in 1975 it had risen to 31%. In addition the state became responsible for three-quarters of exports, half of imports, more than half of fixed investment, two-thirds of bank credit, and a third of employment in the corporate sector. E.V.K. Fitzgerald, 'State capitalism in Peru', in McClintock and Lowenthal, *op. cit.*, pp. 70–71. In *Dependent Development* Evans discusses in detail the growth of the state sector in Brazil. For example, p. 224, the share of state enterprises in the assets of the 100 largest corporations in Brazil rose from 67% in 1970 to 79% in 1974.

52. Martin Walker, 'The big bluff that rules Brazil', *The Guardian*, 11 August 1983.
53. In addition to technical differences over, for example, the role of the exchange rate: Carlos Diaz-Alejandro, 'Southern Cone Stabilization Plans' in William Cline and Sidney Weintraub, *Economic Stabilization in Developing Countries* (Brookings Institute, Washington D.C., 1981), p. 123.
54. Remner and Merxk, *op. cit.*, p. 25.
55. Arturo Valenzuela, *Six Years of Military Rule in Chile*, Working Papers no. 109, 1982, Latin American Program, The Wilson Center, Washington, D.C., pp. 8–9.
56. Pedro-Pablo Kuczyinski, 'Latin American debt', *Foreign Affairs*, Vol. 61, no. 2., Winter 1982/3, p. 347.
57. For an overall analysis see Alejandro Foxley, 'Stabilization policies and their effects on employment and income distribution: a Latin American perspective' in Cline and Weintraub, *op. cit.* For an analysis of Chile, see the author's 'Pinochet's Chile: back to the nineteenth century?', *The World Today*, January 1982; and the subsequent exchange with the Chilean Ambassador in the same periodical for March 1982.
58. 'Even a perfectly rational constellation of prices and investment incentives cannot fully convince entrepreneurs that such an edifice will be in place tomorrow. When economic rationality is built upon an arbitrary political regime, which may depend upon one general's heartbeat, entrepreneurs will not be easily persuaded that today's relative prices are good predictors of future ones. While the economic team builds policy on the assumption that households and firms behave rationally and process information intelligently, the political team assumes citizens cannot be trusted to choose their leaders nor to read an uncensored press.' (Diaz Alejandro, in Cline and Weintraub, *op. cit.*, p. 128).
59. Handelman and Saunders, *op. cit.*, p. 218.
60. Simon Barrow, 'Europe, Latin America and the arms trade' in

Jenny Pearce (ed.), *The European Challenge* (London, Latin America Bureau, 1982), pp. 177–83.
61. *Latin America Weekly Report* (London), 4 June 1982, p. 9.
62. Samuel Huntington, *Political Order in Changing Societies* (Yale University Press, New Haven, 1968).
63. Finer, *op. cit.*, p. 243.

7 Notes on Elites
Donald G. MacRae

I think that I first met Finer in Balliol in late 1946 or 1947; and I did not
know what to make of him except that he was enormous fun and was
engaged in simultaneously reading all the books I had intended to read
plus a very large number of new ones from a rediscovered Europe –
books of which I had never heard. I found his combination of
enthusiasm with the prose of S.J. Perelman, learning and originality
vastly attractive. He has gone on attracting me ever since.

For Sammy the borders of political science and sociology are exactly
where one wants to make them or where one's investigations have
found them. Is *Anonymous Empire* political science or sociology or
both? I don't think it matters. *The Man on Horseback* is about a subject
which no one at that time would admit to respectability – politics,
comparative history, political sociology? *Pareto: Sociological Writings*
is clearly what it says and clearly sociology. It is also the best guide to
Pareto ever made available to the English-speaking reader – although
perhaps today one might wish to add to it Placido Bucoli's *The
Unknown Pareto*.

The word 'elite' originally referred to goods or groups of special and
selected excellence: in the English saying, 'the pick of the crop'. With
time its general usage was confined either to military or intellectual
excellence – elite troops, the artistic elite, etc. – as manifested in specific
social groups or contexts. In late nineteenth and early twentieth century
America the 'elite' was a phrase of snobbery and slight vulgarity,
referring to those who had the *entrée* to the most exclusive areas of
upper-class society. By transference, elite could apply either to the
upper classes in general or specifically to the hereditary nobility. To a
large extent the word always carried with it the idea of exclusion, and
therefore of the power to exclude. In the theories of social Darwinism
and biological sociology, the ruling groups of a society, chosen by
natural and/or social selection, formed an elite, and were sometimes so
described.

In political science and sociology the usage of elite has been more troubled by logical confusions and ambiguities and emotional ascriptions of virtue than is true of most technical terms. Underlying all the usages, however, is a criticism of the social and political optimism which believes that a perfect, just, and entirely open democracy is possible, either in the present or in the future. The core of the theory of the elite is that, whatever the presence or absence of economic classes, a minority political class will exist and be characterised by a self-conscious awareness of its position, by a considerable degree of internal coherence and consistency, and will stand in a relation, therefore, or exclusion and, probably, of hostility, to the rest of society. Meisel's formula of 'consciousness, coherence and conspiracy' errs only in being too strong, but it is a useful guide to the implications of elite theory.

I

The theory of elites has gone through three well-marked phases. In the first, which stretches from Plato to the Abbé Saint-Pierre (1658–1743) and even to Saint-Simon (1760–1825) and Comte (1798–1857), the theory of the elite is essentially bound up with utopian schemes for the more just and perfect government of society. The archetypal idea is that of the Platonic guardians: the disinterested, philosophic rulers of the *Politeia*, More's *Utopia* (1516), Campanella's *Citta del sole* and Bacon's *New Atlantis* (1627) are all examples of this kind of elitism. By the time of Saint-Pierre's *Discours sur la polysynodie* (1718) the idea of the elite came to be associated with the idea of the desirability of a rational bureaucracy. In Saint-Simon the Baconian concepts of a technocratic elite combine with those of Saint-Pierre on bureaucracy and a recognition of the new marriage of applied science and capitalist economic enterprise which is industrialism. Saint-Simon anticipates a just and rigorous society with a plural elite of property owners and scientists, to be joined by technologists, entrepreneurs and financiers. This elite, efficient, informed, and fair, would exercise a dictatorship which would end all social disharmonies, including the class struggle. In the last phase of his thought Saint-Simon gave his elite a theocratic form which emerges in Comteanism in the rule of the priests of humanity through the religion of humanity. We are not concerned here with Comtean positivism.

The second phase of the theory of elites is involved with the emergence of modern sociology as an attempt to understand the relations of society as they are, without anger or desire, and by methods as objectively scientific as is possible. This endeavour was however coloured by the historical circumstances of political experience in Europe from 1848 to

1939, especially the experience of parliamentarianism and of Fascism. It was also more than any other sector of sociology affected by and involved in debate with the postulates of marxism – in particular with the forms of marxism and the varieties of social democracy of the period before 1917. All subsequent discussion and research into elites is dependent on and involves a criticism of this phase of the history of elitist theories.

The dominant names are those of Vilfredo Pareto (1848–1923) and Gaetano Mosca (1858–1941). The relations between the two men were not friendly; they disputed priorities of discovery. As a result both the similarities and the differences in their analyses are often concealed by mere variations of vocabulary, which in Mosca's case may have been deliberately employed to separate his work from that of Pareto. Nevertheless, their work is largely complementary. The core of all elitist political sociology is the claim that societies, merely because they are organisational structures, are dominated by minorities. As Robert Michels (1876–1936, see below) said, 'who says organization, says oligarchy'. Pareto and Mosca are alike concerned to work out the implications of some such proposition.

Both writers, though they drew greatly on classical and comparative sources, depended on the same political experience. Both were disillusioned by the parliamentarianism of a united Italy. Both were deeply concerned with the politics of the French Third Republic (Pareto was a Dreyfusard) and both were impressed by the ideas of Sorel, a personal friend of Pareto. Both reflected on the teachings of Machiavelli, in particular those of the *Discorsi* rather than those of *Il Principe*. Both were rationalists who recognised the importance of non-rational behaviour in society, and in elitist politics. Both believed in individual freedom, including the freedoms of classical economics. Mosca in his latter years seems to have believed that the least evil of attainable forms of politics was parliamentary party democracy. The reputation of both men, and of the theory of elites, suffered from the claims of Mussolini – who attended some lectures by Pareto – that their concepts underlay the ideology of Italian fascism. This is nonsense. Finally, and this is characteristic of all thinking about elites, both writers are pessimists. They reject the optimism of both classical liberalism and marxism: in no society can the majority actually rule; even if economic differences of classes were abolished, political differentiation and domination would remain. At the best, according to Mosca, a 'representative has himself elected'. (*Sulla Teorica dei governi e sul governo parlamentare*, p. 106).

Pareto's theory of elites is part of a total sociological system of the largest kind, a system in which the scale is so large that much of the detail of social life disappears. It is not completely consistent, and though modern sociology has incorporated a great deal of it, it has done this by selection and criticism. A Paretan elite is in the first place a quantitative fact: in every specialised grouping of men some few command the differential skill of the specialism more than the others. The greater this command, the smaller the proportion. Thus there is an elite of chess players, of electrical engineers, of card-shapers, and so on. When this group is internally organised, that is, is more than a descriptive category, and involves relations of order and leadership, then there is an elite in the full politico-social sense. The elite in the first sense is essential to the illustration of Pareto's belief that both for intrinsic reasons of intrinsic capacity and because of social selection, training and opportunity, practical abilities are unevenly distributed. Given this inegalitarian fact, then the significance of the second kind of elite is established. (But, cf. Mosca and Michels.) Pareto further divides the politico-social elite into those, the governing elite, directly engaged in politics, and the non-governing elite, from which, however, the governing elite is most easily recruited.

In governing elites two elements are present. The domination of one or the other of these elements determines the character of the elite. These elements in the terminology of Pareto's sociological system, are innovatory ('Class I residue: combinations') and conservative ('Class II residue: persistence of aggregates'). Those dominated by Class I rely largely on political skill and propaganda; those dominated by Class II rely rather on force, inflexible rigidity and the inertia of social forces. Often, but this involves a cross-cutting classification, elites dominated by Class I are comparatively open, while the Class II dominated elite is primarily hereditary. Pareto makes less of the urge to nepotism than either Mosca or Michels – to whom it is one of the two prime factors perpetuating oligarchy – but he does see nepotistic recruitment as one of the factors which, producing a regression to the biological mean, results in an elite becoming inefficient and so divorced from the masses that it must either revise its recruitment, be forced to do so, or be overthrown by war or revolution.

The masses of the ruled are dominated by conservatism and inertia (Class II residue) and by a readiness to accept and collaborate in verbal, mythical and ideological action ('Class III residue: manifestation of sentiments by external acts'). In consequence the masses are attuned to an elite dominated by conservative sentiments, but are open to the guile, rhetoric and skill of an elite where Class I tendencies are pre-eminent. What is constant about the masses is that they are always to some measure despoiled. By saying this, Pareto does not exclude economic exploitation, but goes beyond it to assert that a degree of political, legal, cultural and social deprivation is a universal feature of societies.

Ruling elites must in time either change or be replaced. If they are changed by the entry of upwardly mobile social elements we have the 'circulation of elites'. Elites are replaced by wars or revolutions under two major sets of circumstances. An elite where Class I residues are predominant relies too little on force, too much on guile and argument, and the disequilibrium between authority and power either permits the penetration of the elite by forceful elements from below, or results in revolution led by men who will impose their authority with massive force and form a new elite. What can threaten such an elite, like that of Calvin's Geneva or post-1917 Russia? After it has installed its new arrangements it becomes dedicated to their maintenance and petrified in an order which is increasingly feebler *vis-à-vis* competing societies where Class I residues are more important (this is Pareto's explanation of the defeat of the Central Powers in the 1914–18 war: *Fatti e Teorie*, p. 335 *et seq.*), or they will be permeated and replaced by new elements of whom they have need. These are the technically and economically skilled: people who represent Class I residues. The fact of elite rule is universal; so also is the movement, the circulation, the replacement of elites in an unceasing social tide.

Pareto's theory is only a part of a general sociology. Its exposition could only be faithful and complete in the context of an exposition of the total system. Nevertheless sociologists and political scientists have fragmented the system, and even so the fragments have given useful analytical insights into the tendencies of political events, not least the consequences of the perpetuation of Communist autocracies.

Mosca, unlike Pareto, confined himself to political sociology and the history of political conceptions. He talks of the *ruling class*, not the elite. By it he means essentially both the few who actually govern, and what he calls 'the political class' or 'the second stratum of the ruling class', who are those without whom power could not be exercised. These necessary men in modern societies are the higher bureaucrats and the politicians who run the machinery of parties and elections; sometimes they include publicists of all kinds and affiliated intellectuals. The Italian marxist, Antonio Gramsci, is not far wrong when he says that Mosca's political class, 'is only the intellectual section of the rulers'. He forgets, however, what Pareto analysed and Mosca sometimes remembers, that these intellectuals can become dissident and that what Crane Brinton (*Anatomy of Revolution*, 3rd edn., 1966) calls their 'transfer of allegiance' is a harbinger of revolution, particularly in strongly aristocratic societies. Both Pareto and Mosca take as given that men are moved by what they perceive to be their interests – Pareto takes this so much for granted that he hardly mentions it – and these interests make up most of what Mosca calls 'social forces'. These social forces may play with different strength on different sections of the ruling class, and in this is both the origin of political change and a protection for the ruled. As with Pareto, the elite is in constant change, but the fact of elite rule is constant.

Every ruling class has its legitimation in a 'political formula'. (This is *not* analogous to Sorel's concept of *myth*.) This formula is an ideological profession to justify power – being the voice of the people, the agent of the supernatural, the chosen of history, the wave of the future, the representative of the race, are all political formulae. Such formulae are not usually deceptions, but correspond to the need of rulers and ruled to be governed, and to be governed in accord with a transcendent principle. In no society, however despotic, however democratic, does authority flow merely down or merely up through the political structure. Nevertheless, most societies have in fact tended towards the despotic end of the spectrum, for all its rigidity, all its denial of aspiration and creativity. Yet, though democracy cannot realise its political formula, it is of all regimes that in which 'the rulers will be most affected by the sentiments of the majority . . . it is the rule of liberty to the extent in which that word can be really meaningful in our epoch of superstates with immensely complex structures'.

With Mosca the theory of elites had moved from the wide generality of Pareto towards its third phase, based on detailed historical and contemporary research and the use of quantitative techniques of analysis. In addition, in this phase political experience has also changed: the era of tyrannies made the study of elites of urgent practical importance.

The detailed study of political parties as a branch of sociology began with M. Ostrogorski's *La democratie et l'organisation des partis politiques* (2 vols. 1902), but R. Michels in 1908 made the first study of parties as elite-dominated mass organisations, with *Il proletiato e la borghesia nel movimento socialista Italiano*. His information was drawn mainly from the Italian Socialist Party and the German Social-democratic Party. Both professed internal democracy on a mass basis. Both were self-perpetuating oligarchies in which the very choice of serious and long-term commitment separated the official and the leader from the led, and which had to be commanded by an indispensable elite of superior culture and capacity if the structure and activity of the party were to be maintained. The very fact that representative government involves a struggle between parties ensures that to keep themselves in the arena the parties must be quasi-military in their real structure, whatever the demands of their ideology and the beliefs of their supporters.

Meanwhile Max Weber was clarifying the context of elite theory by three analyses: of the ideal types of authority, of increasing rationalisation, and of bureaucracy. The relevance of these was to reinforce the importance of political formulae and their variations in different kinds of social system and to show how the very demands of life in industrial, scientifically-oriented, complex societies imposed rationality as a principle of legitimation and bureaucracy as its impersonal instrument. Michels' phrase about organisation meaning oligarchy was now more than an epigram, and Mosca's 'second stratum' revealed as the technicians and administrators of power. The idea of an elite, operating through rational bureaucracy, supported by a mass party, and legitimated by charismatic authority does not occur in Weber. Nevertheless by the time of his death in 1920 he had given the world some of the most essential concepts and organising ideas for the understanding of modern elite systems, in particular those of fascism and communism.

The empirical and statistical study of elites began in 1912 with M. Kolabinska's historical *La circulation des elites en France* and has been pursued for many societies and periods (see bibliography). For democratic societies – specifically the USA – the initiator of many of these studies, H.D. Lasswell, has objected to elitist theories on the grounds that (i) there are insufficient restrictions on the numbers of decision-makers to justify the term elite; (ii) power is very impermanent; (iii) powerholders are too incoherently organised to perpetuate an elite; (iv) they are not conspirators in the interests of their own power; (v) they compete for suffrages they do not control; (vi) the ruled, when they feel their interests deeply involved, expect (demand?) power. These theses certainly modify any narrow interpretation of the American situation, but they do not carry complete conviction: rather they suggest an elite very dependent on Mosca's second stratum, highly segmented, and with a high velocity of circulation. Michels' theory of oligarchy remains intact. There is no empirical study of the chances of multiple office-holding in a lifetime or in a kin group.

In an influential book C. Wright Mills argued that the US now possessed a 'power elite' of those in 'the command posts of the major institutional hierarchies', which are business, politics and the military. This elite is united not so much because it is drawn from an upper class, though Mills argued that this is the case, but by a coincidence of interests. The very plurality and 'organized irresponsibility' of American social structure permits elite power. As will be seen, Lasswell and Mills, both empiricists, cannot both be right. What is important in

Mills is (i) his stress on the role of the military (though no French or German observer would be surprised by this) and (ii) his argument that social pluralism, usually and justly thought of as a countervailing power to despotism and extreme elite rule, may in certain circumstances so fragment society as to create a situation favourable to extreme and unchecked elitism.

On the whole the comparative, empirical and quantitative study of elites has proved disappointing in comparison with the results of institutional analysis and more theoretical investigation. It has probably been most successful in the historical field, involving aristocracies (see, for example, A. Goodwin (ed.), *The European Nobility in the 18th Century*, London 1953), and for the elites of newly independent ex-colonial states (see, for example, T. Kerstiens, *The New Elite in Asia and Africa*, New York, 1966) where history has sharply delimited the problem, and where the new elites consist of an amalgam of marginal men become political organisers and an intelligentsia of recent, alien formation. The idea implicit in the work of Karl Mannheim that the intellectuals might form, connected with but independent from the 'second stratum' a kind of countervailing elite seems to have a good deal of long-term truth even in modern despotisms. It depends in his analysis on the claim that while other elitist concepts ascribe elites to mere power hunger, in fact elites are functional groups, necessary in increasing number and variety to modern industrial societies. But such elites are remote from the concepts of Pareto and Mosca.

II

We now turn to elites and elite theories *vis-à-vis* marxism and communism. If socio-economic classes are to be explained in terms of their economic interrelationships, and these interrelationships are interpreted in a marxist way, then the whole of elite theory either is redundant or belongs to an analysis of a different social dimension. If, however, classes, though they can often be described in a marxist terminology with some accuracy (and Marx himself, particularly in his writings on France from 1848 to 1851, was only loosely a marxist in his account of classes in politics), are taken as variables in a total sociological analysis which does not give social primacy to the economic order, but which is functional, then an elite theory congruent with class theory is logically possible; though none of the major writers on elites nor researchers into their empirical content have in fact produced such a unified scheme.

Marxists are hostile to elite analyses. Their thought-world on the one hand repudiates as needless an account of minority rule in society which is not based on a theory of economic class. Blanqui said that who has iron has bread: marxists must say that who has bread will have iron. On the other hand their utopianism rejects any suggestion that elites are or can be permanent features of social relations and politics in all complex societies. Marxist utopianism is bifurcated. It is a utopianism about the USSR and the communist states as now existent; it is also a utopia of the future. To admit elites into either utopia would at once destroy the credenda of communism. Trotsky, who early confronted this situation, was forced to produce a theory of suspension in the revolutionary development of the USSR to preserve the former utopia, and to will the destruction of Stalin to preserve the latter. Despite his intentions the analysis in *The Revolution Betrayed* (1936) is extremely like the one that a Paretan would offer in terms of social equilibrium and the theory of elites.

The situation is made further paradoxical by the fact that communist parties, which at the least possess many elitist features, are specifically entrusted with the task, once the revolution has taken place, of eliminating elitist features from communist societies. What is more, even in pre-revolutionary situations communist parties, organised around cadres, guided and administered by 'democratic centralism', are yet supposed to be on guard against elitist tendencies within themselves. Such tendencies are supposed to threaten their aboriginal virtue – *c.f.* such terms as 'careerism' – and militate against their *élan*, their tactical flexibility, and their success.

Such paradoxes are among the strengths of communism, which operates through tensions, antinomies and contradictions. A real flexibility is gained, the system as such can hardly be falsified, but it is scientifically untenable. The central paradox of communism and marxism, in history and today, is indeed that marxism can explain neither itself not its political formations.

The doctrine of the party – it is a doctrine, a teaching, and not a theory – in communism is identical for all countries and situations. The *de facto* differences are very great between countries where the party rules, where it is a serious political factor, and where it is a sect. In addition there are real differences which result from the degree of industrialisation and variations in cultural heterogeneity between countries. But for all these variables the doctrine and the facts embody elements which are essentially elitist along with a dogma of the mass basis of the organisation. In both doctrine and fact, too, is a component which deserves comparative and sociological study: this is the image of the mass party as a military organisation. (Michels had acutely observed that 'Bebel and Engels, and especially the latter, may even be considered as essentially military writers.') Unfortunately social scientists have neglected this area of research so important for the understanding of politics in modern society and the basis of contemporary elites.

The doctrine of 'democratic centralism' provides communist parties with their ideological justification both for elitist practices and for their rejection of elitist aspersions. According to the *Great Soviet Encyclopaedia* (1931), the elements of democratic centralism include the duty and right of party members independently to discuss disputed questions within the party, indirect election to party organs at all levels at party meetings and congresses, the periodic accountability of party organs to their electors and the iron duty of instant, efficient, obedience by all members and lower organs of the party to decisions from above. The phrase was first used by Lenin in 1906: it should be seen in the context of his remarks (*Letter on our Organisational Tasks to a Comrade*) attacking 'broad democracy' – i.e. what is usually meant by democracy – in the party as useless and dangerous.

Despite endless polemics against all suggestions that the Bolsheviks and all communist parties derive their organisation and tactics largely from Blanqui and Tkachev and the conspiratorial experience of Narodnaya Volya, it is difficult to believe that these were not operative. Again there is need for historical and comparative study of conspiratorial parties and associations from, at least, the Risorgimento, to establish how much of communism is the institutional consequence of conspiracy and illegality in complex societies. What is certain is that such bodies are elitist: membership in them involves self-election out of society; their intention is that the chosen few shall prove the elite of political revolution. In such organisations, as in communist parties, there is theoretically a flow of initiatives up and down the hierarchical structure. In fact their nature necessitates that the flow is one way – downwards. They are therefore dominated by strong elites.

These elites are involved in the fact and theory of cadres, at once elites and the instruments of elites, in communism. Cadres are the framework (what the word, otherwise unknown in English, means in French) of both an ongoing communist party and the nucleus for the mobilisation and creation of such a party. (Stalin's famous and oft-repeated 'Cadres are everything' is a slogan with many uses – not least that of decision from above as to who are the real cadres at a given place and time.) *Vis-à-vis* other party members the cadres are fellow travellers, guerrillas, the proletariat and the peasants, quite simply an elite, but only the 'leading cadres' are a genuinely political elite, for to be such an elite some measure of political autonomy is required.

But indeed communist parties, by their nature, are making the claim to be elites. Lenin's attacks on *khvostism* (leadership from behind, waiting for the masses, dependence on democratic majorities) are unambiguous. By putting the *future* majority on the side of communism, communist eschatology is the fig-leaf of elitism now. Stalin's four claims for the party confirm this point: (i) the party is the *vanguard* of the workers; (ii) it is the *organised* sector of the working class; (iii) it is the highest (i.e. most on the side of the future) organisation of the workers; and (iv) it is the instrument of the proletarian dictatorship (*Foundations of Leninism*, VIII, 1924) After all, as Lenin said, the proletariat of itself can develop only a trade union consciousness.

The real problems of elites under communism in power have been dealt with by communist writers only marginally or heretically. The important names are Bukharin, Trotsky and Djilas. The essential points are still that of the relations of Mosca's first and second strata of the ruling class and Michels' epigram that organisation involves oligarchy. There are two orders which provide the hierarchies and tensions of communist societies: the political order (the party), and the economic order which theoretically the people, but in fact the party, owns. Both are administrative and bureaucratic orders. (In addition, there are the soviets, but these have always been what Pareto might have described as manifestations of sentiments by external organisations.)

Bukharin in 1920 saw that in political, administrative, technical and economic institutions there is a 'purely technical objective logic' of differentiation. This must involve status and authority. These are justified because their work produces not a system of profit, but one whose 'surplus product' is the property and advantage of communist society as a whole. He later argued that the uneven development of the sectors of the working class explained and justified 'more or less stable groups of individual "leaders" and the emergence of a "permanent organisation of leadership"'.

Trotsky explained the situation, with its elite, through the 'moral degeneration' of the party, caused essentially by the machinations of Stalin, and a consequent 'moral decay of the uncontrolled apparatus' (cf. *The Revolution Betrayed*, 1936). The consequence is the 'Soviet Thermidor . . . a triumph of the bureaucracy over the masses'. His account, apart from the personal role ascribed to Stalin, is congruent with a Paretan analysis in terms of social equilibiation and the circulation of elites (cf. above). Although Trotsky constantly introduces comparisons with the Jacobins, his account is not genuinely comparative, for his history is merely illustrative. He detects no inherent sociological logic at work.

Milovan Djilas (*The New Class*, 1957) introduces overtly and by implication two additional factors into the explanation of the dominance of communist countries by permanent elites. These are (i) that the elites of these societies have used their power to destroy the institutional being of their rivals and regard themselves as legitimated by being the repositories of truth and right. They are therefore not subject to any risk of change or, normally, replacement. The elite (ii) under communism *owns*, not merely administers and manipulates, the total economy. There are therefore no sanctions on the elite, it controls its own recruitment, there is no mediation – except chicane – between the dominant political order and the economic order.

All three see no logical or actual disjunction of party and state bureaucracy. Together these form, in Trotsky's phrase, an 'uncontrolled caste'. Within marxism there is no real explanation of this phenomenon. The elite of communist societies cannot be explained by communists. As a result we have the situation described, in which only the heretical and defeated at all recognise and attempt to deal with the facts. It is also one in which any major circulation of elites can proceed only by a policy of purges and mass violence.

The sources of communist elites have undergone research. The data are widely diffused, often the official information is suspect, sometimes detail can only be acquired from defectors, no single body of material is complete as a temporal record: for all this, we may have a good deal of confidence in this research. It has gone on for about forty years, and in many countries; the picture revealed shows remarkable uniformity.

W. Sombart in *Der proletarische Sozialismus* (1924) showed from electoral statistics (i) that wage workers in the oldest industrial countries were only marxist to a small – in England and America a trivial – degree, while it appeared that communist parties everywhere contained large *petit bourgeois* and bourgeois components, of which the latter predominated in leadership positions. Figures given *passim* in L. Schapiro, *The Communist Party of the Soviet Union* (1960) and information drawn from T.H. Rigby's thesis for London University, 'The Selection of Leading Personnel in the Soviet State and the Communist Party' (1954) show the non-proletarian component in leading positions to have been consistently high. (By 'non-proletarian' is intended both people of middle and upper-class ancestry and those with higher educational formations.) Similar analyses can be found for the military in I. de Sola Pool *Satellite Generals* (n.d.), for Moslem countries in W.Z. Laqueur *Communism and Nationalism in the Middle East* (1956), for east Europe in R.V. Burks, *The Dynamics of Communism in Eastern Europe* (1961), for the Ukraine in J.A. Armstrong, *The Soviet Bureaucratic Elite* (1959), and so on.

But the importance of this evidence should no more be over-estimated than the fact that after 1917 the Soviets employed many elements from the Czarist bureaucracy. The point is really more straightforward. If elite theory is correct, then to join the elite by rising in the party, the administration, the army, or the economy itself ensures a change of attitudes in the new position which of itself estranges the rulers of the apparatus from the ruled. Communism provides within itself no countervailing force to this. It must therefore try to explain away the facts that at the least a political class is inescapable in complex society. Communist ideology and party doctrine and structure provide none of the pluralism by which men can avoid the tyranny of an elite. Even populism – cf. the Chinese Red Guards – is a weapon of the elite, and populism exists almost only in Chinese communism. (It may also operate in small sect-type communist parties such as that in Britain. Research is needed on this point.) The one escape-clause in the system is the result of the actual incoherence of the elements of the communist polity, economy and society under the sway of the party.

Bibliography

Armstrong, J.A. *The Soviet Bureaucratic Elite: A Case Study of the Ukranian Apparatus*, New York, 1959

Aron, R. 'Classe sociale, Classe politique, classe dirigeante', *European Journal of Sociology*, I, 1960

Aron, R., 'La signification de l'oeuvre de Pareto', *Cahiers Vilfredo Pareto*, No. 1, 1963

Aron, R., 'Social Structure and the Ruling Class', *British Journal of Sociology*, I, 1950

Avakumovic, I., *History of the Communist Party of Yugoslavia*, Vol. I, Aberdeen, 1964

Baker, E.J., 'The Philosophical "Refutation" of Pareto', *Mind*, LXIX, 1960

Borkenau, F., *Pareto*, London, 1936

Bottomore, T.B., *Elites and Society*, London, 1964

Bousquet, G.H., *Pareto*, Lausanne, 1960

Brinton, C., *Anatomy of Revolution*, 3rd edn., New York, 1966

Bucolo, P. (ed.), *The Unknown Pareto*

Bukharin, N., *Economic Theory of the Leisure Class*, London, 1927

Bukharin, N., *Historical materialism*, London, 1925

Burks, R.V., *The Dynamics of Communism in Eastern Europe*, Princeton, 1961

Burnham, J., *The Machiavellians*, New York, 1943

Clifford-Vaughan, M., 'Some French Concepts of Elites', *British Journal of Sociology*, XI, 1960

Committee on Foreign Affairs, *Five Hundred Leading Communists*, Washington, 1948

Djilas, M., *The New Class, An Analysis of the Communist System*, New York, 1957

Eisermann, G., *Vilfredo Pareto: System der Allgemeinen Soziologie*, Stuttgart, 1962

Fainsod, M., *How Russia Is Ruled*, Cambridge, Mass., 1953

Finer, S., *Anonymous Empire – A study of the Lobby in Britain*, 1958/66

Finer, S., *The Man on Horseback: The Role of the Military in Politics*, 1962/76

Finer, S., *Pareto: Sociological Writings*, London, 1966

Ginsberg, M., 'The Sociology of Pareto', *Reason and Unreason in Society*, London, 1947

Goodwin, A., *The European Nobility in the Eighteenth Century*, London, 1953

Granick, D., *The Red Executive*, London, 1960

Guttsman, W., *The British Political Elite*, London, 1963

Hodgkin, T., *African Political Parties*, Harmondsworth, 1961

Inkeles, A., 'Social Stratification and Mobility in the Soviet Union', *American Sociological Review*, XV, 1950

Ionescu, E., *Communism in Rumania, 1944–62*, London, 1964

Keller, S., *Beyond the Ruling Class*, New York, 1963

Kerstiens, T., *The New Elite in Asia and Africa*, New York, 1963

Kolabinska, *La Circulation des élites en France*, Lausanne, 1912

Langer, S., *Beyond the Ruling Class*, New York, 1963

Laquer, W.Z., *Communism and Nationalism in the Middle East*, London, 1956

Lasswell, H.D., et al., *The Comparative Study of Elites*, Stanford, 1951

Lasswell, H.D., and Lerner D. (eds.), *World Revolutionary Elites: Studies in Coercive Ideological Movements*, Cambridge, Mass., 1966

Lipset, S.M. *Political Man*, London, 1960

MacRae, D.G., 'Foundations for the Sociology of Politics', *Political Quarterly*, XXXVII, 1966

Mannheim, K., *Ideology and Utopia*, London, 1936

Mannheim, K., 'The Ruling Class in Capitalist and Communist Society', in *Freedom, Power and Democratic Planning*, London, 1951

Marsh, R., *The Mandarins: the Circulation of Elites in China*, Glencoe, 1961

Marvick, D. (ed.), *Political Decision Makers*, New York, 1961

Matthews, D., *Social Background of Political Decision-makers*, New York, 1954

Meisel, J., *The Myth of the Ruling Class, Gaetano Mosca and the Elite*, 2nd edn., Ann Arbor, 1962

Merriam, C.E., *Political Power*, Chicago, 1934

Michels, R., *La sociologia del partito politico nella democrazia moderna*, Turin, 1912

Michels, R., *Zur Soziologie des Parteiswesens in der modernen Demokratie*, 2nd edn., Leipzig, 1925

Mills, C. Wright, *The Power Elite*, New York, 1956

Moore, B., 'The Communist Party of the Soviet Union 1928–44', *American Sociological Review*, IX, 1944

Moore, B., *Soviet Politics: The Dilemma of Power*, Cambridge, Mass., 1950

Mosca, G., *Elementi di scienza politica*, Turin, 1896 (4th edn., Bari, 1947)

Mosca, G., *Partiti e sindacati nella crisi del regime parlamentare*, Bari, 1949

Mosca, G., *Teoriea dei governi e governo parlamentare*, Torino, 1884

Nicolaevsky, B., *Power and the Soviet Elite*, London, 1963

Ostrogorski, M., *Democracy and the Organisation of Political Parties*, 2 volumes, London, 1962

Pareto, V., *Cours d'economie politique*, Lausanne, 1896

Pareto, V., *Fatti e Teorie*, Florence, 1920

Pareto, V., *Manuel d'economie politique*, Paris, 1909

Pareto, V., *Les systemes socialistes*, 2 vols., Paris, 1902

Pareto, V., *Transformazione della Democrazia*, Milan, 1921

Pareto, V., *Trattato di Soziologia generale*, 3 vols., Florence, 1916

Petersen, W., 'Soviet Society under Stalin: The Prototype of Totalitarianism', in W. Petersen (ed.), *The Realities of Communism*, Englewood Cliffs, 1963

Pisacane, C., *Saggia sulla Rivoluzione*, Bologna, 1894

Rigby, T.H., 'Social Orientation of Recruitment and Distribution of Membership in the Communist Party of the Soviet Union', *American Slavic and East European Review*, XVI, No. 3, 1957

Schapiro, L., *The Communist Party of the Soviet Union*, London, 1960

Sereno, R., 'The anti-Aristotelianism of Gaetano Mosca and the Elite, 2nd edn., Ann Arbor, 1962

Smythe, H. and M., *The New Nigerian Elite*, Stanford, 1960

Sombart, W., *Der Proletarische Sozialismus*, Jena, 1924

Trotsky, L., *The Revolution Betrayed*, New York, 1936

Weber, M., *Gesammelte Politische Schriften*, 1921

8 The Internationalisation of Political Science: Promises and Problems*
Hans Daalder

In the last thirty years or so, we have witnessed a strong trend towards the internationalisation of political science, both in organisational terms and in substantive developments. I shall summarise these two developments in *staccato* fashion. At the same time, however, this internationalisation process also faces a number of obstacles which in some cases seem to be growing larger rather than smaller. I shall argue that these obstacles ought to be faced squarely and that steps should be taken to remove them. Is not a maximum of interchange of theoretical thought and empirical findings between different countries and societies a *conditio sine qua non* for a discipline which claims to chronicle and understand political man and political society?

I. Internationalisation: outward indicators

The flowering of organisations
The study of politics has come to be affected by the rapid flowering of a large variety of international organisations. Some of these are chiefly intergovernmental; e.g., UNESCO and other specialised agencies of the United Nations if one is to think in terms of universal organisations, or OECD and the European Communities if one instead thinks in regional terms. Others are based on specific government institutions, e.g., the Interparliamentary Union, the International Union of Local Authorities or the Institute of Administrative Sciences. Yet other organisations are based on associations of political scientists, as is the International Political Science Association (although IPSA also has individual members), or the Nordic Political Science Association. The

* This chapter builds on certain thoughts which I first developed in an address at the Joint Sessions of the European Consortium of Political Research on 19 April 1979, when I finished a three-year chairmanship of that organisation and was close to finishing a three-year appointment as Head of the Department of Political Sciences at the European University Institute in Florence.

European Consortium for Political Research is one of the few international organisations which is directly grounded on university departments (even though the ECPR seeks to activate individual staff members and advanced students as much as their corporate members). Some organisations are based on individual membership only, as are such bodies as the *Institut de Philosophie Politique*, or the Association of Professors of International Relations. Most of these bodies sponsor meetings, and many claim to promote research. Anyone who wishes this can quickly become an almost full-time international 'organisation man' in politicial science.

The explosion of publications and documentation

One need not dwell long on that other outward sign of the inter-nationalisation of the political science discipline: the almost exponential growth of books and journals. Inevitably, English tends to be the dominant *lingua franca*. Abstracts in English in national journals are now a matter of course and many national political science commun-ities find it useful to set up their own 'translation' journals. And if national journals, or authors, do not provide such abstracts, the 'powerhouse' of 27, Rue St. Guillaume in Paris, will see to it that at least the existence of political science publications in languages other than English gets known world-wide.

In the field of journals alone developments are explosive. Not so long ago, a few 'national' political science journals such as the *APSR* (*American Political Science Review*), *Political Studies*, or the *Revue Française de Science Politique* seemed all one needed. But they were soon followed by journals especially oriented towards comparative studies – general ones such as: *World Politics, Comparative Politics, Comparative Political Studies, Comparative Studies in Society and History*, or more regional journals such as the *European Journal of Political Research, West European Politics* and *Scandinavian Political Studies*, or *mutatis mutandis* journals on other specific areas such as *Soviet Studies*, the *China Quarterly, South-East Asian Studies* or *African Studies*. And as if this were not enough, one has simultaneously seen a profuse growth of specialised journals in different sub-fields of the profession, or in the interstices of political science and other disciplines, or on specific political topics and issues. One need only check the list of journals published by Sage Publications alone to become aware of a world of bewildering specialisation.

With the spate of books and journals, bibliographic works have become of increasing importance. We do not only have our *International Political Science Bibliography* and our *International Political Science Abstracts*, but a host of more specialised tools not to speak of new computerised publications such as the *Political Science Thesaurus* or the *Social Sciences Citation Index*, the various automatic data-banks which are becoming accessible on-line world-wide, etc. And not only publications are increasingly documented and shared internationally, so are actual data of great variety. What was begun as a courteous gesture by the Almonds and Verbas of this world, who offered the data of their *The Civic Culture* study to other interested scholars, or the actions of the Michigan entrepreneurs who set up the Inter-University Consortium for Political Research, has now developed into an essential infrastructure for research on widely-varying subjects in many different lands.

The increased mobility of people
Among the outward signs of increased internationalisation one should finally mention the increased mobility of scholars. Do not international workshops breed ever more workshops? Do not international congresses get larger and larger? Are not (some) academics among the best clients of airlines? Do not so many visiting professors arrive in other countries once the spring sets in, that one may speak of a seasonal trek – with more guest lectures offered than students would like to attend?

II. Internationalisation: substantive developments
Some fifty years ago, there seemed to be mainly two traditions in political science. First, there was the philosophical one, dealing with the great thinkers, the main ideologies, and to some degree with current philosophies and problems of methodology; and second, the comparative-institutional approach, that attractive blend of history, constitutional law, and a layman's perception of social structures which was so well represented by a generation of learned scholars exemplified by James Bryce, Leon Duguit or Robert Redslob.

The profession had a few highly visible intellectual centres: Paris, London and Oxford, Vienna and some German cities, notably Berlin, Frankfurt and Munich. The subject also seemed to have a common core: a concern with the functioning of democratic institutions and a normative analysis of democratic rule. European countries and a few white settlements overseas (including the USA) formed the 'universe', and beyond them 'comparative' study and contemplation moved back in time, to historical experience rather than to other geographic areas.

This somewhat self-confident intellectual world was soon eroded by the advent of three interrelated political revolutions: the arrival of totalitarianism, the phenomenon of world war (which did not end in 1945), and the rise of the Third World. These developments had large-scale consequences in the world of political studies:

1. They forced a recognition of the need of new sociological and psychological approaches, to account for forces which could destroy political institutions once deemed the embodiment of stable democratic rule.
2. They demanded a new concern with the comparative method. For how else was one to account for the fact that national socialism or fascism triumphed in some European countries, but not in others?
3. A concern on the one hand with totalitarianism, and on the other hand with the politics of the new states, inevitably forced political scientists to seek a wider geographic coverage than Europe or the white settlements overseas had traditionally provided. Hence, the rush into new descriptive works, the rise of new area specialisations, the need (and lure) of new theoretical conceptualisations, and of large-scale developmental theories (whether of a structural-functionalist or a neo-Marxist kind).
4. A concern with new theories, and new countries, also pushed some towards seeking empirical tests. Political scientists began to rival the economists, and often to surpass the sociologists, in an attempt to collect time-series data, aggregate data and survey data for an ever-widening number of countries.

For a time it seemed as if political science was really making a decisive breakthrough as a *science* in that sense of the word which in English or American is coloured so heavily by natural science. From 'parochial', political science would become 'universal'. From merely descriptive – or in a nicer word 'configurative' – it would become truly theoretical. 'Testing' was to provide the linkage between theorising and empirical research. Cumulative growth of knowledge seemed a real possibility. A genuine political science could no longer be bothered by political boundaries: 'international' and 'comparative' seemed pleonastic terms, as they became implicit in the very definition of social science itself.

At the same time as the 'general' claim for political science grew, so did its degree of 'specialisation'.

The discipline became a labyrinth of theories, concepts, approaches and methods. The subjects expanded from a limited number of countries to an ever-increasing number not only of (new) states, but also of political experiences in other units than the sovereign nation-state – ranging from international organisations to local polities, from formal models to small-group laboratory testing. In the process, the discipline inevitably lost a great deal of its earlier coherence.

But this apparently did not cause great damage to its increasingly international character. On the contrary: the very existence of international communication helped to foster the process of specialisation. Each new specialisation, or so it seemed, produced its own academic market and its own specialised public.

If communication *within* the discipline has often become more difficult through its increased variety, not so the communication across national boundaries by those of like minds and interests.

III. Internationalisation: some fundamental problems

If organisations flourish; if the infrastructure of publications, documentation and data exchange is becoming better and better; if scholars move and take note of one another's work across boundaries; if the intellectual diversity of the discipline becomes richer; if the number and kinds of political units available for analysis expand; if the temper of political science becomes more 'scientific' – is there, then, any reason for concern? Let me confess to feelings of uneasiness which accompany sentiments of satisfaction and exhilaration.

The preponderance of American political science

One possible problem is the dominant role of American political science. I mention this factor first, not because I wish to place myself on the side of its superficial detractors. Those who speak lightly of American political science (in the singular), are generally not aware of its richness, its versatility, or its quality in virtually all sub-fields of our profession. No other political science community has been so broad in the variety of its orientations, so open to scholars from other countries, so generous in its willingness to share in research – let alone to pay for collaborative efforts. Even what one could term the (renewed) Europeanisation of political science in our part of the world owes a great deal to American intellectual as well as financial generosity. Would it be far from the truth, to argue that the backbone of 'European' political science in the period between say 1955 and 1975 was formed by those then young scholars who were stimulated in their 'European' work by their confrontation (on a Ford grant, or a Rockefeller grant, or other American money) with American scholarship?

If I single out the dominance of American political science as being a problem, nevertheless, I do so because it causes certain difficulties on both the American and European side.

American scholars have not always shown a full appreciation of the contextual political realities of countries that were the object of American scholarship. Models were thought to 'apply', data were thought to 'prove' things, without a careful check of the actual political context. Many European scholars have reacted to such trends, generally by offering what we think to be more correct interpretations of the political experience of our own countries. But to the extent that we have done so in a one-to-one dialogue – 'our' country *vis-à-vis* America-based theories or concepts – we have *not* done much ourselves to promote true comparative study even within Europe. Paradoxically, Americans have probably done more to advance multilateral research enterprises in Europe, and with Europeans, than Europeans have done on their own accord. It would seem high time that we Europeans draw at least even with our American colleagues, in the multilaterality of contacts and the generosity of funding.

I shall not dwell long on one other disadvantage of the strong American presence in our discipline – not least because there are many signs that its worst period is now over. Large numbers of Europeans who do not know the versatility of the political science community in the United States – and who clearly know even less about the political record of our American colleagues in the days of McCarthy in the 1950s and of Vietnam in the 1960s and early 1970s – have allowed a cheap anti-Americanism to colour their judgement about the intellectual integrity and quality of the work of American political scientists – and of all those in Europe who have learned from that rich fund of learning across the Atlantic. To the extent that this happened to scholars of a younger generation, one positive asset of the internationalisation of political science was lost to them, through their own blinkers and to their own detriment.

The expansion of national political science communities

'National' political science programmes have rapidly expanded in European countries, both in teaching and research. The wish to emulate developments elsewhere had undoubtedly contributed to this development. Yet, this very expansion seems also to increase the 'national' element in the practice of political science. There is a natural concern for the national factors in the life of the national polity: national history, national institutions, national political forces, and national policy problems. Expanding teaching and research tasks often threaten to exhaust national energies, while growing size makes national political science communities also more self-sufficient and self-supporting.

Was it not always true that – and also easy to explain why – political science in the larger European countries – France, Germany, Britain, Italy – tended traditionally to be more inward-looking than political science in smaller European countries, an element which affected for instance the origin and development of the ECPR in its first decade? Paradoxically, however, political science in some of the smaller European countries is now reaching the dimensions that political science had in larger European countries some twenty years ago. In the line of Karl Deutsch's communications paradigm, this might now turn these smaller countries also more inward-looking – national demands outstripping the rival communication demands of international contacts.

Differences in different parts of the discipline

So far I have argued too much in terms of political science in general, and too little in terms of different sub-fields. Yet, in actual fact different parts of our discipline 'travel' very differently in international contacts. Some cross national frontiers easily, for example all kinds of formal theory (like theories of public choice, game theory, systems theory, organisation theory), problems of general methodology and quantitative technique, theories and findings based on general psychological or sociological properties, some part of international relations studies, and certain basic issues in political philosophy. Others, however, are in an entirely different situation: for example, institutional analysis, more value-oriented parts of political philosophy, political culture-studies, true theories of political development, the study of comparative bureaucracies, concrete policy analysis. The different degree to which different parts of the discipline lend themselves to actual internationalisation is one important blocking element in communication, within national political science communities, and even within the same university department.

One might argue that this very real fragmentation unfavourably affects our understanding of politics itself. Some of us are true experts in the international development of rather specialised parts of our discipline, others know relatively well how different political factors intertwine in our own country alone. But how many professional political scientists really understand the complexities of politics in general – whether across countries, (synchronically) or in a developmental perspective (diachronically)?

The costs of professionalisation

Do we, then, find ourselves face to face with some real costs in the process of present-day professionalisation? If I compare the education of my generation with that of the present young generation, there is no question which is the more professional. Many European political scientists were educated by scholars who were not themselves professional political scientists (even though they might occupy Chairs of Politics). We received an education, rather than a training, and to this day some of us have considerable difficulty in coping with clear defects in our professional make-up. Not unnaturally, we have tried to do better, by enhancing the professional element in the training programme for which we have been – to a greater or lesser extent – responsible. More and more departments now reach the stage in which they can claim some *expertise* in at least most of the sub-fields of political science.

Yet, our gain in professionalism may have been made at the expense of the general character of our educational programme. Do we offer enough understanding about historical factors which determine our polities? Do we cover the range of present-day political systems well enough? Do we equip new generations with a sufficient knowledge of other disciplines, so as to make them at least know why these could be relevant in specific instances? We can be happy about the internationalisation of large parts of our discipline. But who can still speak with sufficient credibility for the profession as a whole – within our own department, within our national communities, and also within Europe or the world generally? Is the relative absence of the 'general' scholar not a dangerous symptom for our profession, for true international growth and cooperation, for a genuine understanding of politics?

IV. Can we surmount the obstacles?

If this diagnosis is correct, there are no easy remedies. We should *not* forgo the clear advantages of professionalism and specialisation. We should *not* moan the stronger position that our field (or should I rather say fields?) have begun to occupy in the national life of our own countries. We should *not* fall for the easy temptation of the rhetoric of international meetings and say that all will be well if we only meet more, and do more, together. Yet there *is* a genuine need to do something, lest the highly selective internationalisation of some parts of our discipline, fragment and fracture the 'whole'.

I can only offer the following suggestions which all point to the hard way – which in my view is the only way.

1. We should probably begin by reviewing our present teaching programmes, to see whether their professional character is well matched to what I have somewhat diffidently called the more 'general' and the more 'cultural' component. How much attention do we pay to the general functioning of politics in specific societies, in the past and in the present, in our country and across countries? How wide does our training run across our own discipline? And how well aware are we – and do we make our students – of the possible relevance of other disciplines?

2. We should ask ourselves the honest question, how well our future graduates understand the politics of at least one other country than

their own reasonably well. I am thinking of at least *one* other country, rather than of a great many ones. Only a few scholars can genuinely hope for a real knowledge and understanding of the politics of more than a few countries. But there is undoubtedly no better way to begin understanding even one's own country than by truly immersing oneself in the politics of another society.

3. For the more advanced young scholars (whether already employed in teaching themselves or not) we should demand with greater force that they spend a substantial time in another country than their own.

   There are obvious difficulties in the way of such a suggestion. It raises problems of financing extensive periods of study abroad. It runs against an understandable, if disconcerting tendency, for younger scholars to 'play safe', given shrinking job opportunities. Yet, the possible pay-off would seem to be so substantial that both university departments and national educational authorities would be well advised to take special steps. Ideally, a substantial period of research in another country should be a *conditio sine qua non* for academic appointments and/or promotions.

4. For those who cannot get away for longer periods, shorter international training programmes could be a partial substitute. Summer schools such as the ECPR Summer School on Methodology at the University of Essex, and the European University Institute Summer Schools in Florence, which have been oriented rather more towards analyses of substantive political developments in Western Europe, are playing an important role in socialising new generations of political scientists in the possibilities and promises of comparative study. But perhaps we should be even more ambitious than that. Would it not be advisable for a few prominent centres of political study in Europe to join forces across borders, and to establish an international graduate programme – at a minimum at the master's level, but preferably leading to an advanced doctorate with an international faculty and a student body which might rotate among the institutions participating in such a programme?

5. There is a clear need to strengthen genuine comparative research projects. Again and again, we have experienced how few scholars move as yet easily in that area, and how tempting it is to escape from some of the real dilemmas of comparative politics into overly-specialised, technical ventures. Nonetheless there is no better way to understand politics than to raise important questions – and to do so by raising them in the context of different societies. Perhaps, we should be a little braver than we often are, and have international teams of scholars face important political issues in joint seminars and research projects.

6. Finally, there might be merit in a project in which experienced scholars of different countries would join to offer a critical assessment of the state of the discipline, facing clear weaknesses as much as possible strengths. Such a project should deal with general issues, but also move into specialised fields. Such a venture might well reveal that we are 'richer' on many points than we ourselves would have suspected. This might help us to avoid the easy pitfall of believing that only the newest work, and the newest 'fad', is the best and the most exciting. But it could also help scholars in individual countries to learn from each other's strengths and weaknesses. It could assist us in planning programmes of education and research in which the 'combined wisdom' of the profession might provide a counterweight against the all too visible dangers of traditional routines, overspecialisation, passing fads, or the expediencies of government policies – which are often not less self-confident for showing great fickleness. In a period where governments tend at one and the same time to cut expenditures in the social sciences, and to offer in return at most contracts for research according to political rather than academic criteria, well-grounded priorities established by prominent scholars cooperating across European borders, both in general and more specific fields, might well provide a welcome counterforce.

At the same time one should continue to raise the banner of individual excellence at the top of our mast. In a book which is published as a tribute to such an unplannable individualist as the retiring Gladstone professor S.E. Finer, it is as well to emphasise what is, alas, in many countries no longer a self-evident view. Perhaps one should make the special issue of *Government and Opposition* (Vol. 15, no. 3/4, 1980; published under the title *A Generation of Political Thought*) in which among a number of other distinguished scholars Finer analysed his own intellectual development under the characteristic title 'Political science: an idiosyncratic retrospect' – required reading for aspiring young political scientists and policy-makers in universities and governments alike! One could not find a better case, if one wishes to argue that political science requires above all insatiable intellectual curiosity, a wide-ranging political knowledge of different times and places, and profound analytical skills. Or should we simply say genuine learning?

9 Participants and Controllers*
Geraint Parry and George Moyser

Introduction

Political participation is again an issue of importance in discussions of British politics. Like most other advanced industrial countries, Britain shared in the participatory mood of the 1960s – sufficiently for Samuel Beer to devote a substantial part of his recent gloomy review of the British political scene to 'The Romantic Revolt' and 'The New Populism'.[1] The participatory impulse affected academics as well as citizens and a literature on the subject began to emerge[2] without, however, resulting in a major empirical study. In Britain, as elsewhere, the 1970s saw an apparent decline of interest in participation, possibly symbolised by the failure to enact devolution to Scotland and Wales which some saw as an exercise in stimulating greater involvement.[3] Yet if participation no longer formed a central part of the political agenda, it did not disappear entirely; at the beginning of the 1980s it re-emerged in a less dramatic but still substantial form, despite the hegemony of the distinctly non-participatory Tory Party.

Within the Labour Party the campaign for party democracy was successful in securing wider participation in the reselection of MPs as candidates and in the selection of the leader. It is always premature to proclaim the overthrow of Michels's Law but its ironclad quality has at least been called into question. Tony Benn's 'arguments for socialism' were largely built around the twin themes of participation and accountability. Although the breakaway Social Democratic Party is conventionally placed at the opposite end of the socialist spectrum from the Bennites its chief ideologue, David Owen, was no less convinced of the volume of participation.

He laid claim to the heritage of William Morris, the syndicalists and the Guild Socialists by criticising the centralist, Fabian tradition:

* We wish gratefully to acknowledge the financial support of the British Social Science Research Council under grant no. E00220003.

> The momentum towards participation has its roots in the very educational advances for which socialists and others have striven.[5]

The Liberal Party, would, clearly, have no difficulty in absorbing the participatory strands in the SDP's thinking. It had a long-standing commitment to such policies as industrial partnership and profit-sharing, devolution and decentralisation. Additionally, it had gained a number of electoral successes at national and local level by its commitment to 'community politics'[6] – the mobilisation of political interest in local issues or, as cynics would have it, making politics out of cracked paving stones.

In this respect the Liberals were, however, merely employing a vogue language of 'community' which has paralleled the language of political participation. Like the language of participation, it is capable of exploitation by the established powers. 'Community' used as an adjective appears to imply an institution as much created by leaders as provided for recipients. In Britain in the 1970s there appeared, throughout the length and breadth of the land, community workers, community leaders, community industries, community action groups, community sports organisers, etc., appointed from above at least as frequently as generated from below.

Beyond the level of party politics there are those who have detected since the 1970s a 'crisis of legitimacy' facing Western democracies in general. Britain's proclaimed political stability has been called into question in the face of a record of government failure to prevent economic decline.[7] Falling electoral turnout and increased electoral volatility have been accompanied by calls for extensive political and constitutional reforms – A Bill of Rights, proportional representation, devolution.[8] In summer 1981 came inner-city crowd disturbances which some interpreted as an expression of frustration at existing channels of political action and of alienation from the political authorities. These disturbances were identified with the communities in which they occurred but opinion has differed as to how far they arose out of national issues, such as employment, or out of the conditions of the particular community or sub-community.

It is in this context that some critics have argued that a genuine solution to the growing problem of legitimacy can only come through forms of extended participation. Colin Crouch has argued that if the price of survival for the modern welfare state in conditions of severe economic constraint is self-restraint in the demands of the working class, then in return the working class may have to be offered more opportunities for participation in political decisions.[9] As Crouch puts it:

A suitable slogan for this development would be 'no moderation without participation'[10]

One response of the state might be the corporatist embrace of the elites of the peak associations with little in the way of wider involvement. An alternative model is based on a plurality of participatory institutions and processes. The effectiveness of this model depends, to quote Crouch again,

> on the extent to which viable authentic communities (usually, that is, residential, occupational and professional) form the units at the base of the organisations.[11]

Such participation is seen less as an alternative to existing modes of electoral politics than as a means of renewing their vitality. At the theoretical level these concerns appear to preoccupy the doyen of pluralism, Robert A. Dahl, in his recent *Dilemmas of Pluralist Democracy*. Dahl points to what he regards as an irreversible shift of power towards corporatist institutions and away from elected institutions.[12] But he also argues for the need for greater and more varied decentralisation and participation if the potentialities of pluralist democracy are to be realised. In Britain a similar balancing act is performed by Labour, combining a quasi-corporatist policy of a 'national economic assessment' of economic growth, prices and wages between government and unions with Bennite proposals for worker participation. Similarly, Social Democrats like Owen profess a preference for participation and decentralisation whilst stressing the need for that basic corporatist device – incomes policy.

The 1980s are far from the heady atmosphere of the late 1960s which inspired earlier studies of participation in Western Europe and elsewhere. There has been a renewal of academic interest in participation and it is linked to an interest in the relationship between community and changing patterns of political activity.

The politics of participation and control
It will come as no surprise that given the breadth of his interests, S.E. Finer has made an important contribution to the study of political participation.

Any study of political participation at national and community levels faces an immediate problem in that the very description of the subject matter involves the use of what philosophers have recently come to call essentially contestable concepts. These are concepts whose meaning can only be understood by reference to a whole complex of associated ideas and values, whose meanings must equally be grasped before one can claim to have given an account of the original term which one was studying. The terms 'political' and 'community' have good claims to be prime instances of contestable concepts.

It has also been argued, more questionably, that 'participation' also falls into this category. For it may be suggested that one can only be described as 'participating' in any activity when one is doing so voluntarily, or with some sort of likelihood of being effective. This would exclude various political activities on the grounds that they are 'mobilised' rather than participatory, symbolic rather than effective. Thus voting in general elections in a liberal democratic country would not count as political participation, either on the grounds that a single vote can have only an infinitesimal effect on the outcome or on the grounds put forward by some radicals that elections as such provide no effective choice. Similarly, many schemes for community participation on such matters as planning proposals have been rejected with scorn as not fulfilling the requirement of effectiveness or 'reality' necessary for genuine participation. Instead they have been regarded as symbolic gestures – the participatory stage is said to come too late in the process for the basic issues to be debated. A different but related argument is that participation in such schemes shores up a system which is biased in its structure and should be rejected. Participation, then, is held only to be genuinely possible in an alternative society which will have provided not merely the appropriate procedures but also the social and economic preconditions in which participants will have approximately equal opportunities to make their views heard.

As with other political concepts there are participation theorists who seek to reject the contestability thesis and argue that a neutral definition which does not presuppose that any particular normative standpoint can be formed. By defining 'participation' as 'taking part' they seek to distinguish the definition of the term from any attempt to designate the activity as effective or ineffective.[13] Even in this approach there must be some point at which one wishes to reject the designation 'participation' to describe a person's involvement in an activity. Something more positive than merely living in a society or being a purely passive member of a group appears to be required to be a participant. If one then incorporates a voluntary conscious character into the definition of participation it becomes incumbent on the researcher to establish that the participant is indeed aware of what kind of activity he is engaged in. But this in turn presupposes a conception of the activity itself – a conception which may not be that shared by the researcher. This problem is particularly acute when it is participation in politics with which one is dealing.

In his essay on 'Groups and political participation' we find Finer grappling with just these problems. He favours the broader definition of participation:

> By 'political participation' I stipulate: sharing in the framing and/or execution of public policies.[14]

Like the 'neutral' definition, Finer's incorporates the view that participation must be voluntary. However, he adds a further element which places his position somewhere between the two extremes of definitional neutrality and contestability. He argues that to count as participation the activity must not only be effective but be seen by the actor as having been influential.

> In short: for someone to feel that he is a participant, it would not be sufficient that such and such an outcome were produced, but that they should *be seen to have been produced in a certain way* – that a causal connection between the individual's action and the final outcome is manifest, and manifest *to him*.[15]

Thus the regular loser is not a participant in the outcome, i.e. in the framing of public policies – (but does the loser still participate in a recognisably public and political process?) A person is also not a participant if the small part he or she plays in the collective decision is such that it cannot be recognised as his or her personal contribution or responsibility.

Now, one effect of such a definiton is to draw the boundaries of those who would qualify as the participants much more narrowly. It would be wrong to conclude that participants are to be identified with decision-making elites but the range of participants stretches no further than those who can claim to have made an impact on the outcome either individually or, it must be noted, collectively through group involvement.

The second effect of the definition is on the way in which the politics of regimes are analysed. In *Comparative Government* Finer reserves the term 'participation' for those procedures in which the general public takes an effective part almost comparable to that taken by the elite;[16] this is consistent with the position he adopted in the article published two years later. The referendum and the popular initiative are clear instances, the election of judges is another, as is serving in executive office in a voluntary capacity. Following equally consistently from his account of participation, Finer then argues that this would be too strong a word to describe the dominant form of political activity in which citizens are involved in liberal democracies. Instead, elections should be viewed as the means by which the public *controls* the rulers. Elections permit the exercise of a broad veto power over rulers through the process of re-election or rejection. Finer therefore proposes a continuum of popular involvement in government stretching from genuine participation to popular control and then on to the most common conditions of the political world – mere acquiescence or even submission to coercion.

Researchers into participation are thus faced with a range of definitions which may affect both the choice of activities which they study and the terms in which they describe and analyse them. When one adds to these definitions the range of meanings of 'political' the problems are multiplied. Finer's definition is traditional in directing attention to policies 'propounded for, or administered on behalf of, the public as a whole'[17] When this definition of 'political' is coupled with the definition of participation the researcher should immediately be alerted to a set of intriguing conceptual and methodological problems. A political participant is one who is voluntarily and consciously engaged in the framing and/or execution of public policies. For the central core of participants who are fairly close to the decision-making this presents no problem. There may be some, however, who would not describe themselves as participating politically, yet might be described by others as so doing. Radicals sometimes describe many institutions and their employees as political because they see them as supportive of the regime or as carrying out its policies, whereas the occupants of these roles view their own activities as neutral or *apolitical*.

The problem occurs most explicitly in respect of participation in the 'output' side which Finer, rightly in our view, includes within the range of political participation. Voluntary social workers, members of a quango, members of an industrial tribunal may regard themselves as performing a political role in executing directly, or in surrogate fashion, public policy. Others may think of their activities as advancing their careers, earning some extra income or helping improve their social lives. Some trade union members have been included in surveys as political participants because they report that their branch was engaged in trying to affect local community dcisions. Others were excluded because they did not report such involvement.[18]

Within the realm of what has come to be called 'uncoventional' participation – demonstrations, boycotts, riots – the problem is again acute. The relatively stable world of pressure groups and party activities does in fact generally provide us with fairly straightforward, or at least workable, definitions of the political. But the world of unconventional political activity is less predictable, more spontaneous, and situationally defined. Whether a crowd disturbance is seen by those involved at the time as a political act (as distinct from retrospective interpretations), or as engaged in for 'fun and profit', to use Banfield's notorious phrase[19], can be hard to determine and can in any case vary from one person to another. One guideline may be the target against which the disturbances are directed. If the target is a political elite, interpreted broadly, one may conclude that one is dealing with a political act which the wide definition of participation would incorporate. However the situation can be more complex. A disturbance prompted by police harrassment could be regarded as being directed against the execution of public policy by officials who are central to the maintenance of the state. Not only local factors may be involved, there may also be a reaction against a style of law enforcement which has implications for the public as a whole. Alternatively, of course, the disturbances may indeed be parochial with virtually no implications for general policy, let alone for the legitimacy of state institutions.

To a considerable extent Finer is right in arguing that these crowd phenomena are generally of political significance when they occur with such sufficient regularity and permanence of membership that they gain a structure and organisation which permits them to have a continuing effect over time, i.e. when they approach the character of a group. Otherwise, he argues, a major crowd event, such as occurred in France in 1968, has a once and for all effect which may not be that intended by those on the street.[20] In another respect Finer's assessment made in 1972 may require slight revision. He points out that the level of involvement in any form of direct action is low and only intermittent. Nevertheless, there is some indication that the milder forms of action – petitions and lawful demonstrations – are becoming sufficiently part of the ordinary repertoire of the citizen's political acts[21] that they must be incorporated into an integrated account of political participation. Increasingly, it would appear, there are citizens for whom signing a petition or taking part in a demonstration are as likely forms of political action as writing to their MP or local councillor. For those below voting age, but at the age when they may feel deprived or discriminated against, the repertory of potential political actions will necessarily include relatively more 'unconventional' forms. Thus, the boundary between 'conventional' and 'unconventional' may need to be re-drawn.

This is one major reason why future research on participation can no longer separate the study of these two forms of conduct as strictly as has so far been the case. If, as Finer rightly argues, we must look at participation at least as much from the subjective viewpoint of the actor as from the observer's standpoint then the probability is that different actors in different contexts will think of the unconventional-conventional distinction very differently and also assess the various modes of action very differently – as effective or ineffective, as indeed participating, controlling or non-participating acts. The researcher is faced with a dilemma in that to pursue the implications of the 'subjective' side of the definition may lead to acceptance of highly idiosyncratic and non-comparable usages. Alternatively, to impose a definition is to risk missing the signficant political dimension which the respondent may perceive in his or her own life.

The distinction Finer drew in *Comparative Government* between a politics of participation and a politics of control does not, of course, turn on the subjective assesment of the activity but on its proximity to actual decision-making. It betrays an instrumental view of political involvement stemming from Bentham and James Mill rather than from Rousseau. The prime object of political activity is to promote or to defend one's interests. The actual level of involvement will be influenced by the costs of the activity in the light of the anticipated benefits accruing from one's own contribution. One major impetus to action is provided by the assumption of this theory of politics that others are as self-interested as oneself. One cannot be certain that any other person's pursuit of self-interest will benefit oneself. Even if one were disinclined to leap into the political arena one would regret one's inaction if the outcome turned out to be contrary to one's interests. (Rather like regretting not going for a job after one reads of the appointment of one's peer.) So, at the least, there is the incentive to minimise one's regret[22] At the most, there is the prospect of making a decisive intervention to promote one's interests.

Notoriously, however, the theory requires that the activity does produce a recognisable benefit. Downs and Olson have shown that in modern large-scale political systems the chances of one person making a decisive difference by his or her vote or group membership is minute. We have the paradox that the democratic rights to vote or to join unions, for which generations struggled, are construed by the theory as costs which so outweigh the benefits as to make the exercise of the rights irrational. This is not the place to go further into the criticism of the theory or into the attempts to amend it to meet the objections.[23] The fact remains that citizens in liberal democracies have not concluded that politics is so costly as to make involvement irrational. A sense of duty or, as Hardin suggests, a desire to be part of the history of the age may motivate them rather than a purely instrumental calculation. Nevertheless, levels of political activity are sufficiently low as to suggest that most people are also fully aware that it only makes sense to spend a limited time on politics and that this time should be made to count. In other words they may see their role as typically more towards the 'control' position on Finer's continuum. The professional politicians and pressure group activists 'participate' and are permitted fairly considerable room for manoeuvre. The limits are set by control mechanisms of which the most signficant are elections. Others would include public enquiries and appeals to an Ombudsman.

In their survey of aspects of political participation in five democracies, Barnes and Kaase found such low levels of activity that they wondered how democracy was to be sustained.[24] Whilst this is a reasonable question for a participatory conception of democracy, the problem is less puzzling if democracy is based on mechanisms of control with only intermittent bursts of political activity on the part of the population as a whole. If British citizens believe in a division of labour between the professional participants and the citizen controllers there is less reason to worry about the vitality of democratic institutions. In fact, we still know relatively little about such attitudes. Quiescence may be the result of satisfaction, deference, alienation or indifference. It may stem from a sense that the political system is incapable of handling the economic problems which face people, or else that these are problems which are not within the province of government but belong to the private sphere.[25] Research into participation or non-participation must examine not merely the bald 'facts' of levels of activity but the meanings attached to them by the respondents.

The line from participation to control is a genuine continuum. The pursuit of a politics of participation or of a politics of control is also a matter of strategy as well as of disposition. From an instrumental view, the decision as to strategy will turn on an assessment of costs and benefits. It is, however, important to recognise that what may start as a strategy of control may end up with unexpectedly high levels of political involvement – levels associated more with a participatory conception of democracy. One may illustrate the point with James Mill's *Essay on Government*. Here representative government is proclaimed as the 'grand discovery of modern times' because it is the device by which the public may most effectively control governments which are presumed to be composed of self-interested persons who, left alone, will manipulate power to their own advantage. Mill focuses immediately on the issue of control:

> All the difficult questions of Government relate to the means of restraining those, in whose hands are lodged the powers necessary for the protection of all, from making bad use of it.[26]

Mill goes on to argue that what is required is a 'checking body' with sufficient power for its purpose and with a sufficient identity of interest with the community. Because government also has the capacity to do good, Mill does not favour the limitation of its powers by some system of checks and balances, although this is consistent with a theory of control. Nor was there any impartial and effective means of punishing politicians who had broken trust. There would be problems in defining a punishable offence as distinct from an abuse and there would be difficulties in establishing proof. The experiences over the impeachment of President Nixon may be taken to confirm Mill's argument. The alternative was to limit the duration of office in order to minimise the representative's capacity to do harm. Elections should be as frequent as possible while allowing for the performance of the functions of government. (The Chartists and other radicals in the nineteenth century campaigned for annual elections.) The American House of Representatives for example, operates on a two-year cycle. In each case the expectation is that the political elite will be kept on its toes and be forced to respond to the public at large.

Although conceived of as a method of control, a system of frequent elections may involve a high level of activity. This did not worry Mill:

> With respect to the inconvenience arising from frequency of election, though it is evident that the trouble of election, which is always something, should not be repeated oftener than is necessary, no great allowance will need to be made for it, because it may easily be reduced to an inconsiderable amount.[27]

But political involvement would presumably not stop at getting the electorate out for frequent general elections. Firstly, there is every reason to extend the principle in American fashion to a host of local public offices from school boards to community relations organisations. Secondly, to exercise control through such electoral mechanisms presupposes a pretty intensive level of interest in politics. One must be sufficiently knowledgeable to determine whether the candidate has promoted or defended one's interests or is likely to do so during the next year or two of office. Whilst it would be misleading to take measures of political interest – reading newspapers, discussions – as measures of participation, the level of interest required might almost attain the intense level an advocate of participatory democracy would desire. In this way, although the motivation for, and justification of, political activity is a concern for control, and although the activity is still somewhat removed from the point of decision, the actual level of activity could be closer to what one would anticipate in a radical democracy.

A politics of control has to contend with a number of major problems, some conceptual and others practical. Mill's version was excessively simplistic in supposing that the interest of the community was something definable in terms of the interests of an (enlightened) majority. The more pluralistic a society the more problematic it is to discover what constitutes majority control. Majorities are to a considerable degree an artefact of the particular electoral system employed. A simple majority system with only two parties gives a result which overcomes many of the logical problems associated with the construction of a collective choice. However, it does so at the cost of forcing all the possible policy alternatives into two packages between which the elector must choose without being able to distinguish those parts of the package he or she approves from those which he or she disapproves. A proportional representation system may more accurately reflect the balance of preference between the available packages, but at the risk of transferring the production of a final policy to coalition building by representatives. It may be less easy to attach responsibility to these representatives at the subsequent election and enforce the appropriate check. A satisfactory checking system involves much more than Mill's device of limiting duration of office but also some mechanism of eliciting the public will in the name of which the control is to be exercised.[29]

A second major issue for any theory of control (and, indeed, for most alternatives) is to ensure that the elites do indeed respond to the pressures placed on them by the public. Participation rapidly becomes pointless if it is seen to be ineffective. Mechanisms of control will atrophy if it is discovered that they are no longer capable of performing this function. From the standpoint of the elites ineffective public participation can be manipulated as a form of legitimation. Malfunctioning control mechanisms can even reduce the need to modify conduct so as to anticipate and prevent defeat. This is why the study of participation and of elites must be taken in tandem.

The theory of political control operates on the assumption that it is in the interests of the elites to respond to the demands of the public. The threat to the elites is that they will be thrown out of office if their policies deviate too far from the interests of the public – and that they do not wish to be thrown out. This last assumption seems reasonable at first sight. However, it ignores two difficulties. Firstly, there are those public-spirited elites who see their role as enacting policies in the 'objective' community interest rather than as securing re-election only on terms that they regard as sacrificing their principles. Some even try to make an electoral virtue out of the pursuit of principles rather than of votes. The threat of defeat would not lead them to deviate from their chosen course, although it would prevent them or their successors from continuing in it. Such Burkean representatives are more likely to be found in non-partisan (and non-competitive) communities. To the extent that party now dominates politics at both national and community level this difficulty may be regarded as relatively insignificant.

The second difficulty is much greater, and far surpasses anything that a James Mill would have anticipated: bureaucracies are not subject to electoral defeat. The traditional Millian mechanism of control – short duration of office – does not apply. The original assumption was, of course, that political control of the bureaucracy would suffice to ensure that it could not develop policies at variance with the will of the electorate. One does not have to labour the point that things have changed and that in most advanced industrial societies civil servants have considerable influence (to put it at its mildest) on the policies which are enacted. The logic of the control theory has to be extended into the relations between ministers and civil servants and into the whole realm of the execution of public policy. It may imply a wide range of reforms – increases in ministerial control, open government, public inquiries, decentralisation.[30]

The importance of establishing the extent of elite responsiveness to control mechanisms or to participation is reinforced by some recent work which has challenged the control theory on both empirical and moral grounds. In what may be described as a revival of classical elitism in modified form, Lowell Field and Higley in a number of writings, and Nordlinger in a study of the autonomy of the democractic state, have criticised contemporary political science for over-emphasising 'societal' explanations of politics and policy outcomes and for under-playing the degree of initiative possessed by elites.[31] According to this view, elites operate only within very broad constraints laid down by the non-elite. To a very considerable degree elites need not anticipate that they will be faced with severe sanctions enforced by the public. The resources available to elites mean that they largely determine the agenda. The policies that are debated are mainly initiated by them. The public at large often has no fixed policy priorities, in which case the elites define the issues. But even where powerful counter-elites do have policy preferences the elites in public office have substantial resources to enable them to direct or overcome the sanctions which are threatened. Consequently, it is on the elites that political science should concentrate rather than on the control mechanisms or the channels of participation:

> Look at least as much to the state as to civil society to understand what the democratic state does in the working of public policy and why it does so; the democratic state is frequently autonomous in translating its own preferences into authoritative actions, and markedly autonomous in doing so even when they diverge from those held by the politically weightiest groups in civil society. These two far-reaching assertions are what this book is all about.[32]

In line with the classical elitists these writers not only argue for the 'realism' of this approach to political science but also for the political and moral value of an elitist stance. Acceptance of the determining voice of elites should, in the view of Field and Higley, lead one to concentrate on encouraging elites in their self-confidence in handling national and international problems. Nordlinger argues that autonomous elites may often be seen as defenders of the public interest against powerful but biased interest groups. It may also, he argues, be as essential to consider the success of elites in the skilful management of crises as the degree of their responsiveness to the often changing demands of social groupings.

Clearly, any assessment of the instrumentality of either participatory or control strategies needs to generate some measure of elite responsiveness. In their classic study, Verba and Nie developed an indirect measure of elite-citizen linkage by examining the degree of concurrence between them on community problems and priorities. In doing so one must, of course, attempt to determine whether this concurrence is brought about *by* the elites as a result of some form of mobilisation or agenda manipulation – as would be suggested by some of Nordlinger's theories.[33] Secondly, it is necessary to specify more precisely than is done by the new (and the old) elitists the distinctions between subsets of elites. Verba and Nie draw a broad division between elected and non-elected elites. But one needs to go further than this. Amongst non-elected elites public officials differ from business leaders, trade union officials or community leaders in their channels of contact and communication with the general public. It would be surprising, although an important question for research, if all these notables showed similar patterns of concurrence with the non-elite on policy priorities. Even if they did – for example, by regarding unemployment as the chief problem for the community – it would be surprising if they agreed on the solutions, which is an equally important, yet sometimes neglected topic of academic enquiry into elite-mass linkages.[34]

Concurrence is not the only measure of linkages between elites and non-elites. A more direct procedure is to ask those concerned what they think of interactions in the past. From the non-elite viewpoint, one major factor affecting the estimate of the rationality of present or future participation is its past effectiveness. Nothing is more likely to deter participatory ventures than the sense that the elites have not responded in the past or that the elites have in fact decided the issue in advance and that 'putting out to participation'[35] is merely symbolic. Most members of the public will not wish to waste precious time on such exercises as attending inquiries on local housing schemes or road proposals in these circumstances. Some argue that less time is spent on the politics of control, but the failures of the mechanisms to ensure elite responsiveness can lead to a similar degree of cynicism amongst the public. Indeed, the cynicism may be *more* serious as the next stages on the continuum are acquiescence and submission. Enquiry into recent experience of elite responsiveness and into the likelihood that the respondent would again involve himself or herself in some form of political action seems essential if the study of participation is to shed light on the vitality of democratic institutions.

Studying the public attitude to the effectiveness of conventional and unconventional political involvement has to be matched by research into the attitudes of the elites themselves. To the degree that elites regard some forms of participation or control as illegitimate or as merely a nuisance, they may set greater barriers to contact and render these ineffective. It is a forceful criticism of pluralist politics that, although it is formally open to any groups to press for their interests, nevertheless disadvantaged groups such as ethnic minorities, the homeless or battered wives are not recognised as legitimate by the elites to whom they direct their claims.[36] The frustration that could arise from this has potential consequences for democracy depending upon what such groups might decide is the instrumentally rational response to the situation. Will they press on in the conventional participatory modes – campaigning, contacting officials, attending meetings? Will they instead resort to the unconventional modes of direct action ranging from demonstrations and boycotts to various forms of violence? Or will they withdraw into acquiescence, submission or a condition of discontented but relatively powerless alienation? The 'moderate' option of using the control mechanisms is the one which may be less instrumental because, as minorities, they lack the political leverage to make the notables listen and respond. It is only where minorities are relatively large, or are capable of forming coalitions with other groups, or happen to be in a position to swing the balance between competing power blocs that the possibility of control will arise.

The positions of black minorities in British and American cities illustrate the differences. In a city such as Chicago the blacks constitute such a large proportion of the electorate that a massive and solid vote can swing a local election almost on its own, certainly with the support of any other ethnic minority groups and particularly when the opposition is split – hence the victory of a black mayor in Chicago in 1983. In Britain, despite concentrations in particular areas, in no city taken as a political whole do blacks form anywhere near such a substantial grouping. The competing political leaders cannot be made to respond as a consequence of *needing* the support of the black minority alone. The effectiveness of a politics of control must then vary according to the relative power positions in a community. In Chicago it may be true that

Blacks may have learned that *powerlessness* does not demand attention. To demand more, one must participate more.[37]

but in Britain the inference cannot be made with the same confidence, even if the first part of the statement were true.

The rationality of adopting a participatory or a controlling strategy must then depend on the relative power positions within a community. Verba and Nie also pointed out that the rationality of political activity will depend on its particular mode and target.[38] Thus, whatever the rationality of voting, contacting a politician or an official about a personal or a local community problem might have an early and recognisable pay-off. Beyond this, however, it is to be expected that different community contexts will affect whether any particular form of political pressure is likely to make sense in instrumental terms. This raises certain problems as to the most appropriate design for a comparative study of participation. In particular, should one seek to study a large number of communities or a few communities in greater depth – a 'large-numbers' or a 'limited numbers' strategy?

Studying participation and control

In assessing this issue one must consider closely the nature of the theory being employed for on that hinges the question of choosing the most appropriate research design to generate the necessary information. In this particular instance, a primary concern is the balance that is struck between the individual actor on the one hand and his or her social and political context on the other. The so-called 'instrumental approach' which has been discussed in this essay seems to have given greater weight to the former, making, as Curry has put it, 'an assumption of methodological individualism'.[39] Within the rational choice variant, this stress can be seen in the highly atomistic mechanism employed to explain why decisions about whether to participate, or merely to seek control, or to remain inactive, are made. Such decisions are essentially construed as a matter of individuals weighing utilities either through a personal utility maximisation procedure or, more controversially, through minimising perceived disutilities ('regrets').[40] A similar emphasis, albeit to a lesser degree, can be seen in the social psychological approaches commonly adopted by those concerned with empirical patterns and inductively derived instrumental theory. Particularly in earlier studies, their explanations were couched in terms of individual resources, individual attitudes and values and individual life-experiences.[41]

We would argue that this focus on the individual as the major object of analysis has led, possibly unconsciously, both to a failure to give adequate attention to the operating context within which individuals make their decisions about political action, and to the selection of a research design which exacerbates this situation. Thus, the sample survey is uniquely powerful and efficient in generating information about individuals in the population at large. One of its key virtues is that, for relatively low cost, it allows generalisations to be made about national populations so long as the sample is fairly drawn as to be representative. At the same time, however, the very procedure which allows such inferences tends to divorce each individual from the social and political context within which he or she operates. Individuals within such samples do not interact with each other, contextual characteristics (for example, local normative climates) cannot readily be measured and added to the theory-testing process.[42] The net effect, as Clark has noted, is further to reinforce, or give impetus to, those types of research question surveys are very good at – making individualistic generalisations about large, national populations.[43]

Increasingly, however, there has been an attempt to remedy what has been seen by some at least as an imbalance between individual and context. Thus, Verba and Nie gave at least some recognition to the role of community political characteristics and to mass-elite linkages.[44] But it was at best a minor theme of their study and the community design was no more than a very limited exercise tacked on to the main national sample survey. The end product was, therefore, a set of communities that had the virtues of being relatively large in number and, in some senses, representative but also had serious defects as an attempt adequately to locate individuals in their local milieux. For example, only twenty-five or so mass respondents and seven elite persons were interviewed in each of their research localities. In these circumstances it is not surprising that the individualistic bias in their explanatory model was not substantially challenged or altered. On the other hand, in a subsequent volume more stress was laid on the collectivistic nature of resources and the effect of institutions (and by implication elites) on political participation.[45] But, equally, the local community element, along with elite-mass linkage analysis, disappeared. The other major empirical study in the related area of political protest, published about the same time,[46] referred to normative climates and the repressive stances of political authorities, but as these authors also depended solely upon national sample surveys no real shift in theoretical balance was accomplished or even intended.

Hence, in recent years, commentators have continued to call both for a better balanced (and more realistic) explanatory model and for a more appropriate research design. Thus, Uhlaner, in a recent review, has argued that

> In order to account satisfactorily for political participation, the nature of the relationship between individual and community must be moved to the center of the inquiry.[47]

Somewhat more specifically, and germane to the points we have been making earlier in the paper, Uhlaner concludes that

> The integration of the individual as an autonomous rational utility maximizer with the individual as a member of social and political communities will give us a better and richer account of political participation, and one which rings truer to observed political phenomena.[48]

Intregrating these two theoretical aspects brings with it the necessity of focusing on groups, community structures and cultures as well as on elite behaviour. Only in this way, we would argue, can the instrumentality of participation and control be treated adequately. To cite again an example referred to earlier, such a re-orientation would allow fuller cognisance to be taken of inter-group power relativities within the local or national polity. This is clearly an essential ingredient, in an era where so much mass political participation is necessarily collectivist in nature, for the understanding of participatory decisions at the individual level. The same might equally be said of control decisions and the perceived respective utilities of the two strategies.

To accomplish this shift, it is not sufficient in our opinion merely to tack on to information about individuals whatever contextual data are available. This merely makes a nod in the appropriate direction without fundamentally altering the 'individualistic bias'. What is needed is a true multi-level design. This involves, at a minimum, samples of mass citizenry, as well as contextual data on community characteristics, and organisational leaders and elite activities in sufficient depth as to constitute a separate data-gathering task. These would then be harmonised, or brought together, within a common analysis and theoretical framework. In proposing this, we would concur with Uhlaner's remark that

> a study design as a series of city samples instead of a national sample[49]

would be far more feasible, although we ourselves would argue more in terms of a series of *community* samples than restricting the scope solely to large urban contexts.

This implies, more specifically, that a number of communities should be included, each carefully selected so as to ensure that, between them, as many important contextual situations would arise as would be compatible with the resources available. How many precisely is, of course, a matter whose working out can only be judged in the light of particular research situations. But if the complex web of group identifications, elite mobilisation tactics and so forth are to be mapped out thoroughly enough then it would seem likely that, with the sort of resources usually made available for projects of this sort, the number of research sites must necessarily be small. Hence, this line of argument would seem to lead, to a recommendation of the 'limited numbers' selection strategy.

Such a recommendation or conclusion has been echoed by others who have been concerned by the quality of, and apparent biases in, earlier theories and research designs. Two examples may suffice to illustrate the point. Knoke points to the need to give greater attention to the local political cultural setting of participation.[50] He argues, as have many other writers, that political culture has a mutually influencing relationship with political structures, and both help to shape mass and elite political action. Yet, despite the concept's rich theoretical potential (a potential which he explores in a preliminary way reminiscent of Mansbridge's work[51]), he concludes that

the research evidence on political culture . . . is exceedingly sparse.[52]

To remedy the situation, he explicitly suggests, like us, a limited numbers design. For, as he points out,

To collect adequate information on community residents' political beliefs requires samples of considerable size if the responses are to be broken down by sub-culture.[53]

Resource constraints would then limit the number of communities within which this cultural mapping operation could be carried out to no more than a 'representative handful'. Equally, he underscores the limitations of national sample surveys in performing this kind of task. Such surveys are very good at identifying and describing those subcultures which are, in the national populations as a whole, numerically significant and geographically fairly widespread. They are very poor if used as a basis for analyses performed at the local level, or amongst sub-cultures which may be weak at the national level, but significant in particular localities or neighbourhoods. At most, as a typical rule, national surveys will generate twenty or thirty interviews in any one primary sampling area. This sort of data base cannot be used to make anything but the crudest representations of the relevant areas and then only with unacceptable degrees of unreliability. What is needed, therefore, is a design that breaks with the deeply-embedded notion of a national sample by building from the local level upwards, rather than from the national level downwards. This may well entail compromises over the issue of representativeness, but we would argue that it is a compromise well worth making for the sake of acquiring research data sufficiently well-grounded as to enable more valid and reliable answers to be developed even if they are applicable only across a limited range of locales. Indeed, it is a compromise which must be tolerated if progress of the sort we have been describing is to be made.

Schumaker, in the second of our two illustrations, stresses another important aspect of the local context, that of mass-elite linkages.[34] Further, he also seems clearly to argue for a research design along lines similar to ours. In his view, it is important in studying political participation (and control) that it be linked to elite responsiveness both through an intensive study of citizen preferences across a wide variety of political issues, and through systematic study of the agenda setting, enactment and implementation stages of local public policy-making. For responsiveness, it need hardly be added, is also an important, if not crucial, ingredient in determining the instrumentality of different forms of participation, and of the relative efficacy of a 'participatory' as opposed to a 'controlling' strategy.

In reviewing what needs to be done in this field, the conclusion Schumaker comes to is that

> large-scale cross-community investigations are currently feasible only through the utilization of crude surrogate measures of important components of policy responsiveness.[35]

In other words, a design that attempts too firmly to maintain the notion of a national sample of communities, inevitably does so at the price of undermining to an unacceptable degree the measurement of those contextual features through which participation must be understood. At best, all it can achieve is to highlight possible aspects or areas where properly rooted investigations could be conducted in a follow-up study. Such an activity might well, therefore, have 'important heuristic functions', but, like ourselves, Schumaker is under no illusion that this is in any way a substitute for properly conducted research. Indeed, he seems firmly convinced that only through the linked case-study approach, whereby a small number of in-depth investigations are coordinated by some common theoretical rationale, will

> rapid development and validation of theory . . . occur.[36]

Knoke's emphasis on including a range of communities representative of different types, and Schumaker's preference for a series of crucial cases, clearly implies their support for what we too see as the virtues of the 'limited numbers' strategy over its 'large numbers' rival. At the same time, however, there would seem to be a difference of emphasis between them which in turn highlights two important possible variants in how the limited numbers option could in practice be implemented. In this respect, one might select communities according to some typology of communities created so as to ensure variation in two or three key characteristics. Frankenburg has made some suggestions as to how a typology of communities based on sociological criteria might look in Britain.[57] Other examples are available in which a typology has been created inductively through the analysis of a large number of areal data so as to produce either a limited number of descriptive 'factors', or a small number of 'clusters' of the areas concerned.[58] The problem, however, is that in the sort of investigation we have in mind, either the appropriate information may not be available (one thinks of cultural criteria, for example) or there may well be so many important criteria to build in that the resulting typology has too many 'cells' for 'representative' communities to be studied in the requisite depth.

An alternative approach, therefore, is to give less emphasis to some putative, and possibly contentious, notion of representativeness, and to concentrate instead on how communities might be selected so as to highlight particular contextual conditions that are interesting for the way in which they shape participation at the mass level. This would seem to be more what Schumaker had in mind. Under this heading, one might include a community that had faced, or was about to face, some politically relevant threat such as a factory closure, a major environmental threat, or a large-scale riot. Such a context would then facilitate the study of instrumental, and other, theories of participation as well as throwing light on normative debates about democracy. Another illustration might be a highly solidaristic mining town in which the sense of community was particularly pronounced. Such a 'one-interest' area might in turn reflect in relatively extreme form, a consensual climate in which mass participation and elite response was conducted – though the extent to which this was in fact the case would, of course, be a matter for empirical investigation. In this way, through inclusion of a number of discrete community studies that share a common data-gathering programme and substantive agenda, a picture might be built up which would be stronger and larger than the constituent elements taken separately.

There would, of course, also be dangers to be reckoned with. Thus, the selection of deviant or atypical communities might over-emphasise the degree of political activity, ideological articulacy, elite responsiveness, etc. present in the population as a whole. But this might be guarded against to some extent by eschewing inappropriate national generalisations, or even by including a community or communities that did not exhibit any particular extraordinary or deviant characteristics relevant to participation so that it would function as a sort of 'control' community. Finally, some check or restraint might be possible through the combination of this case-study approach with the typological alternative previously discussed.

In either strategy, however, the primary goal, as we see it, would be more likely to be accomplished than if a design was constructed calling for large numbers of 'representative' but necessarily superficial community studies.[59] This goal is to develop an account of participation and control that breaks out of the limitations imposed by too narrow a view of instrumentality and does so by taking much more seriously than heretofore the political, social and cultural context in which citizens actually operate.

Conclusion

This essay has concentrated on the instrumental approach to the politics of participation and of control. It is probably fair to say that Finer has maintained a somewhat sceptical attitude to those who argue that participation can have an educative effect on the participants which will stimulate still further participation. He points out that

> it cannot be said that the existing evidence proves that this permanent self-conscious interest *does* exist, but in latent form, hemmed in by constrictive institutions, and only waiting to be liberated from these to bound joyfully into full participation.[60]

In fairness to the educative theorists Finer acknowledges that they might reply that one cannot expect to discover evidence of this political interest in societies where political practice does not encourage it. Are we absolutely condemned to regarding the educative hypothesis as an act of faith, as Finer concludes?

The very reasons that Finer adduces largely explain the fact that no major study of participation has sought to test the educative hypothesis. Yet some approximations to a test can be mounted if citizens are asked about their experiences of participation. What have they learned about the political process? Are they as a result more aware, as J.S. Mill hoped, of the needs and aspirations of others? Do they appreciate the very cut and thrust of politics, discovering what R.H.S. Crossman called its 'charm'? Alternatively are they disillusioned, less trusting, newly convinced of the ineffectiveness of political action? Ideally, of course, one would wish for a series of studies over time – before and after an intervention – rather than the cross-section which is all that most studies of participation can afford. Even then one would not satisfy fully either the educative theorists or entirely meet Finer's scepticism, since one is still working within the context of existing structures. What would be gained is some guidance to the potential of such structures to adapt to new levels of involvement and a suggestion as to how citizens might react to new opportunities for participation.

The strategy of control does not expect any change in human nature nor any great upsurge of interest in public affairs. Nevertheless, to function it does require, as was suggested earlier in commenting on James Mill, a degree of knowledge and information as to how one's interests are best defended and promoted. It also requires sufficient power relative to others for control to become possible. Finally, it evidently supposes that the elites can be made responsive. Although there is good reason to hold with Finer that the politics of control characterises modern Western democracies, it is also clear that it currently faces severe difficulties. The forces of centralisation and bureaucratisation, the size and complexity of the public sector all make the mechanisms of control more intricate, unwieldy and politically less effective. The elites, though not necessarily excessively centralised, at least in Britain, tend to rely on horizontal communication and pressures rather than on linkages with a mass public whose political involvement may not even meet the levels considered appropriate to control, let alone participatory democracy.

In such circumstances the politics of control risks breaking down on its own terms. It is this situation which Finer addresses in *The Changing British Party System*.[61] The prevailing political formula remains one of government by the people, but practice increasingly deviates from the formula. Finer is too much of a realist to suppose that myth and reality can ever entirely coincide but he also recognises the dangers in their diverging too far. The need is to bring them more into line by making control more effective. What Finer's argument then suggests is that the logic of what is accepted as the prevailing political formula should drive one towards a radical position. Amongst the reforms required are proportional representation, primary elections, the popular initiative and the referendum. It would be too much to claim Finer for the ranks of the participatory democrats. There are, for instance, no proposals for direct community governments. Nevertheless, these reforms are much more demanding of the citizens than anything currently required, although they could be regarded as implicit in James Mill's instrumental position. No doubt participatory democracy, like socialism, takes up too many evenings. But controlling the controllers can also be a strenuous, but it is to be hoped, a rewarding activity.

Notes

1. *Britain Against Itself* (Faber, London, 1982)
2. For example, C. Pateman, *Participation and Democratic Theory*, (Cambridge University Press, Cambridge, 1970); G. Parry (ed.), *Participation in Politics* (Manchester University Press,

Manchester, 1978).

3. M. Kolinsky (ed.), *Divided Loyalties* (Manchester University Press, Manchester, 1978).

4. *Arguments for Socialism*, (Penguin, Harmondsworth, 1980).

5. D. Owen, *Face the Future*, (Jonathan Cape, London, 1981) p. 26.

6. P. Hain (ed.), *Community Politics* (Calder, London, 1976).

7. W. Gwyn and R. Rose (eds.), *Britain: Progress and Decline* (Macmillan, London, 1980) and J. Alt, *The Politics of Economic Decline* (Cambridge University Press, Cambridge, 1979).

8. D. Kavanagh, 'Political culture in Great Britain: the decline of the civic culture' in G. Almond and S. Verba (eds.), *The Civic Culture Revisited* (Princeton University Press, Princeton, 1980).

9. 'The state, capital and liberal democracy' in C. Crouch (ed.), *State and Economy in Contemporary Capitalism* (Croom Helm, London, 1979) pp. 46–56.

10. *Ibid.*, p. 46.

11. *Ibid.*, p. 47.

12. R.A. Dahl, *Dilemmas of Pluralist Democracy* (Yale University Press, New Haven, 1982) p. 80.

13. G. Parry, 'The idea of political participation' in G. Parry (ed.), *Participation in Politics* (Manchester University Press, Manchester, 1972) p. 59.

14. S.E. Finer, 'Groups and political participation' in G. Parry (ed.), *Participation in Politics* (Manchester University Press, Manchester, 1972) p. 59.

15. *Ibid.*, p.74 (emphasis original).

16. S.E. Finer, *Comparative Government* (Allen and Unwin, London, 1970), pp. 40–42..

17. 'Groups and political participation', p. 59.

18. S. Verba and N. Nie, *Participation in America* (Harper and Row, New York, 1972), pp. 176–83, 353.

19. E.C. Banfield, *The Unheavenly City Revisited* (Little, Brown, Boston and Toronto, 1974), chapter 9.

20. 'Groups and political participation', p. 74.

21. S. Barnes and M. Kaase, *Political Action: Mass Participation in Five Western Democracies*, (Sage, Beverly Hills, 1979).

22. See J. Ferejohn and M. Fiorina, 'The paradox of not voting: a decision theoretic analysis', *American Political Science Review*, Vol. 68 (June 1974), pp. 525–536. See also W. Peak, 'Conceptualizations of political participation: a critical examination of the rational participation literature', *American Political Science Association Annual Meeting*, Chicago, 1983, esp. pp. 8–9.

23. Still one of the most succinct criticisms is in B. Barry, *Sociologists, Economists and Democracy* (Collier Macmillan, London, 1970), chapter 5. For a sensitive discussion of the problems and possible solutions see R. Hardin, *Collective Action* (Johns Hopkins University Press, Baltimore and London, 1982).
24. *Political Action*, p. 84.
25. See K. Schlozman and S. Verba, *Injury to Insult: Unemployment, Class and Political Response* (Harvard University Press, Cambridge, Mass., 1979) for the subtle ways in which such issues can be tackled by a combination of survey and in-depth interview methods.
26. *Essay on Government* in J. Lively and J. Rees (eds.)., *Utilitarian Logic and Politics* (Oxford University Press, Oxford, 1978), p. 58.
27. *Ibid.*, p. 76.
28. These issues have of course been widely discussed and received stimulus from Finer's work and even from the very fact that it represented a change of position on his part. See S.E. Finer (ed.) *Adversary Politics and Electoral Reform*, (Antony Wigram, London, 1975). Note the Dedication.
29. Necessarily a matter of considerable compromise given that there is no logically satisfactory solution to the problem. For a recent discussion of the vast literature see W. Riker, *Liberalism versus Populism* (Freeman, San Francisco, 1982).
30. For exposition and discussion of some implications for the party system in Britain see S.E. Finer *The Changing British Party System, 1945–1979* (American Enterprise Institute, Washington D.C., 1980) chapter 6, pp. 194–203.
31. G. Lowell Field and J. Higley, *Elitism* (Routledge and Kegan Paul, London, 1980); E. Nordlinger, *On the Autonomy of the Democratic State* (Harvard University Press, Cambridge, Mass., 1981).
32. Nordlinger, *On the Autonomy of the Democratic State*, p. 203.
33. See also S.B. Hansen, 'Participation, political structure and concurrence', *American Political Science Review* **69**, 1975, pp. 1181–99.
34. For a brief discussion, with findings, although in a different context, see K. Hill *et al.*, 'Mass participation: electoral competitiveness and issue attitude agreement between congressmen and their constituents', *British Journal of Political Science* **9**, 1979, pp. 507–11.
35. The official phrase when participation was the vogue following the Skeffington Report. See A. Barker and M. Keating, 'Public spirits: amenity societies and others' in C. Crouch (ed.) *British Political Sociology Yearbook: Vol. 3 Participation in Politics* (Croom Helm, London, 1977), p. 143.

36. See K. Newton, *Second City Politics* (Oxford University Press, Oxford, 1976).
37. M.B. Preston, 'The election of Harold Washington: black voting patterns in the 1983 Chicago mayoral race', *P.S.* **XVI**, 3, 1983, p. 488.
38. *Participation in America*, chapter 7.
39. G.D. Curry, 'Utility and collectivity: some suggestions on the anatomy of citizen preferences' in T.N. Clark (ed.), *Citizen Preferences and Urban Public Policy: Models, Measures, Uses.* Sage Contemporary Social Science Issues, no. 34, Beverly Hills, 1976, p. 75.
40. For the controversy over the 'regret' decision-making rule, see the discussion on 'Participation, coalitions, vote trading', *American Political Science Review*, Vol. 69, no. 3, 1975, pp. 908–28.
41. For a review from that period, see L.W. Milbrath, *Political Participation*, 1st edn. (Rand McNally, Chicago, 1965).
42. See A.H. Barton, 'Bringing society back in: survey research and macro-methodology', *American Behavioral Scientist*, 1968, pp. 1–9.
43. See T.N. Clark (ed.), *Urban Policy Analysis: Directions for Future Research*, Urban Affairs Annual Reviews, Vol. 21 (Sage Publications, Beverly Hills, 1981).
44. *Participation in America*, chapter 13 and part III.
45. S. Verba, N. Nie and J-O. Kim, *Participation and Political Equality: A Seven-Nation Comparison* (Cambridge University Press, Cambridge, 1978).
46. Barnes and Kaase, *Political Action*.
47. C.J. Uhlaner, 'The integration of individual and community in political participation', *American Political Science Association Annual Meeting*, Chicago, 1983, p. 1.
48. *Ibid.*, p. 16.
49. *Ibid.*, p. 15.
50. D. Knoke, 'Urban political cultures' in Clark (ed.), *Urban Policy Analysis*, pp. 203–26.
51. See 'Urban political cultures', pp. 212–19 in which Knoke contrasts a private-interest oriented, conflict-inducing 'pluralistic' sub-cultural type with that of a collectivist-oriented common value based 'unitary' sort. cf. J. Mansbridge, *Beyond Adversary Democracy* (Basic Books, New York, 1980).
52. 'Urban political cultures', p. 219.
53. *Ibid.*, p. 220.
54. See P.D. Schumaker, 'Citizen preferences and policy responsiveness' in Clark (ed.), *Urban Policy Analysis*, pp. 227–44.

55. *Ibid.*, p. 228.
56. *Ibid.*
57.. R. Frankenberg, *Communities in Britain: Social Life in Town and Country* (Penguin, Harmondsworth, 1969).
58. See, for the application of factor analytic techniques, C.A. Moser and W. Scott, *British Towns: A Statistical Study of their Social and Economic Differences* (Edinburgh, Oliver and Boyd, 1961), esp. chapters V and VI. For the use of a clustering approach see R. Webber, *Parliamentary Constituencies: A Socio-Economic Classification* (Office of Population Census and Surveys Occasional Paper no. 13, London HMSO, 1978).
59. Since the 'large numbers' strategy has been used quite extensively, we have focused more on its disadvantages than advantages. The latter include, beside representativeness, the capacity in principle to undertake macro statistical analyses in which the communities are themselves the constituent units of the investigation. This is, in general, preferable to the more limited comparative analysis possible within the limited numbers alternative. For an application, see Verba and Nie, *Participation in America*, part III.
60. 'Groups and political participation', p. 79; see also *The Changing British Party System*, p. 231.
61. See pp. 189–231.

10   Comparing Constitutions
Gillian Peele

Political science is a relatively young university discipline in comparison with related subjects such as law and history. In asserting its intellectual autonomy it has – rather like some wayward adolescent – sometimes gone to extremes to underline its independence and has frequently experienced fierce debates about the scope and methods of the subject. One of its excesses both in the United States and in Europe was the enthusiasm with which in the 1950s and 1960s it adopted behaviouralism and rejected the formal institutional approach to the study of government. This movement was symbolised by David Easton's advocacy of the need to remedy what he saw as the sorry state of a discipline which suffered from 'theoretical malnutrition' and a 'surfeit of facts'.[1] Writing in 1953, Easton had directed much of his fire on Lord Bryce whom he accused of having been averse to system-building to an extent which had damaged the development of American political science.[2]

As a result of the strictures of Easton and others, political scientists did turn their attention to the somewhat thankless task of trying to construct general theories of political behaviour, although in the United Kingdom and especially in Oxford the change of fashion was slow to make itself felt. Thirty years after Easton's attack, political scientists on both sides of the Atlantic have experienced a reversal in the intellectual mood surrounding their subject; accordingly they have rediscovered the importance of studying institutions and of accepting that there are a number of legitimate approaches to the subject of politics. One area which must surely benefit from this renewed interest in the formal and institutional aspects of politics is the general field of constitutional analysis.

Political developments have themselves contributed to this renewal of emphasis on the need to keep the study of constitutions at the centre of the discipline. The study of government in British universities had for long been influenced by lawyers and historians; and perhaps because some of the works of British political scientists in this tradition were associated with efforts to export the 'Westminster model' to newly independent Commonwealth countries, they are unjustly neglected. Yet if one now returns to the work of Sir Kenneth Wheare, for example, what is striking is not that it is in any sense dated but rather that recent political experience has thrown up so many new constitutional problems even within the boundaries of the Commonwealth. Thus, for example, the role of the Governor-General in Australia, the repatriation of the Canadian constitution and the role of the Crown in the Grenada invasion have all occasioned major political disagreements in the past decade.[3] So far from being a footnote to our imperial past the constitutional legacy of the Commonwealth has continued to insert itself in contemporary British political debate, although it is probable that this phenomenon will decline.

Inside Britain itself the re-emergence of constitutional issues on the country's political agenda in the 1970s caused divisions within the major parties and highlighted the extent to which such major re-appraisals as those entailed in the devolution debate, for example, were unusual in the nation's political life.[4]

The precondition of any serious study of constitutions is, of course, a familiarity with the basic documents in which a country's constitution is contained. Professor Finer has made his own contribution to reviving the study of constitutions by producing his own imaginative and carefully cross-referenced edition of the constitutions of the United States, of France, of the Federal Republic of Germany and the 1936 and 1977 constitutions of the Soviet Union.[5] And he has done so in a way which encourages the consideration of those texts in a comparative manner. In this essay, however, I want to suggest some ways in which political scientists should try to go beyond the bare bones of the text of any constitutional document and approach the more familiar questions about the basic political structure of a country's government from a slightly different angle. In short, I want to suggest a set of questions that might be asked to try to understand the character of a country's constitutional culture or style.

Two points should perhaps be made at the outset of this endeavour – which is in effect a plea for reintegrating the study of constitutions into a broad comparative context which can take account of the varying political, social, intellectual and legal influences on a particular constitution. First, it should be clearly understood that the questions and topics suggested here are by no means intended to be exhaustive or definitive. Secondly, although there are a number of difficulties associated with the concept of culture as a tool of political analysis, I believe that it captures as well as any other concept that might be used –

such as political environment – the phenomenon under review. For the primary concern of this chapter is the complex set of values, attitudes and assumptions, political prejudices and practices that interact with the more formal elements of a constitutional system. Kenneth Dyson has drawn attention to the way in which recent German scholars both in the field of jurisprudence and in the wider fields of social science have struggled to integrate the insights and assumptions of their several disciplines.[6] What I am suggesting is that his careful examination of the development of the idea of the state tradition in Western Europe underlines a gap in our whole approach to the study of the area where law and politics intersect.

A constitution may usefully be defined as the body of rules and norms that govern the relationships between the institutions of government and between those institutions and the individual citizens and private groups.[7] In many countries the most important of those rules are contained in a single document which is the 'constitution'. However it would be a rare political system which could codify all its constitutional rules into a single document; all political systems therefore supplement their basic constitutional text with a variety of statutes, judicial pronouncements, opinions of academic authorities and custom. And in those countries without a written constitution – such as the United Kingdom and Israel – there is a very different mix of sources of constitutional norms and rules. (Israel, it should be noted, while it does not have a comprehensive written constitution akin to that of the United States or France does, however, have a set of basic constitutional laws which govern specific areas of political life.[8] As in the Federal Republic of Germany there was insufficient agreement about the nature of the state to make a comprehensive constitution possible, although in Israel's case the difficulties related to religion rather than territoriality.) What must be emphasised at this stage is that to speak of the American or the French constitution is to speak of something much more complex and subtle than the simple framework enacted in 1789 or 1958 and that of necessity an element of doubt will surround some aspects of even the most stable of constitutional systems.

The constitution of the United Kingdom, when this definition of a constitution is used, appears somewhat less mysterious than has sometimes been supposed. Although it lacks a single central constitutional document, the United Kingdom has a series of charters and statutes which taken together add up to a substantial amount of written constitutional law. Moreover, there is a considerable body of case law which would be germane to a wide range of constitutional debates. Sometimes Parliament has had to legislate when custom and convention have broken down or been the subject of dispute. Thus, for example, when the relationship between the two Houses of Parliament became the subject of party controversy after the House of Lords had rejected the 1909 budget, legislation was passed to clarify the powers of the Upper House. The Parliament Acts of 1911 and 1949 thus form a statutory basis for a major constitutional relationship, although clearly the mere passage of these statutes has not settled all the issues that arise in connection with the powers and functions of the two houses, and some doubt about the constitutional position of the acts has been expressed by various legal and constitutional authorities. The legal position of local authorities in the United Kingdom now rests wholly on statute, although, as a recent case concerning the Greater London Council's planning powers revealed, there is still room for disagreement about the interpretations of the powers granted under the relevant acts.[9] And debate continues to surround the extent to which local authorities should exceed the performance of their statutory obligations by offering other services, for example those that can be financed under s.137 of the Local Government Act of 1972.[10]

The entry of the United Kingdom into the European Community in 1972 also had a major impact on the character of its constitutional framework. For by entering the Community by signing a Treaty which under Article 177 established a source of authority superior to that of the British Parliament within the United Kingdom, and by acknowledging the power of the Court of the Communities to pronounce on the compatibility of domestic and European legislation, the United Kingdom took a step, admittedly of its own volition, which shattered whatever was left of Dicey's doctrine of parliamentary sovereignty.[11] Experience since British entry into the Community suggests that European directives with politically controversial consequences – for example the introduction of tachographs in lorries – will be followed only after substantial discussion in the U.K. The point, however, is that the theoretical hierarchy of laws has been changed, and Dicey's statement that under the British constitution 'no person or body' has a right to set aside or override the legislation of Parliament no longer holds.[12]

What the United Kingdom's constitution exhibits more than any other, though, is the importance of the role of those norms and precepts derived from political practice and experience. Where the practice has hardened and the rule to be gleaned from it is clear the convention, as it is called, can be stated explicitly; where there is doubt or difficulty writers and commentators may either doubt whether there is a convention at all or what is its effect.

This preliminary discussion serves to underline the point that all constitutions derive from a number of sources and that those sources can best be understood as body of norms which range from the transparently clear to the ambiguous and perplexing. And because conventions and practices, customs and usages are subject to the specific political circumstances which they are meant to govern (rather than vice versa) it is often when they are most needed that they will be most elusive. Thus there was much difficulty over the publication in 1975 of the diaries of Richard Crossman in contravention of the customary rules of cabinet confidentiality. Yet it was the courts which alone could step in to articulate a rule capable of controlling the situation which arose when a minister refused to accept what had generally been thought to be the agreed conventions of British political life, although even there it may be doubted how effective the extended law of confidentiality would be if similar circumstances arose in future.[13] Similarly, the advent of a genuine multi-party situation in the United Kingdom potentially could re-open discussion about the role of the monarch with regard to the appointment of a prime minister and the refusal of dissolution of Parliament, questions which most commentators have thought settled.[14]

The British constitution is thus one which, although it has acquired an increasingly significant legal framework, relies very heavily for its interpretation and its operation upon the norms which are contained in the conventions and practices of everyday politics. And it relies also upon the constitutional culture in which both the institutions of government and the politicians themselves interact. In seeking to broaden the approach to constitutional issues, six general areas of interest will be identified. These topics are not intended to preclude others but rather are an indication of the kinds of questions that need to be borne in mind when seeking to understand a constitution in its entirety.

The extent of consensus

Constitutions when written may represent a fragile agreement which the politicians and the judges and indeed all those who have to operate the constitutional system may need to preserve. Mention has already been made of the difficulties that the nascent state of Israel encountered as it sought to define the role of Judaism in the polity and its constitutional framework reflects the uneasy compromise reached between those who wanted a theocratic state, those who wanted a secular Jewish state and those who for religious reasons wanted no Jewish state at all. Germany's division has never been acknowledged as legitimate in her constitutional arrangements, although the preamble to the constitution speaks of 'those Germans to whom participation [in the Parliamentary Council of 1949] was denied'.[15] By claiming to cover the whole island the constitution of the Republic of Ireland provides a way of compromising between those who wanted to see the establishment of a working Irish state and those whose nationalism rejected such a pragmatic accommodation with the United Kingdom.

Federations that entrench minority rights or polities with marked social cleavages over religion or language exhibit different features from homogeneous societies, and those divisions in turn affect the constitutional culture. Once a balance is struck between the claims of competing groups or factions within a political system that accommodation frequently will be constitutionally protected from change or amendment for fear of upsetting beleagured minorities. But it may be – and the constitutional arrangements for Northern Ireland were an example of this in the early twentieth century – that one or other feature of the constitution is so unpalatable to the majority that it will not rest until it is eliminated. For instance in Northern Ireland the proportional representation provided for in elections to Stormont was dropped at the insistence of the majority Protestant population.[16]

The role of the judiciary

The role of the judiciary or other constitutional arbitrator, such as the *Conseil d'Etat* or *Constitutional Council* in France reveals much about the constitutional culture of a country. Three questions immediately arise about this role. The first is the extent of the role accorded to the guardians of the constitutions. How much influence can they have on the workings of the body politic and how visible is that influence.

Secondly, how legitimate is that role seen to be by the various strands of opinion in the society. The question of legitimacy is one which of course affects countries with the explicit form of judicial review found in the United States and the Federal Republic of Germany (though not in earlier German constitutional regimes such as the Weimar Republic outside Bavaria) particularly severely; but it also affects countries that think they do not have judicial review in the American sense.[17] Judicial review is perhaps best thought of in terms of a spectrum of court-located powers ranging from the ability of a court to strike down a legislative act in its entirety – as in the United States (though as in *Buckley* v. *Valeo* the Court may simply strike down a part of a statute deemed incompatible with the constitution) – to the subtle process of review which occurs in the ordinary process of statutory interpretation.[18]

The extension of administrative law remedies in the United Kingdom in the period after 1964 and the admittedly somewhat idiosyncratic exercises in judicial law-making by Lord Denning ought to have brought home to observers of the British constitution not that a set of judges was acting improperly but that judicial review is a practice which occurs naturally as a by-product of the judicial process and that in certain spheres it may bring the judges into conflict with the administration.[19]

Thirdly, what are the results of any crisis of confidence in the methods for resolving constitutional disputes?

The legitimacy of the judiciary and its actions is of course a question which has arisen from time to time in a particularly acute form in the United States as in the mid-1930s when the Supreme Court struck down much of Franklin's Roosevelt's New Deal legislation. At that point the Supreme Court and the more democratically based elements of the American governmental system came very close to a constitutional confrontation. But personnel changes on the Court itself and a strategic retreat by the President averted a crisis. Slowly thereafter the Court adopted a two-tier standard of interpretation which initially at any rate appeared to limit the occasions on which it might find itself in conflict with an elected legislature or an elected President. This two-tier standard of judicial review suggested that it would defer to the policies of the more political branches of government except where the rights of discrete and insular minorities were concerned.[20]

Yet the Supreme Court's concern with protecting individual rights and those guarantees of civil liberties contained in the Constitution (and especially the first ten Amendments of 1791 and the Fourteenth Amendment of 1868) has increasingly meant that the American judiciary as a whole has been drawn into the centre of political controversy. Indeed the Supreme Court's explication of the Fourteenth Amendment's equal protection clause and its involvement in such major issues as desegregation after *Brown*, reapportionment after *Baker* v. *Carr*, the reform of criminal procedure and legal aid after *Miranda* and *Gideon* v. *Wainwright* and the availability of bilingual education after *Lau* has meant that the United States has witnessed a situation in which so far from striking down acts as unconstitutional the courts have been setting positive policy standards for governmental agencies to adopt – frequently with financial consequences.[21]

Perhaps it was inevitable that the Supreme Court of the United States should become a politically controversial body, for the clashing principles of majority rule and constitutionalism seemed to have been built into the fabric of the political system established in 1787 and made explicit in Chief Justice Marshall's enunciation of the doctrine of judicial review in 1803.[22] Certainly if anyone doubted that those principles were still in conflict he or she need only glance at the debates that have surrounded the role of the Court in recent years. The *Brown* v. *Board of Education of Topeka* decision of 1954 signalled the start of a new era of controversy and underlined the Court's delicate position in a political system where its need to act suggested that the other branches of government could not or would not do so.[23] And of course *Brown* and its progeny also revealed the dilemma of a court which had to rely on the political organs of government to implement its decisions because it itself had neither the power of the sword nor that of the purse.[24]

Over thirty years since the *Brown* decision Presidents have had as previously the opportunity to influence the character of the Court throught the power of appointment. Yet even the determination to reverse the allegedly unorthodox jurisprudence of the Warren Court and the general reaction against some of its more liberal policies has not produced a Court any less controversial. The major abortion decision – *Roe* v. *Wade* – in 1973 was the product of a Court under the more conservative leadership of Chief Justice Warren Burger.[25] However the reasoning behind its affirmation of an absolute right to an abortion in the first trimester of pregnancy was as novel as anything in the *Brown* decision. Indeed it could well be argued that the decision was constitutionally more innovative (or suspect) than *Brown* since it was grounded in an implicit right to privacy which the constitution allegedly recognises but nowhere makes clear, whereas the Fourteenth Amendment had itself been passed in the aftermath of the Civil War and clearly had some direct relevance to the rights of negroes in American society.

The Court's decisions in the desegregation cases and in the abortion cases have not merely aroused political opposition; they have also caused doubt to be cast on the legitimacy of the Court's role in the whole political system. Strangely that doubt does not come from simple conflict with the executive or the legislature. Indeed the resolution in 1983 of the debate about the constitutionality of the legislative veto in *Chadha* v. *Immigration and Naturalization Service* had the bizarre effect of mutilating at one time far more Congressional legislation than the Supreme Court struck down during the New Deal.[26] The doubts about legitimacy seem rather to arise when the arguments which the Court uses and its style of decision-making seem inappropriate.

It would be convenient if the observer could say that the Court loses legitimacy where it employs arguments that depart from precedent and are too result or policy-oriented; but unfortunately the matter is not quite so simple. Clearly the American public does expect more than a strict application of existing law from its Supreme Court since it assumes that the Court will be wrestling with problems of constitutional principle and values. It is the manner in which it does so that determines the legitimacy of its actions. Phillip Bobbitt, in an original and stimulating examination of the modes of constitutional argument used by the Court, addresses this problem and distinguishes between the legitimacy to be obtained from the employment of certain legal conventions and the justification which derives from a social or political philosophy.[27] The point to be made in this context is that the particular mix of modes of argument which will command legitimacy is not something which, to use Lord Reid's phrase about natural justice, is cut and dried or can be nicely measured.[28] It reflects the nuances of a legal culture and the varying weight placed on such values as equality, procedural justice and fairness as well as broad assumptions of social policy.

The fact that a court may appeal to a variety of values in the wider society and that the particular mix that will give it legitimacy may change with the passage of time is then one which makes it necessary to look beyond formal legal doctrines for an understanding of how courts interact with the polity. It is also this which makes crude comparisons between courts as worthless as crude comparisons between political parties. The United States Supreme Court, for example, has utilised in recent years the equal protection clause of the Fourteenth Amendment as the doctrinal support for a number of changes in public policy and to promote substantive as well as procedural equality.[28] This 'new equal protection' doctrine was, as one constitutional authority has shown, very much the result of the 'egalitarian zeal' of the Warren Court and it contained two ideas: that there existed certain fundamental interests which the constitution ought to protect and that any governmental action which created classes of persons based on suspect criteria (such as race) was to be subject to the strictest standard of judicial scrutiny.[29]

Yet that egalitarian zeal was not maintained, and during the 1970s and 1980s public opinion in the United States has become less sympathetic towards liberal egalitarian initiatives. Certainly, as the experience of the Reagan administration's reductions in domestic spending has underlined, the United States's attitude towards welfare provision is still highly ambiguous and America probably has the least developed and comprehensive welfare state of the advanced Western democracies. The change shows how attitudes and values can be reversed in a political system though whether the Court should move with public opinion or act as a steadying or corrective mechanism is a moot point. Inevitably, however, a Court with significant policy responsibilities will be attuned to swings of public mood if only to gauge whether its decisions are likely to prove controversial. In fact, of course, although the American Supreme Court has developed constitutional support for integration through the application of such remedies as busing, it has stopped short of using those remedies to counter *de facto* as opposed to *de jure* segregation.[30] And while – as a result of state court decisions – it seemed at one stage in the early 1970s that the inequalities that resulted from the differing tax bases of school districts might be remedied judicially, the Supreme Court has refused to give priority to equality of wealth in education over the rights of local school districts to spend their money as they please.[31]

The legitimacy accorded to a Court is also crucially affected by its ability to perform the tasks which it has undertaken. Here again the United States offers some pertinent examples of the difficulties and dilemmas that may confront a legal system that seeks to use its judiciary for political functions that are outside the normal capacity of either the courts or the judges. Desegregation involved the lower court in making orders relating to local school systems and individual schools. To some extent the initial supervision by the courts was necessary to ensure compliance; but even liberal supporters of integration have queried whether the long-term goal of good race relations inside a school is well served by frequent judicial intervention. From the courts' perspective perpetual monitoring of such matters as racial mix is a burden which they are not well fitted to discharge. And in the case of *Pasadena* v. *Spangler* the Court declined to take on the task of reviewing annually the percentage of minority race pupils in each school once it was satisfied that an effective desegregation plan had been implemented in the Pasadena school district.[32]

The character of constitutional argument

A third indicator of the legal and constitutional culture is the nature of constitutional argument not merely in the courts themselves as discussed earlier but in the wider political system. One of the surprising features of British politics in the 1970s was that a range of fundamental constitutional debates appeared on the country's political agenda including, *inter alia*, discussions of the territorial divisions of power within the United Kingdom, the question of a bill of rights, the related issues of the EEC and sovereignty and the role of the House of Lords. Yet the manner in which these issues were discussed displayed the depth of the United Kingdom's attachment to *ad hoc* solutions and its lack of interest in general constitutional issues. It equally displayed the degree to which all political questions in the United Kingdom inevitably become cast in the mould of adversary politics.[33]

Many examples could be given to bear out the assertion that the British are reluctant to treat what are manifestly constitutional issues in terms of general principles. But three relatively recent ones may be mentioned since they also underline the extent to which the attitudes of left and right on these questions corresponds hardly at all to what may be found in other political systems.

In the 1970s there was some discussion about whether Britain needed a bill of rights and further discussion about whether, if it were thought desirable, it should be a specially designed charter or an adaptation of the European Convention on Human Rights.[34] (Britain was one of the first countries to sign the Convention but has never incorporated it into British law, although from 1966 individual British citizens have been allowed to apply directly to the Commission of Human Rights.)

In most European countries, and certainly in the United States, the assumption is that while lawyers may not necessarily be natural allies of the working class, they will be able to implement fairly and impartially a code of rights designed to protect individuals from the errors of the state. But when the question of a bill of rights was discussed in Britain – culminating in a report from a Select Committee of the House of Lords – it was evident that both the right and the left of the political spectrum had objections to the idea.[35] Many Conservatives were opposed to the idea for reasons which reflected an instinctive dislike of change rather than any rational reflection on the merits of the argument, an attitude which was in some ways also exhibited in the devolution debates of the later 1970s.[36] On the left, however, the opposition was inspired almost entirely by the realisation that any enactment of a bill of rights might mean an enhanced role for the judiciary. The trade union movement in particular has a long history of hostility to the judiciary which has its roots in the early decisions on trade union powers at the beginning of the twentieth century and was reinforced by the experience of the courts' role in the implementation of the industrial relations legislation of 1970–74.[37] In relation to civil liberties issues, however, it also had reason to look with suspicion at the role of the European Court of Human Rights which had been unsympathetic to some British trade union practices, most notably the closed shop.[38]

On the left hostility to the idea of a bill of rights extended beyond the ranks of the Labour Party itself. Thus the National Council for Civil Liberties, which recognised the need to strengthen the protection of the citizen against the possibility of such threats to liberty as police malpractice, also rejected the remedy of a bill of rights preferring instead strengthened specific parliamentary legislation directed at the abuses it criticised.[39]

The question of protection against police malpractice was raised again in 1983 in connection with a bill which the Conservative government introduced to give the police additional powers while at the same time providing for a strengthened means of reviewing complaints against them.

The first version of the bill had few supporters and its critics suggested the need to make the complaints procedure completely independent of the police authorities. This position was one which the Police Federation itself came to take since it was persuaded that, however honest an internal inquiry, the public would only be reassured once an open and independent review of any allegation had occurred. The Conservative government refused to amend its bill in this respect even when doubts were raised within the party.[40] The principle of independent review was clearly subordinate in the Government's view to considerations of economy and efficiency despite the fact that independent reviews – through National Health Service Commissions and Local Commissioners for Administration as well as through the Parliamentary Commissioner for Administration himself – had become routine in the British system of government.[41]

A final example of Britain's particular approach to constitutional issues and an indication of the lack of receptivity of the culture to such questions is the general topic of open government. It might be thought that a democracy as old as the United Kingdom's and with as long a tradition of freedom of speech might be anxious to implement modern demands for a greater openness of style in the management of government, even apart from the specific concerns of scholars who would like to have early access to official documents and of critics of particular pieces of restrictive legislation such as the Official Secrets Act.[42] In fact the mentality of secrecy so criticised by the Fulton Committee in the late 1960s continues to pervade Whitehall and has now been additionally justified by concern for the cost of providing information on a regular basis to the public.[43]

Attitudes towards the state

One factor in the character of a country's constitutional culture – indeed perhaps the factor at the very centre of it – is the attitudes that a country's population has towards the state itself. Professor Dyson, in a rich and illuminating examination of the differences between the varying conceptions of the state which can exist in Western Europe, has shown how individual nations have developed their own peculiar constellations of attitudes towards the state and political authority.[44] France's tradition of highly centralised state authority – contained in the polity's definition of itself as a Republic 'indivisible, secular, democratic and social' – has had a marked effect on its style of administration.[45] By contrast the British tradition is oddly schizophrenic. The idea of the state is foreign and unfamiliar. Powers when granted to the executive are vested in the Crown, in particular individuals such as secretaries of state or other ministers, or in designated bodies.[46] On the other hand, the remnants of prerogative powers which the monarch has are extensive in foreign affairs and, although customarily exercised on the advice of ministers *and* with Parliamentary approval, constitute a degree of discretionary power available to the executive which is formidable indeed.

It is of course true that the functions of a modern government demand a substantial degree of legislative and rule-making activity by the executive and the bureaucracy and that in many ways the only democracy which has recognised the logic of the modern state is France which has constitutionally given its executive an extensive autonomous rule-making power.[47] This has been done by defining the field where Parliament may legislate and by proclaiming under Article 37 that 'matters other than those that fall within the domain of legislation shall have the character of regulations' – i.e. executive made rules.[48] In the British case treaties of the most sweeping kind can be entered into without reference to Parliament, although, as with the Treaty which took Britain into the European Community, legislation may have to be passed to integrate its provisions into British domestic law.

The power of British central government is further increased by the absence of any strong centres of opposition to it. Whitehall has increasingly eroded the autonomy of local authorities and neither the Conservative Party nor the Labour Party appears to have any consistent theory of the role which local government ought to play in the constitutional system. The courts, it is true, have over the past twenty years attempted to develop a coherent system of administrative law to govern situations where the citizen could come into conflict with a governmental agency and through such cases as *Ridge* v. *Baldwin* (1964) and *Padfield* v. *Minister of Agriculture, Fisheries and Food* (1968) has attempted to limit the discretion of the executive by making it at least conform to principles of law.[49]

Attitudes to the state in a country's political tradition inevitably have implications for the individual and for organised groups. In the United Kingdom, as has been shown, the reliance on Parliament and on the ordinary courts has created a climate hostile to any formal codification of civil liberties and perhaps a certain insensitivity to those liberties themselves.[50] Yet in France, where the Declaration of Rights of 1789 forms an important symbolic part of the country's political heritage, many have claimed that the actual protection afforded to civil liberties, at least until the advent of President Mitterrand, seems to have been questionable at best.[51]

As far as voluntary associations are concerned, the heritage of Britain once again contrasts very markedly to that of other countries. It has been a peculiarity of Britain's historical development that the trade unions, instead of seeking legal recognition of their status, have tended to demand immunity from the law and the normal procedures of its operations. Thus the suggestion in the late 1960s that the trade unions should be governed by a comprehensive statute which specified their rights and obligations was received as a direct attack on the trade union movement. The Conservative Government of 1970–74 found that its Industrial Relations Act could not be implemented and the combination of the political role played by unions in bringing down the Heath government in the United Kingdom and of Ulster's unions in bringing down the power-sharing executive made many commentators wonder whether the conditions of twentieth-century society effectively gave unions a veto on the actions of the elected government. The need to involve trade unions in the implementation of an incomes policy earlier in the 1960s and the cooption of their representatives into administering some agencies connected with manpower and employment also led to much speculation about the extent to which Britain had become a corporate state.

Experience since the Heath period – and particularly since the advent of the Thatcher government in 1979 – has been curiously ambiguous with respect to relations between the trade unions and the law. On the one hand unions such as the Post Office Workers have been willing to recognise the extent to which political opinion has moved since the early 1970s; and that union has complied with judicial directions in connection with its industrial actions. However in 1983 serious disagreement arose when the National Graphical Association refused to accept the courts' control of its tactics during a dispute with a printing firm in Warrington. Thus, although the attitudes of trade unions towards the law is by no means as uniformly hostile as it was during the 1970–74 period, there is still sufficient antagonism to make compliance by no means certain.

The idiosyncracy of the British tradition of regulating trade union activity can be seen if it is compared with practice in the Federal Republic of Germany. There the trade unions were almost coopted into the wider constitutional system and although it could be argued that the period since Herr Schmidt's departure has seen a weakening of industrial partnership, there has been no suggestion that the trade union movement should operate outside the norms of constitutional government.

The attitude of the media
In any society the attitudes of a country towards its government and the whole constitution will be crucially affected by the media. Obviously a society in which the government is able to censor press reporting or television coverage is the other end of the spectrum from a society like the United States where the major limitations on freedom of speech are the ability to pay for television time or fear of public disapproval.[32] In

between, however, there is a range of problems which are not always easy to resolve but which may well affect the public's perception of issues. For example to what extent is self-censorship by a television network influenced by fear of governmental disapproval and perhaps the imposition of a financial sanction? To what extent should monopolies in the press and broadcasting be broken up by government as the Mitterrand government tried to do in 1983? How far should fear of libel laws limit political journalists? And to what extent should the large journalist and printers' unions be allowed to censor the material they will publish or even destroy the ability of a newspaper to survive?

Such questions are clearly of crucial political importance, but they are frequently not given the special consideration which their position in the maintenance of a democratic system deserves.

Procedures for constitutional change

The analysts of constitutions have spent much time on questions relating to how certain kinds of laws may be entrenched or given special protection. They have given less thought to the more political problem of how demands for political change can be accommodated. The demand for devolution in Britain, the problem of how to cope with referendums and whether they should be used on subjects other than issues which threaten party unity, the topic of proportional representation all give rise to the question of how one breaks a constitutional impasse or the grip of the two major parties? In the United States constitutional change could be effected against legislative inertia or resistance by the Supreme Court, but the treatment of the Equal Rights Amendment shows that even the Court may find itself in a dilemma. There the Court has resisted efforts to get sex declared a suspect category for the purposes of judicial review, and it has done so no doubt on the grounds that extending the scope of the Fourteenth Amendment in this way would be unwise given that the matter was one which the political process might be expected to handle itself. But what happens when the process of constitutional ratification is stymied? Does the Court have to adopt a hands-off policy for the next decade or may it act more quickly? Does the very idea of constitutional change itself threaten to destabilise the political system or seem such a threat, as until recently in France, that it could be used as a major political weapon on behalf of the incumbent majority?

Conclusions

These remarks have been made to suggest the need to look at constitutions not simply as documents or formal sets of rules but as phenomena which reflect the attitudes, traditions and biases of the wider societies in which they exist and the polities they are supposed to constrain. Many of the subject areas that have been mentioned are difficult to research because they include questions about popular values, elite assumptions and political behaviour; and they are accordingly resistant to methodologies that aim to provide precise information. Yet the student of politics must be aware that the subject is fundamentally affected by forces beyond measurement and influences which, even if they cannot be totally explained, should be acknowledged. The constitutional texts are perhaps the province of legal scholars; the political scholars must operate both with the texts and the penumbra where law and politics meet.

Notes

1. Quoted in J. Blondel, *The Discipline of Politics* (Butterworths, London, 1981), p. 174.
2. See D. Easton, *The Political System* (Knopf, New York, 1953) for a full exposition of this approach.
3. See for example, K.C. Wheare, *The Constitution of the Commonwealth* (Oxford University Press, Oxford, 1960) as well as his *Modern Constitutions* (Oxford University Press, London, 1951).
4. On this generally see M. Beloff and G. Peele, *The Government of the United Kingdom* (Weidenfeld, London, 1980).
5. S.E. Finer (ed.), *Five Constitutions: Contrasts and Comparisons* (Penguin Books, Harmondsworth, 1979). In addition to reproducing the texts of the French, West German, American and two Soviet constitutions of 1936 and 1977, Professor Finer has included a long essay on the nature of the British constitution.
6. K. Dyson, *The State Tradition in Western Europe* (Oxford University Press, Oxford, 1980).
7. An earlier article of mine used a definition of the constitution which drew attention to the relations between the institutions of government and the individual but not to the relations between the government and corporate or sectional groups within society. I now think that this aspect of the constitution should be made more explicit, particularly because of the questions raised by trade union activity in recent constitutional debate in Britain. See G.R. Peele, 'Britain's developing constitution' in J. Ramsden and C. Cook (eds.), *Trends in British Politics Since 1945* (Macmillan, London, 1978).
8. On the constitution of Israel see A. Peaslee, *Constitutions of the World*, Vol. 2, pp. 488–517.
9. See, for example, *R* v. *Secretary of State for the Environment ex parte Greater London Council* (*The Times*, 2 December 1983).

10. On the scope of the s.137 powers see A. Alexander, *Local Government in Britain Since Reorganization* (Allen and Unwin, London, 1982).
11. Dicey's statement of parliamentary sovereignty is contained in *Introduction to the Study of the Law of The Constitution* (10th ed., Macmillan, London, 1959).
12. *Ibid.* For a recent discussion of the impact of Europe see John Usher, *European Community Law and National Law – The Irreversible Transfer?* (Allen and Unwin, London, 1981).
13. On the Crossman diaries case generally see H. Young, *The Crossman Affair* (London, 1976); also *Attorney-General* v. *Times Newspapers Ltd.*
14. Many of these issues are discussed in V. Bogdanor, *Multi-Party Politics and the Constitution* (Cambridge University Press, Cambridge, 1983).
15. Quoted in Finer, *Five Constitutions*.
16. On the constitutional arrangements of Northern Ireland see D.C. Watt, *The Constitution of Northern Ireland* (Heinemann, London, 1981).
17. For an overall view of judicial review in West Germany see D.P. Kommers, *Judicial Review in the Federal Republic of Germany* (Sage, London, 1976). For a more general discussion see H. Mosler (ed.), *Constitutional Review in the World Today: National Reports and Co-operative Studies* (Heymans, Cologne, 1962). Max Planck Institute: *Beiträgen zum ausländischen öffentlichen Recht und Volkrrecht. Band 36.*
18. *Buckley* v. *Valeo* 424 U.S. 1 (1976).
19. For a radical view of Lord Denning's constitutional role see P. Robson and P. Watchman, *Justice, Lord Denning and the Constitution* (Gower, Farnborough, 1981). For his own legal philosophy see Lord Denning, *The Discipline of Law* (Butterworths, London, 1979) and the same author's *The Due Process of Law* (Butterworths, London, 1980) and *What Next in the Law?* (Butterworths, London, 1982).
20. For a general view of the role of the equal protection jurisprudence see P.G. Polyviou, *The Equal Protection of the Laws* (Duckworth, London, 1980).
21. *Brown* v. *Board of Education of Topeka* 347 U.S. 483 (1954); *Baker* v. *Carr* 369 U.S. 186 (1962); *Miranda* v. *Arizona* 384 U.S. 436; *Gideon* v. *Wainwright* 372 U.S. 335 (1963); *Lau* v. *Nichols* 414 U.S. 563 (1974).
22. *Marbury* v. *Madison* (1803) 1. Cranch 103.
23. *Brown* v. *Board of Education of Topeka* (1954). For a history of the

Brown decision itself see P. Kluger, *Simple Justice: The History of Brown v. Board of Education* (Andre Deutsch, London, 1977).

24. The argument is Alexander Hamilton's in the *Federalist Papers No. LXVIII*.
25. *Roe* v. *Wade* (1973) and its companion case of *Doe* v. *Bolton* 93 S.Ct. 705.
26. *Chadha* v. *Immigration and Naturalization Service* (1983) 103 S.Ct. 2764.
27. P. Bobbitt, *Constitutional Fate: Theory of the Constitution* (Oxford University Press, New York, 1983).
28. Lord Reid in *Ridge* v. *Baldwin* (1964) A.C. 40.
29. See Polyviou, *op. cit.* Polyviou makes the case that the now equal protection doctrine was only really expounded in 1968; see *Schapiro* v. *Thomson* 394 U.S. (1968).
30. On busing generally see G. Orfield, *Must We Bus?* (The Brookings Institution, Washington, D.C., 1978).
31. See *San Antonio School District* v. *Rodriguez* reversing *Serrano* v. *Priest*; also J.E. Coons, '*Serrano* among the social scientists', *The Educational Forum*, March 1977.
32. *Pasadena City Board of Education* v. *Spangler* 427 U.S. 424 (1976).
33. The phrase is taken from S.E. Finer (ed.), *Adversary Politics and Electoral Reform* (Antony Wigram, London, 1975). Some of the arguments are developed in N. Johnson, *In Search of the Constitution* (Pergamon, Oxford, 1977).
34. See House of Lords, *Report of the Select Committee on a Bill of Rights* H.L. 176 (1978).
35. On implementation and its problems see J. Jaconelli, *Enacting a Bill of Rights: The Legal Problems* (The Clarendon Press, Oxford, 1980).
36. For an excellent overview see V. Bogdanor, *Devolution* (Oxford University Press, Oxford, 1979).
37. On this period see M.T.S. Holmes, *Politics and Economic Policy* (Butterworths, London, 1982).
38. For a forceful statement of the left's case against the judiciary see J.G. Griffiths, *The Politics of the Judiciary* (Fontana, London, 1977).
39. For the evidence of the NCCL see Minutes of Evidence, H.L. Select Committee on a Bill of Rights. Sessions 1976/77 and 1977/78.
40. See, for example, K. Warren and D. Tredinnick, *Protecting the Police* (Conservative Political Centre, London, 1982).
41. The Parliamentary Commissioner for Administration and its off-

shoots themselves represented substantial modifications to the theory and practice of British constitutional life. See R. Gregory and P. Hutcheson, *Britain's Parliamentary Ombudsman* (Allen and Unwin, London, 1975); see also N. Lewis and B. Gateshill, *The Local Commissioner for Administration: A Preliminary Assessment* (Royal Institute of Public Administration, London, 1978). cf. F. Stacey, *Ombudsmen Compared* (Oxford University Press, Oxford, 1978).

42. On the Official Secrets Act see D. Williams, *Not in the Public Interest* (Hutchinson, London, 1965).
43. On open government see G. Wraith, *Open Government* (Royal Institute of Public Administration, London, 1977).
44. Dyson, *op. cit.*
45. J. Hayward, *Governing France: The One and Indivisible French Republic* (Weidenfeld, London, 1983).
46. For a general review of British attitudes see Dyson, *op. cit.* and G. Marshall, *Constitutional Theory* (The Clarendon Press, Oxford, 1971).
47. See Hayward, *op. cit.*
48. Finer, *Five Constitutions.*
49. *Ridge* v. *Baldwin* A.C. 40 (1964); *Padfield* v. *Minister of Agriculture, Fisheries and Food* A.C. 997 (1968).
50. For a useful discussion of the general British attitude towards civil liberties see F. Stacey, *A New Bill of Rights for Britain* (David and Charles, London, 1973).
51. Hayward, *op. cit.*
52. D. Halberstam, *The Powers That Be* (Chatto and Windus, London, 1979).

11 Adversary Politics, Public Opinion and Electoral Cleavages
David Robertson

Introduction

Probably the best known of Professor Finer's contributions in the last ten years is his thesis that British politics is characterised by an 'adversary' style of competition. In itself this might be little but a truism, rather like pointing out that the British judicial process is accusatorial rather than inquisitorial. Of course British politics is adversary in nature; it is supposed to be. The duty of Her Majesty's Opposition is, after all, to oppose. It is Finer's particular explanations for why the system is adversary, how it might be made less so, and why there is too high a cost attached to adversarial politics which make them interesting, important, but theoretically more complicated than he has sometimes seemed to see himself.

Finer's version of the adversary politics thesis first appeared just before the second of the near deadlock general elections of 1974. It was developed, with others, in his book *Adversary Politics and Electoral Reform*[1] in 1975, and repeated as the single major objection in his 1980 work *The Changing British Party System, 1945–1979.*[2] It is not without significance that the *New Society* article in which it first appeared, in September 1974, was called 'In defence of deadlock'; his overwhelming objection is, in fact, to large and safe one-party majorities in the Commons. The February 1974 election had produced a minority Labour government, and even Wilson's improvement between then and October only produced an overall majority of three. The thesis can be stated, initially, as a set of simple propositions.

(1) The two-party system in Britain is held up by an electoral system, the simple plurality system, which magnifies the parliamentary lead a party gets compared with its lead in the popular vote.

(2) This fact combines with a sensitivity to small changes in electoral popularity to produce rapid and disproportionate shifts in relative numbers of MPs, thus leading to alternating governments with 'safe' majorities.[3]

(3) The electoral system combines with the purely contingent fact that Liberal (we can now say Alliance) voting support is very evenly spread across constituencies, compared with uneven Labour and Conservative support. This ensures third parties do not get elected in an even remotely proportionate manner.

So far the thesis is unarguable, and, except for those who object to some sense of 'unfairness', unremarkable. We have always known that this was the case, and used to glorify it with the notion of a political 'pendulum' which swung the country from left to right and back every few years. Indeed survey data from the 1960s showed that public opinion, at least in abstract, favoured the idea of alternation in power. The next set of propositions are the core of the thesis, and they are neither empirically unarguable nor normatively neutral.

(4) The two major parties need to keep the 'extremists' amongst their parliamentary delegations happy, and adopt party policy accordingly, so that the actual policy sets that alternate in office are more widely opposed than they would be were the average position in the House to be followed. This is a complex argument and will be shortly studied in detail.

(5) Party discipline helps to ensure that these unnecessarily extreme policy paths are loyally followed by the majority party, and thus automatically become legislation.

(6) Not only are alternative policies more extreme than the natural parliamentary position, but members of parliament themselves are unrepresentative of the electoral opinion. In the electorate as a whole there is far more consensus, and a more moderate preference distribution than in Parliament, so that the policies enacted consistently tend to be more extreme than those actually favoured either by a majority of the electorate or even a majority of supporters of the party in power.

The implication of the whole set of propositions is that changes of allegiance by a small proportion of the electorate are subject to a political 'multiplier effect' which produces major and radical shifts in government policy, shifts between positions which were never anyway supported by a majority of the electorate. Hence 'in praise of deadlock', and hence the second part of the book title 'and electoral reform'. A deadlocked Parliament should produce more 'moderate' results, if it produces any at all, and proportional representation will have two effects. The first good effect assumed is that, in order to form a coalition, a party will have to forgo the preferences of its extremist wing and offer would-be coalition partners a set of more 'moderate' policies. The second good effect is that proportional representation systems do not multiply the legislative-seating effect of small fluctuations in voting figures, and thus most elections would not much change the power of a ruling coalition. The consequence of the reform of British politics would be to encourage incrementalism and to maintain long-term policy stability along a moderate road supported by a far higher part of the electorate, which is, in fact, seen as highly consensual. At this stage Finer wheels in economists and others to demonstrate that policy consistency of this incrementalist nature would be a good thing, and that Britain has suffered from too frequent and too sharp discontinuities in policy in the post-war world.[4]

My concern in this essay is not particularly with the remedy that Finer prescribes, though some of what I have to say must touch on his hopes for the treatment. Nor is it, specifically, with the illness itself, because I am not qualified to compute the extent to which we would have been better off following an incrementalist policy, if, indeed, we have not been doing so. I am only concerned to ask whether or not the symptoms actually exist, and, if they exist, whether they actually imply the disease Finer and others are concerned with. It is necessary to examine above all the two key propositions of the diagnosis.

Is it the fact that parliamentary delegations are less consensual, because of the force of the 'extreme' wings than they would otherwise be? Is it a fact that electoral opinion is rather more consensual than parliamentary opinion? If these are not true, then either politics is not adversarial or polarised, or it is, but with implications very different from those drawn by Finer and his colleagues. The thesis is mainly one about Britain, but it is held by many to have a general relevance to the British two-party parliamentary model elsewhere. New Zealand, for example, has been held to suffer from the disease, and the writer of one modern textbook on New Zealand politics uses the label as an un-disputed fact about, and explanation for the ills of, that version of the Westminster model.[5] Certainly there is no feature of the thesis, as laid out above, which ought not, in principle, to apply to all simple-plurality political systems with a political culture roughly similar to Britain's. However, we have one interesting and well-documented control case. The USA shares enough features with the UK to use as a partial test of some aspects of the adversary politics thesis, having both a simple plurality electoral system and a two-party system remarkably resistant to third parties. It lacks one crucial ingredient, however, in its absence of tight party discipline. As both congressional opinion and public opinion in the United States are unusually well-documented, we can investigate some properties of both the crucial hypotheses in this comparative test.

What is Moderation?

First, what evidence does Finer himself use? To establish that the British electorate is fairly highly consensual, and that it tends to have policies rammed down its throat with which it does not agree he cites a series of policy examples. Some, like attitudes to the power of the unions, seem well-settled. It is indeed true that more Labour voters agree with the proposition 'The unions have too much power' than disagree, thus making them actually more like Conservative voters than like their own MPs, many of whom have, after all, reached the House from a union post. It is more dubious that this is, as Finer claims, an issue 'on which Parliamentary parties have bitterly opposed one another'.[6] Indeed it is an example of one of the issues in British politics that is peculiarly hard to measure. It is not only true that perhaps over 70% of the population agree with that judgement on union power; it is also true that roughly similar percentages of union members agree with it. However, surveys usually discover that union members make an exception in the case of their own union, which is almost never seen as too powerful. In 1979, for example, only 20% of the electorate thought that the trade unions 'did a good job' for the country as a whole, but 71% thought that they did a good job for their own members, and 64% of union members thought that their own union 'did a good job' for them. Similarly fewer than 20% of union members thought their own union was even 'a little too ready' to take industrial action.[7] As well over 50% of all employed voters are members of trade unions, it becomes somewhat less clear that there is much consensus about union matters in the electorate. Nor would many union leaders see the Labour governments of 1964–70 or 1974–9 as exactly over-zealous in their defence. Indeed Finer quotes the repeal by the 1974 Labour government of the Conservatives' disastrous Industrial Relations Act as an example of the 'repeal readiness' of these adversarial parties. The mere fact that the Labour government, in 1969, tried to put a similar act on the statute book might suggest that the parliamentary dissensus on the issue is less than intense. The second of the three issues he draws particular attention to suffers from similar problems under a more detailed analysis.

This is the whole question of nationalisation. Again, it is true, as he says, that strong majorities have always been against further national-isation of industry since at least the early 1960s.[8] It is also true that nationalisation has remained a major Labour party policy. Some industries have been subject to nationalisation since 1964. In the post-election survey of February 1974, 72% of those who expressed an opinion were against any further nationalisation.[9] Yet one must set against that two facts seldom considered. The first is the sheer unimportance of the issue. In 1974 52% reported that it was 'not very important' to them when deciding how to vote; but as there was no weaker response, one might stress instead that only 8% thought it the 'most important issue'. By 1979 the issue had become even less important. In that election only upper-middle class convinced Conservatives ranked it, on average, higher than ninth out of nine issues in importance.

The second point is that attitudes to nationalisation are, *par excellence*, those that make least sensible a portrait of the electorate. Butler and Stokes demonstrated the enormous fluidity of opinion on the issue over the 1960s.[10] In 1974 38% of the electorate claimed to prefer the Labour party on nationalisation (more of it), which is 10% more than the proportion of those who said they actually wanted more nationalisation themselves. This was not because of any ambiguity about the party's orientation, for nearly 95% of the electorate correctly identified the Labour party policy on the question.

In such a context it is hard to see why a party that takes office should not go ahead with a clearly announced policy of nationalisation. The argument Finer really has is more probably that a responsible party would not *advocate* a policy of nationalisation when it knew that there was no real enthusiasm for it, and yet people would accept the policy as the cost of getting the Tories out that year. There are, of course, many issues on which there is a clear-cut imbalance of opinion in the electorate, a set of values that do represent a real political consensus which a representative electoral and parliamentary system would ensure legislation to enshrine, and where the distribution of parliamentary opinion is directly opposed to public opinion. The most recently demonstrated example is the restoration of the death penalty, favoured by somewhere between 70 and 80% of the electorate *in all socio-political groups*, and rejected by roughly similar majorities in the House. A similar issue in 1979 was a strong popular preference for at least a total ban on non-white immigration, if not for a more Powellite policy.

Two things are true about issues such as these. First, those who characteristically object to adversary politics not only would not condone the application of the populist policies concerned, but would defend MPs by reference to a very different, Burkeian, doctrine of the connection between electoral opinion and legislators' duties. Secondly, there is no electoral system whatsoever that would produce a Parliament prepared to hang, ban all black immigration, or another 1979 example, withdraw the military aid to the civil power in Ulster. This is because a proportionally representative system in itself cannot produce any particular result unless the parties, which means the professional politicians, cooperate. The National Front might get 2% of the seats in a proportionally elected House of Commons, but those twelve or thirteen MPs would be very lonely. There is a shared policy perspective amongst the sorts of people who become politicians, reinforced by experience in office or in the House, and this is just as much to be noted as the *dissensus* between them. What is obvious is that we need to be very clear indeed about the nature of opinion at both mass and elite levels, and equally clear about what we think the theoretical linkage should be between these opinion distributions and policy output before judging our system of party competition. It is such an examination to which this essay is directed.

Does public opinion, on the whole, resemble either of the two sorts of 'consensus' distribution that Finer imagines? I say that Finer offers two different images of electoral consensus, because in fact the argument he offers seems to alternate between a model with a normal distribution of opinion where the 'centre of gravity', the 'moderate' position, is the most populous, and one in which a clear preference on a dichotomous issue is held by a strong majority of the electorate. This latter case is the one he thinks is demonstrated by the data about attitudes to nationalisation, but it is, of course, not at all the same as the 'populous middle' version. The latter would require that, on a scale running from 'massive extra-nationalisation' to 'total denationalisation', the median voter preferred something 'in between'. The problem is partly one of theory, and partly one of measurement. Are there intelligible 'middle' positions on issue, and can they be measured sensibly by political opinion surveys even if they exist?

One of Finer's contributors in the 1975 book, Nevil Johnson,[11] believes that the two-party system is predicated particularly on the idea of there being two, and only two, sides of a debate on any policy issue. He objects to this narrowing of choice. Clearly one can almost always turn an apparent choice-dichotomy into a continuum, though there is no guarantee that 'middle positions' will work, and ultimately no avoiding making a decision of principle about a type of policy. An industrial relations act can be strong or weak, to take a Finer example; one could nationalise 'a lot more industries' or 'only a few more industries' in the words of the standard survey question; one can buy Trident, not buy Trident but keep Polaris, or scrap the lot, but the basic questions are dichotomous. Government interference with unions, with industrial ownership, a nuclear defence policy, or not. If one sees the issues as presented to the electorate in dichotomous terms, then the idea of the electorate being more moderate, more consensual has a quite different meaning from the one attached to the notion of moderation by Aristotleian golden policy means.

From the way he discusses the notion of consensual positions in Parliament, Finer may be thinking of moderation as a set of 'centrist' positions on continua, for he relies heavily on a diagrammatic presentation in the 1975 book. But he may see moderation in a different light. It is worth considering what these mean at this stage, even before discussing parliamentary opinion distributions in general. Figure 11.1 reproduces his diagrammatic presentation of the distribution of attitudes in a Parliament. The upper diagram shows how he thinks parliamentary attitudes are distributed, *taking no notice of party membership*. The lower shows the distribution inside each of the two parties.

Figure 11.1

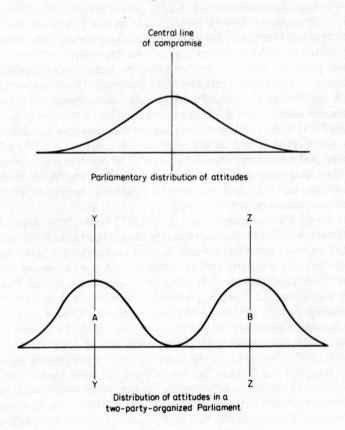

Central line
of compromise

Parliamentary distribution of attitudes

Y   Z

A   B

Y   Z

Distribution of attitudes in a
two-party-organized Parliament

Source: Finer, *Adversary Politics and Electoral Reform*

Technically, this diagrammatic presentation, borrowed from the spatial theory literature, does not work.[12] There could not be a maxima of the curve where he draws his 'central line of compromise' on the upper diagram, if it is supposed to graph the same Parliament as the lower. The latter clearly shows that no single MP, let alone the largest single group, occupies that position on the scale. Nonetheless the point he is making is fairly clear, and I discuss it later. Finer is thinking in terms of some additive scale, of the sort often published by pressure groups in the United States where they grade Congressmen's roll-call vote performances. In these cases moderation is the result of adding together a set of dichotomous positions; the less one is totally committed to one party, the more one will select some preferences from each end, with an 'average' result in the middle of the scale. Thus, with the sorts of issues he has in mind, a voter could be against national-isation, in favour of controls over unions, against cutting the social services, and in favour of a voluntary incomes policy. In October 1974 each of these positions was supported by a strong majority of the population. Unfortunately, two were Labour Party policies, and two belonged to the Tories. An additive index, giving one point for each agreement, and zero for each disagreement would give, were they coded along party lines, a zero score to the Labour loyalist, and a maximum score to the Conservative loyalist (or vice versa). Consistency meant either accepting nationalisation and undisciplined trade unions and a voluntary incomes policy and a build-up of the social services, or holding social service spending down, applying a statutory incomes policy, controlling the unions, and refraining from nationalisation. To get a moderate score, to be in the 'middle' of the spectrum, which is where one would be had he shared the majority opinion on each issue, is to be inconsistent in terms of the policy sets offered by the parties and made intelligible to their members by some general ideology. The feasibility of moderation in this sense is a difficult question, and one I return to later. At this stage it can certainly be admitted that British parliamentarians are indeed unlikely to exhibit moderation in this sense, and that it is at least statistically likely that median scores of this sort would be common, though perhaps not *that* common in the electorate.

One must consider the other sense of policy moderation. Is it true that on important issues there is a roughly normal distribution? Do people tend to hold 'in between' positions if one presents policies as continua? Is there a sense in which parties tend to go for extreme options and voters for moderate ones on specific issues? Available data, from the election surveys in Britain for the elections of 1974 and 1979 are somewhat confusing, in that they tend to show a variety of distributions. The only one that does not seem to occur very much, however, is the one that gives us consensus in terms of the normal distribution with the largest group of voters between the extremes. Instead we get either consensus with most people at one end, as with the populist 'law and order' style issues, or bimodal distributions, rather like the imaginary one in the lower half of Figure 11.1.

One trouble is that such data depend on the way a question is worded, and the number of responses allowed. If there is no moderately worded intermediate position, there will be no moderation; but if one presents sufficiently draconian alternative end points, one will always get it.

Much of the time one is in fact forced to admit that moderation cannot sensibly be measured, or thought of, in terms of intermediary positions on policies. On some, it can. These are typically distribution style issues, where one can either conceive of 'in between' points, or where indifference to a good or its public provision is not meaningless. As these issues are still the bread and butter of politics, it is worth looking at typical opinion distributions.[13]

Table 11.1 gives summaries of three such issues from 1979, all of them dealing with matters of egalitarianism. We need not approach the question of opinion distribution entirely theoretically. We might well want to question the assumption that a concentration around the 'middle' of an opinion distribution is somehow or other 'natural'. *A priori*, there would seem to be two general patterns that we could expect

Table 11.1   Distribution of opinion on three class-related issues, 1979

	Increase workers' control (%)	Redistribute wealth (%)	Establish comprehensives (%)
Very important; Government should	17	26	17
Fairly important; Government should	39	29	19
Doesn't matter either way	12	16	17
Fairly important; Government should not	22	18	21
Very important; Government should not	10	11	26

to observe. One would be given by a highly consensual political culture, the other by a divided culture with conflicting groups. The consensual culture would show most people agreed at one end of a scale, with rapidly decreasing numbers in each category as the positions became less conformist to cultural norms. A divided culture would show a bimodal pattern, because it would be measuring a social cleavage. As political parties in Western democracies exist to fight each other, they will concentrate policies on the cleavage areas. The issues that are actually at stake in major party confrontations should, *ceteris paribus*, exhibit bimodal distributions; the comparative sizes of the modes will depend on the size of the conflicting groups on either side of the cleavage. Some issues, however, will have become so deeply rooted in a social consensus, so much part of the political culture, that they will be nearly unanimous. The issues in Table 11.1 concern the need to abolish grammar schools and replace them with comprehensives, the need to redistribute wealth, and the need to introduce industrial democracy. Each of these shows a roughly bimodal pattern, and the sizes of the modes correspond very roughly with the standard 30:70 middle class: working class breakdown of the British electorate. (The grammar school distribution is, actually, reversed, but that fits with the class mobility aspirations of the skilled manual working social grades for whom comprehensives are seen as even more of a threat than they are by the established middle classes.)[14]

These issues are at the core of class, and therefore party, conflict in modern Britain. But, of course, this conflict is not always symbolically capable of expression. Thus whilst only 45% of the electorate actually believe, in abstract, that wealth should be redistributed, sacred cows abound. Asked if it is important to spend more money on the NHS, 84% think that it is fairly or very important to do so. Ask the question even more emotively and ask how important it is that the government should 'spend more money to get rid of poverty', and 88% think this to be at least 'fairly' important. Sacred cows work in reverse: ask whether the availability of welfare benefits has 'gone too far' and only 17% feel that such provision is inadequate.

What I am suggesting is that opinion distribution in Britain, as long as it is not measured in terms of emotive symbols deeply rooted in the political culture, in fact shows a perfectly predictable class based bi-polarity. Where it does not because of the symbolic value of the issue, as in the examples cited above, it tends towards very high conformity. The other consensual situation concerns the political culture on cases that do not touch the fundamentals of party conflict, issues that are outside competitive arenas because of a consensus amongst politicians, populist issues of law and order, defence, racialism and so on. Nowhere does a 'normal' distribution with a heavily populated 'centrist' position actually show up in British politics. Nor was there any reason to think that it would or should do so.

Even if the adversary politics theorists are wrong about the moderation of public opinion in this respect, it does not follow that they are wrong in another sense of moderation, or that the party system does not exacerbate rather than constrain the conflict. The sense in which they might still be correct in expecting a 'normal' distribution is the one already suggested, that moderation consists in holding a set of opinions which, from the viewpoint of any one major party, are inconsistent. If the population is inconsistent in this special sense, the professional politicians would be more extreme than the electorate. Their insistence on consistent policy sets would mean that the voters were always forced to choose between two extremes, neither of which really fitted their actual preference distributions. We are talking here, as pointed out before, of an additive scale of the sort used to compare US Congressmen. It is a useful point then at which to switch attention primarily from the mass to the elite.

Parliamentary moderation

For lack of serious evidence on what preferences British MPs actually have, Finer has had to write hypothetically when talking of opinion distributions in Parliament, as demonstrated in Figure 11.1. We do have the possibility of comparative analysis with the United States, using real data. Figures 11.2a and b give an actual opinion distribution, for the 96th Congress, which held office between 1978 and 1980. The graphs in Figures 11.2a and b are drawn from data on the 1980 ratings given to each member of the House of Representatives by the pressure group known as ADA, Americans for Democratic Action.[15] They select a set of crucial votes during the legislative session, and give each member of the House an additive score, one point for each time he votes the way they wish. These scores are then expressed as a percentage of the total possible score. ADA represents liberal Democratic philosophy, and is only one way of measuring the party split in Congress. It should be noted that in the diagram I have used only non-Southern representatives, in order to get a tighter cluster for the Democratic party.[16]

Figure 11.2a expresses the number of congressmen falling within a particular score band as a percentage of the total of all the congressmen in the sample. It accords, therefore, with the upper part of Figure 11.1, Professor Finer's expectation of the overall distribution of attitudes in the House, taking no notice of party. Rather than having a normally curved unipolar distribution the US House of Representatives clearly

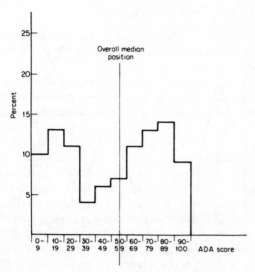

Figure 11.2a   ADA scores across the whole 96th Congress
shows a bimodal distribution. A low point exists around ADA scores of
30–39 where only 4% of the congressmen lie. To the Republican side is
a modal point of scores between 10 and 19, with 13% of the House (and
another 10% with even lower scores). The high mode lies some way
away at 80–89 points, with 14%, with yet a further 9% having still
higher scores. In all, 47% of Congressmen have what might be
described as 'extreme' scores, lying on the opposing modes or being
even further from the centre. The actual median position, the position
on the scale where roughly half of the members would lie on either side,
is 57% (47% have scores lower than 57, 48% have scores higher than
58). This median position is what Finer must mean, in his diagram, by
the 'central line of compromise'. According to spatial theories of
voting, policies near this position are the only ones that will get
through. This is because at any other point on the scale there will be a
majority of members who prefer the policy at the median point; in the
language of game theory, policies at that point 'dominate' all other
strategies.[17]

A system with any great degree of party loyalty in it will never reach
policies at this logically invulnerable point. This is what Finer is getting
at when he offers the second figure, and Figure 11.2b is my equivalent.
Here I have taken each party separately and drawn the distribution of
its members' attitudes. Each point on a lines gives the percentage of
members *of the relevant party* who take up that position. Now the
distributions change. They are each unimodal, but they are *not* normally distributed. Instead they are sharply skewed towards the relevant
extreme. There is overlap, of course. About 18% of Republicans fall

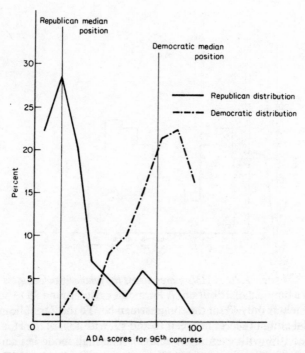

Figure 11.2b   ADA scores inside each party, 96th Congress

into a 'left-wing' group which lies nearer to the *Democrat* end of the spectrum than does a group taking up about 8% of the Democratic party. (All of this, one must remember, is after having excluded the notoriously conservative Southern Democratic faction.) Despite overlap, the picture is quite clear. We can apply the same logic that gave us the overall median position to the separate parties. These points, the party medians, represent the dominant policy positions within the caucus of the parties, the points at which one would expect the parties each to set their own policies, supposing they wished only to choose within their own preferences, and were making no tactical effort to win opposition support. In this case, as shown on the lower graph, the median Democratic position is at point 73 on the scale, and the median Republican position at point 15. Both of these are a long way from the 'central line of compromise' – they are the equivalent to what Finer calls the parties' 'lines of consensus'.

At least according to Finer's theory, these lines are where party policy will generally be set, and it is a series of alternations of these more-than-necessarily extreme policy sets that adversary politics is all about. This is also where his lack of care in defining the sense in which centrist positions are 'moderate' starts to hurt, and where my earlier

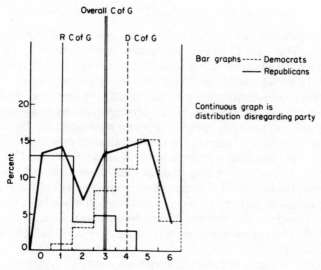

Figure 11.3   80 Senate members in 96th Congress

discussion of the two senses of moderate political attitudes comes in. It is not clear that the 'central line of compromise' is anything of the sort. Certainly, in the American congressional example it is no such thing. Those from the two parties who have similar 'middle range' scores are not at all similar creatures, and do not constitute a cohesive group of compromising non extremists. A Democrat and a Republican may get an identical score of fifty on the 100-point scale. Far from being politically similar, they are likely to be very different political animals. In the American context this is well known, because we are talking about the Liberal Republican from, say, New York City, and the Conservative Southern Democrat. They have the same score, because each slipped from the ideal point of his party the same number of times, but almost certainly not so as to vote the same way on the same issues.

To demonstrate this, consider Figure 11.3. This too is a distribution of US legislators, based on roll-call votes. Here I have constructed a simple scale myself by taking the voting records of 80 Senators (those who served in the 96th Congress and were still in the Senate for the 97th). The recorded votes are six of the votes picked out by *Congressional Quarterly* researchers as key votes in the 96th Congress.[18] I have coded them very simply so as to give a score of 1 for each time the Senator voted in the way that the Senate Democratic Majority finally voted on the issue, and 0 for each time he did not do this. It is therefore a pure party loyalty scale, rather than measuring proximity to some pressure group, or some theoretical ideal of 'Democratic ideology'. The distribution shows the same characteristics as the previous one. We can easily see the 'centre-leaning' group in each party. There are 13 Democratic Senators with a score of three or less, and 12 Republicans with a score of 2 or more. The rest group fairly tightly round median positions. Yet these 'centrist' legislators have nothing substantively in common at all. On one vote, which was intended to restrict federal involvement in bussing cases, the Republican 'centrists' split 9:3 in favour of bussing, the Democractic centrists were 11:2 against. On another, an attempt to call a temporary halt to the building of new nuclear generating plants, the Republican group were split fifty-fifty (though their party as a whole was 80% against the halt) but the Democratic group voted 11 to 2 not to impose the halt. The pattern goes on, predictably. If one takes 25 Senators who comprise this central group, the two party components agree together on their votes no more than the two parties in the Senate as a whole do.

This is not, of course, surprising, but a matter of simple parliamentary logic. When back-benchers do abstain or, rarely, vote against the whip in the House of Commons, they are nearly always agreeing with the official position of the other party, not with the rebels from that party.[19] Nor can one explain the US data by saying that the phenomenon is peculiar to America because of the politics of the South. Of course it is the Southern question in the United States which largely explains the conservative Democrats, but that merely labels one country's version of a general point. The general point is that moderation in parliaments and in mass publics stems from the same cause – a lack of what American electoral sociologists have called 'issue constraint'.[20] This means that to know what someone believes on issue X does not help one predict what he believes on issue Y. It has long been known to be true about mass publics. Since Converse's classic article on 'Belief systems in mass publics' it has been noted that correlations between scores on separate issue question variables in surveys are very low.[21] When dealing with the electorate, this has often been seen as a reason for treating the mass as politically incompetent, as non-rational, even, at times, as a danger to the functioning of democracy.[22] There is no reason to treat 'middling scores' on a parliamentary aggregate scale in any different manner. In general parliamentarians do have much more issue-constraint than voters. For congressmen who score very high or very low on roll-call indexes, knowing how a legislator voted on the nuclear power vote gives a good prediction of how he voted on bussing, and on the other four issues in my mini-scale. This is not true of the Republicans with unusually high, or the Democracts with abnormally low, scores.

I have two empirical points about Finer's theoretical propositions.

One is that consensus does not exist in the electorate on some issues, and that where it does exist on specific issues, this only produces an overall centrist thrust in the sense of low issue constraint. The other is that moderation in legislatures is rarer because of the generally higher level of issue constraint, and those parliamentarians who do slide into centrist positions in parliaments have little in common with each other. By themselves, neither empirical points would suggest that there is an alternative to adversary politics. One might, indeed, reduce party discipline in Britain, so that governing parties would not be able to force through policies that their 'centre-leaning' extremes disliked. Or one might alter the electoral system so that a political party which represented the low issue constraint political middle got its proportion of seats in Parliament. This is a perfectly good way to block legislation, and, by stopping a good many things getting done, necessarily stop an alternation of extremes. It is worth noting that the inability of the US Democratic contingent in the Senate to impose party discipline did indeed result in the 'extreme' policy of federal involvement in bussing cases being stopped by a bipartisan majority. In general there is a very good chance of creating an immobilism in politics by combining a multi-party parliament with a non-consensual electorate through proportional representation. This is not, admittedly, what the adversary politics critics want. They believe in the consensual electorate with a normal distribution along genuine lines of moderation. But where is the cleavage structure in the electorate to produce such a distribution of electoral opinion? Moderation through general consensus on a collection of policies with some internal logic is one thing. One might well wish to argue that this has existed in some political systems since the Second World War, and that where it has existed, a PR electoral system has produced not only stable, but productive and effective government.

A favourite example of this good effect of PR and coalition government is the Federal Republic of Germany. There is no doubt that there was, at least until the early 1970s and perhaps still, a very high degree of consensus amongst all parties on the crucial questions of economic policy and state security. Here the mass consensus was repeated in a parliamentary moderation that the crucial role of the FDP ensured. In contrast the extremely non-consensual politics of Italy, combined with a PR system and a set of centrist parties for coalition fodder, which did not represent moderation in anything but the aggregation sense I have discussed, has produced an appalling immobilism. The interesting question is which of these situations the British system resembles. It is an important problem, and it is also one of considerable theoretical importance in political science, because Finer's thesis happens to contradict one of the few otherwise well established pieces of empirical theorising we have.

Are the parties diverging?

The argument is that because the preferences of the two are far apart, the policies they espouse are also considerably separated. In fact this ought not to be the case, regardless of the shape of the opinion distribution in the mass public. By 'ought not to', I mean that the standard theories of party competition would predict that competitive forces lead parties towards a vote-maximising point in the middle of an ideological spectrum.[23] Not only does theory predict this, but most analyses of British politics until the mid-1970s also suggested this happened.[24]

Finer's view seems to be that the alternating extremes character-isation of British politics is true of the whole post-war period, and especially true of the period from 1964 onwards. Yet many would have thought that what the period up to 1964 showed was somewhat different. Did we not have, partly as a result of the war-time coalition, the creation of a new paradigm in the period 1945–51, continued with only minor changes by the incoming Conservative government? Did not that Government survive 13 years in office, until the Labour party was forced to become more moderate and accept the Butskellite synthesis? Indeed, was the Labour government from 1964 to 1970 not almost a model of moderate, if incompetent, continuation of that synthesis? If one had to date a divergence of the parties in Britain, it would be difficult to make any case for an earlier date than 1970, and even this would involve highlighting a few tendencies of Mr Heath's rhetoric rather than government policy. A more plausible turning point would probably be the election of Mrs Thatcher to the leadership of the Conservatives, along with the growing strength of the Labour left after 1974. These judgements, these historical descriptions, though, are highly subjective. Finer thinks we have a terrible record of reversals of policy:

> The steel industry that has been nationalised in 1950/51 was denationalised in 1953, and then renationalised by the Labour Government in 1966. The Conservative Rent Act 1957 was radically amended by the Labour Rent Act . . . 1965, much of which was in turn reversed by the Conservative Housing Finance Act, 1972, which is in the process of being repealed by Labour's Housing Finance bill, 1975. As far as taxes are concerned SET was introduced by the Labour Party in 1966 and abolished by the Conservatives in 1972. . . . Economic planning has suffered similar vicissitudes: the 1964 Labour Government established the DEA and the Industrial Reconstruction Corporation, both of which were abolished by the Conservatives after 1970.[25]

In vain to say this does not sound too bad. Only one of the 1945–51 nationalisations suffered this reversal. Eight years is quite a long time, given population mobility, for a Rent Act. And housing provision has not changed since the 1920s. In vain to point out that SET, introduced as a *Selective* employment tax was made non selective shortly thereafter by Labour itself, and was quite pointless, or to note that it was Wilson himself who effectively gave back the economic planning role to the Treasury, leaving the DEA with almost nothing to do, shortly after 1966. In vain, not because Finer is right, and I am wrong, but because there are no clear yardsticks as to what would constitute a decent life term for a policy, and because we are both agreed that the history of economic policy, under all governments, since at least the late fifties has been one of disastrous fumbling.

We need some more objective way of seeing when, if ever, the party system shifted from high consensus to polar opposition. One method is to examine the official party manifestos, to see if the publicly espoused policies can be plotted in some way so as to give us maps of party change. The figures below use such a methodology, based on a rigorous content analysis of these official documents. They are quoted with the

Figure 11.4   U.K. Party Manifestos: Movement on a Left–Right Axis

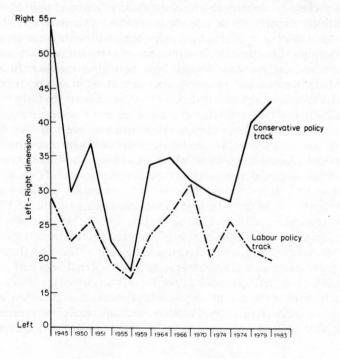

permission of my co-editors, from a forthcoming cross-national study.[26] This work which covers nearly twenty competitive party systems, demonstrates the viability of such a technique. The details are too complex to discuss here. For an earlier application of the technique to British politics, readers are referred to my *A Theory of Party Competition*.[27].

For this purpose it may be acceptable just to describe the diagrams as plotting party policy movement along a basic Left–Right dimension, as indicated by election manifestos, for each election since 1945. For Britain, with which we are primarily concerned, this is given in Figure 11.4. Figures 11.5 and 11.6 repeat the analysis for two other similar countries. Figure 11.5 uses United States party programmes for presidential years, and 11.6 the official election manifestos of the two major New Zealand parties. Naturally the precise meanings of the left–right dimensions vary in each country, but by showing that the technique gives intelligible plottings for countries other than the UK one hopes to establish confidence. More to the point, of the two, New Zealand has also been described as adversary in style since the early or mid-1970s, but such a label has not been applied to the USA.[28] The figures make it pretty clear why this should be so. In both New Zealand and the UK we see the major parties moving in ideological space in fairly close conformity to presumed shifts in electoral opinion until relatively recently. To be sure, there have been swings back and forth between more or less left or right poles, but usually either in concert, or with only a slight time lag. The direction of swing has usually been the same, and the parties ultimately have been close together. In New Zealand, for example, the two parties were closer to each other in the mid-1960s than they were to their own past positions in the early 1950s. Similarly the 1970 positions of the Labour and Conservative parties were very much closer to each other than they were to their 1959 positions, which had also been highly consensual. Very much the same applies to American positions where, in addition, the different nature of the ideological dimension, and the different character of Presidential and party races actually produce the appearance of ideological overlap.[29] But the crucial difference is stark. The map for the USA does not change its character at all during the period. In both the Westminster models, the picture of party competition as displayed by this technique is radically different after the early 1970s. The American map does show a steady rightwards shift by the Republican party after the relatively 'left' positions in the 1960s, themselves the result of a steady climb up from rightish post-war positions. But on the whole, so does the Democratic party. Certainly the rough parallelism continues. For New Zealand, and above all for Britain, the 'policy tracks' show an increasing divergence. Not since 1974 have British parties been consensual, and the direction of changes is to increased, not decreased, conflict. It might, of course, be said that we already knew this, but it is preferable to have some relatively unambiguous data to support the essentially intuitive opinions we would otherwise have to deal with. In the context of the Finer adversary model, the figures give a valuable corrective to a general assumption of adversarial politics throughout the period, an assumption that fitted ill, in any case, with most academic intuitions. For there is no evidence that politics were highly polarised until fairly recently.

Figure 11.5   U.S. Party Programmes: Movement on a Left–Right Axis

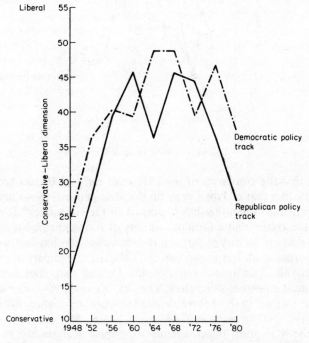

The obvious question to ask, on reviewing these party changes, is what has happened to the electorate? Has it remained, if it ever was, consensually oriented, have the parties been moving to extremes over a static battlefield? If they have, then we may indeed conclude that the party system is ill, and may even require surgery as drastic as a change in the electoral law. We should, however, first check. The alternative thesis would be that the prevailing mood of the electorate was changing,

Figure 11.6   New Zealand Party Manifestos: Movement on a Left–
Right Axis

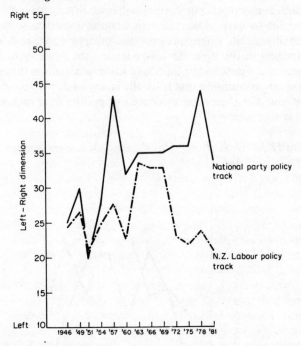

and that the consensus of the 1950s and early 1960s had broken up.
Work like that of Ivor Crewe on the 'dealignment' thesis has already
shown that something has happened to the electorate.[30] It has been
demonstrated that a form of volatility of voting choice has been bred
and that the solidity of partisan and class cleavages has decreased. His,
and other work has shown that the Labour party in particular has lost
from this.[31] In recent elections the Labour party has lost heavily
amongst its earlier safe voters. The 1983 election, with mass desertion
from Labour to the Liberal-Social Democratic Alliance, furthers this
theory.

The SDP itself is perhaps not what most analysts first thought, a
moderate force representing a solid and centrist new political position.
Indeed it is unclear from its performance in by-elections and in the last
election that it represents anything coherent at all. The opinion poll
support, and its by-election successes, were essentially at the cost of the
ruling Conservative party. Yet its general election vote came almost
entirely from the 1979 Labour support.[32] In itself the Alliance almost
certainly is nothing but a new vehicle for the disenchanted to use as a

half-way house for a transfer of political allegiance, as the Liberal party so often has served. Not only is there no evidence that the electorate remains centrist, being deserted by polarising parties, rather there is very strong evidence that electorate is becoming noticeably more conservative. One might simply cite the 1983 election result itself. Whatever those upset by the 'injustice' of underrepresentation for the Alliance may say about the Conservatives not really 'winning' an election in which they got less than 50% of the vote, and less than 40% of the electorate, they did win, in the sense the British constitution gives to that concept. For a party which had already gone, in 1979, further 'right' than at any time since 1945, and had turned even further rightwards, to 'win' an election given its huge economic difficulties is not to be lightly ignored.

We know, of course, that electorates, because of judgements of relative competence, often vote for parties whose political movement is opposite to the thrust of public opinion more generally. The 1980 American election, to take a very good example, is most probably not evidence of a rightwards shift of public opinion, even though Mr Reagan represented a move to the right compared with Mr Ford. The barely 50% turn-out, and the widespread sense of choosing between three men, none of whom deserved the White House, is one way of sensing that. This judgement can be backed up empirically. On most political attitudes which were tested both in 1976 and 1980, the electorate had either moved in a direction away from that represented by Mr Reagan, or not moved at all. Asked, for example, to rank themselves on a seven-point scale running from 'extremely liberal' to 'extremely conservative', samples in 1976 and 1980 reported an average position of, respectively, 4.38 and 4.34 – in other words, they reported statistically *identical* self-placements. Nor does this mean they were politically blind. The rankings they gave to the candidates in the elections fit perfectly well with our intuitions. In 1980 the sample saw Reagan as notably more 'conservative' than the 1976 sample had seen Ford, and also saw Carter as having become less liberal. The electorate knew what it was doing, and it was not moving towards the right in voting for the more right-wing candidate. On the general question of the federal government's duty to see to it that people have secure jobs and a decent standard of living, in other words on government economic interventionism, the electorate had a more 'liberal', more 'interventionist' position in 1980 than 1976. The average score, again on a seven-point scale, had been 4.6 in 1976, but changed to 4.3, that is, towards intervention, in 1980. The change may seem small but it is perfectly statistically significant.[33] Equally the average position on a scale measuring attitudes to women's liberation changed from 3.2 to to 2.9, towards liberation attitudes, and this again is significant by standard statistical tests. Attitudes changed marginally in a liberal direction on abortion, and even on bussing to achieve integration. All these moves are in a direction contradicted by the actual shift towards Reagan. They suggest that there is no reason to see his victory, and the ideological shift at the elite level it portrayed, as meaning that the American electorate itself had turned to the right.

Very similar tests can be applied in Britain for the shift in electoral opinion between 1974 and 1979. We have a host of opinion questions that were asked in identical form in both October 1974 and May 1979. Of seventeen policy or opinion questions that can be directly compared, the electorate moved to a more right-wing average position on 15. Of the remaining two, one, the question already mentioned on redistribution, produced an identical average score (2.58 on a five-point scale) in both elections. The only question to produce a leftwards shift was the highly symbolic one on increasing cash to the NHS. As the winter preceding the election (and the election itself to some extent) had been dominated by unprecedented strikes by public health service workers, this oddity is easily set aside. The brute evidence is that the rightwards shift of the Conservative policy in the seventies was at least matched by a similar shift in mass opinion.

Attitudes to expansion of the social services were measured on a four-point scale, where a score of 1 meant advocating considerable cutting, and 4 considerable expansion. The national average position dropped from 2.75 in 1974 to 2.48, statistically a very significant result. Even the nationalisation scale shifted from an average of 2.80 to 3.17 (that is, away from nationalisation, and again highly significant), though the 1974–79 Government was hardly noted for its massive nationalisation programme, and though the election campaign hardly mentioned the issue.

Similar rightwards shifts occured across the spectrum of policy areas: on welfare in general, on women's rights, racial equality, abortion, defence expenditure, comprehensive schooling, industrial democracy, and many other areas. One study has shown that the connection between this shift and actual vote swing is very clear.[34] A sizeable correlation exists between the size of the ideological shift and the size of the electoral swing in all socio-demographic subgroups of the population. As yet we have no evidence that this trend has continued between 1979 and 1983, but it would be very surprising if it has not. The contrast with North America is marked. There the electorate has not shifted ideologically, or if it has, it is to continue the liberalising trend of the 1960s and 1970s. Nor, though both candidates were to the right, in 1980, of their party's 1976 position, has the party system broken into diverging and polarising tracks. But in Britain a long-term party consensus has shattered, a long-term electoral stability has gone, and both the electorate and the governing party have shifted in a reactionary way.

At the same time the main opposition party, crippled by electoral desertion, has moved towards its own old ideological home, giving up all apparent interest in competitive politics. In this sense, and this sense alone, there is evidence for a special version of adversary politics in Britain, and suggestions that it might be happening elsewhere. (There is not, to hand, adequate survey evidence for New Zealand to back the party mappings, but impressionistic reports suggest a similarity to the UK experience.) We do not have a moderate public opinion in Britain betrayed by permanently adversarial parties who set policy along their own preferences, and thus we do not have a political multiplier effect. I have tried, indeed, to show that the whole conception of the middle ground in politics on which both the diagnosis and remedy of the Finer thesis is based are logically and empirically vacuous. Yet we do seem to have a change to a set of party positions which would indeed, will indeed, if the Labour party is ever re-elected, cause much of what he fears.[35] Why has the whole ground of British politics shifted?

This essay is no place to try to answer so cosmic a question, but in conclusion there are two speculations I would offer, which also bear on the underlying assumptions of Finer's adversary politics thesis.

The first speculation is about the way in which public consensus on policies gets fixed in the first place. At some stages in history the basic ideas of what are desirable or possible goals, and feasible or acceptable means become established. In Britain the 1940–45 coalition and the ensuing Labour government established such a political 'paradigm'. In the United States the New Deal, and very probably also the socio-economic mobilisation for the Second World War established a similar rough set of bounds for public life. In New Zealand it was again the war-time experience out of which the current party system grew. Throughout Western Europe the conditions and imperatives of post-war reconstruction created public expectations and values.

No one could expect these to last forever, and the economic slump of the early and mid-1970s looks as likely a candidate for a new threshold as any. But when the ground of consensus starts shifting, when one party begins to offer, and have accepted, a new definition of the nature of public expectations, one cannot expect its opposition immediately to conform to this. The Conservative party in the election of 1945 did not immediately accept the Labour party programme. The Republicans in 1932 and 1936 hardly made themselves carbon copies of FDR's political paradigm. Faced with a breakdown of the understandings that allowed a good chance of office every other election, with close convergence on what the government has been doing, how can an opposition react? Indeed, how should it, normatively, react?

One obvious answer is that a shift away from consensual politics, when policies manifestly cease to work, has to be asymmetric. The British Conservative party intentionally and publicly has gone right. It appears for the moment anyway to have taken the electorate with it. The Labour party must surely, at this stage, return to its ideological home for a while. To quote a man who tried unsuccessfully to destroy American political consensus in the 1960s, there comes a time when the electorate must be offered 'A choice, not an echo'.[36] Only when the choice has been presented, and made by the voters, can a new consensus appear. There is every sign at the moment that the new consensus, in Britain at least, will be a harder faced and less collectivist one. That choice is for the electorate, and if they make it, the main opposition to the Conservative party, whoever it may be, will have to adapt.

The other speculation comes from the first. There is a sense in which the real consensus in British politics has not been tapped during the last twenty years. I have made the argument for this thesis elsewhere,[37] though it it not a new one. There is a strong case for saying that the British political culture is highly populist. It is not right-wing, because there is a strong sense of class injustice still present, but it is not liberal either. Any party which really convinced the electorate that it would *both* pursue a redistribution of power and prestige as well as wealth, *and* would stand firm on what the current Prime Minister calls 'Victorian' values would probably easily win an election. To cite just two opinion distributions – a majority of the population in 1979 favoured the abolition of the House of Lords, and also favoured a strong military posture, as subsequent enthusiasm for the Falklands war proved. So far no major party has attempted to build a consensus along its natural line in Britain. Perhaps they never will.

My general conclusion is then that Finer is wrong in seeing adversary politics as a natural or endemic feature of the British political system, but that we are in fact experiencing the birth of a new consensual paradigm, and that this process must inevitably be one highly adversarial in nature. A simpler and quite old theory is that we are going through a series of 'critical elections' leading to a re-alignment, though so far we have evidence only for the initial de-alignment phase. This whole process, I suggest, is a natural product of the decay of the post-war paradigm. A move to PR at this stage in our history could be extremely dangerous, because it could delay or halt the birth of a new politics, leaving us struggling in an immobilism rather than in productive moderation.

Notes

1. S.E. Finer (ed.), *Adversary Politics and Electoral Reform* (Anthony Wigram, London, 1975).
2. S.E. Finer, *The Changing British Party System 1945–79* (American Enterprise Institute, Washington, D.C., 1980).
3. Finer cites the famous cube law at this stage, though the development of a much more popular third force, either with the increased vote for the Liberals or the growth of the SDP can only make his point stronger.
4. See, in particular, the essays by T. Wilson and D.K. Stout in *Adversary Politics*.
5. S. Levine, *The New Zealand Political System* (Allen and Unwin, Sydney, 1980).
6. *Adversary Politics*, p. 15.
7. All figures given for opinion in 1974 to 1979 are taken from surveys conducted by the British Election Study at the University of Essex, of which I was, with Bo Sarlvik and Ivor Crewe, Co-Director during the period covered. Detailed analyses of most of these points can be found in either B. Sarlvik and I.M. Crewe, *Decade of Dealignment* (Cambridge University Press, Cambridge, 1983) or David Robertson, *Class and the British Electorate* (Martin Robertson, Oxford, 1984).
8. See, for detailed analysis, David Butler and D.E. Stokes, *Political Change in Britain* (Macmillan, London, 1974).
9. General breakdowns for all questions asked in the four surveys between February 1974 and June 1979 can be found in the official codebooks of the BES project, available from the SSRC Survey Archive, Essex University.
10. Butler and Stokes, *op. cit.*, chapter 14.
11. 'Adversary Politics and Electoral Reform – Need We Be Afraid?'.
12. It is, in fact, a very simple application of the techniques pioneered in political science by Anthony Downs in *An Economic Theory of Democracy* (Harper, New York, 1957).
13. A wider range of such opinions, with more detail, is given in Robertson, *op. cit.*, chapter 8.
14. Attitudes to comprehensive education have been amongst the very best correlates of social class and of Labour party voting since the early 1950s. See Robertson, chapter 9.
15. There is no very good reason for using the ABA ratings rather than any of the other major groups. In fact past research has shown the correlations between ADA, COPE, ACA and OCUS to be so high as to yield one single underlying 'Liberalism–Conservatism' dimension under almost any form of dimensional analysis.

16. The sample I have used for these purely illustrative purposes is actually even more restricted. It includes only those non-Southern Congressmen elected to both the 96th and 97th Congresses. Putting the Southerners back in does not radically change the overall distributions, and I include them in the Senate analysis.

17. This is the central finding of all spatial or economic theories of voting and democracy, but it does, of course, assume that the voter, whether he be a Congressman or a member of the electorate, is voting only to maximise his own preferences on that issue, and is not constrained by any other considerations.

18. The data are taken from R.H. Healy (ed.), *Politics in America – members of Congress in Washington and at home* (Congressional Quarterly Press, Washington, 1981).

19. See P. Norton, *Dissension in the House of Commons 1974–9* (Oxford University Press, Oxford, 1980).

20. P.E. Converse, 'Belief systems in mass publics' in D. Apter (ed.), *Ideology and Discontent* (Free Press, New York, 1964).

21. The best arguments on this are in N. Nie, S. Verba *et al.*, *The Changing American Voter* (Harvard University Press, Cambridge, Mass., 1978).

22. The most famous version of this thesis is chapter 14 of B. Berelson and P. Lazarsfeld, *Voting* (Chicago University Press, Chicago, 1954).

23. See Downs, *op. cit.*

24. This assumption of correspondence was very widely shared in the political science profession until recently. Perhaps the best example is a book like Barry Hindess, *The Decline of Working Class Politics* (McGibbon and Kee, London, 1971) precisely because it so regrets the consensus which Finer denies was there.

25. *Adversary Politics*, p. 17.

26. Ian Budge, David Robertson and Derek K. Hearl (eds.), *Ideology and Party Strategy* (Sage, London, 1984).

27. (Wiley, London, 1976).

28. Levine, *op. cit.*

29. The apparent 'overlap' in Democratic and Republican positions is not surprising when one remembers that there is a considerable gap between the image the Presidential candidates project, and their party programme, which is built by a coalition during the Nominating Convention, and has to cope with the needs of many different sorts of candidates' races at different levels and in different parts of the country. One has to treat the points on the American graphs as showing the rough areas within which a candidate will be found, but the general movements are reliable.

30. I.M. Crewe, B. Sarlvik and J.B. Alt, 'Partisan dealignment in Britain, 1963–1974', *British Journal of Political Science*, 1976.
31. Robertson, *op. cit.*, especially chapters 1–4.
32. One indication of this, which cannot be safely established until the data from the 1983 election survey is published, is the relationship between turnout and Conservative vote percentage. On the whole the Conservatives did slightly less well than the polls had predicted. But where a Conservative was in danger from the attractions of the Alliance, as, for example, in Chelmsford, the turn-out went up, and the Conservative share of the total vote went up. In general the Alliance seems to have polled as nearly as possible all the votes it could, as did the Labour party. The slightly depressed overall turn-out appears to have been the result of confident Tories not bothering to vote.
33. I quote the significant tests, which are seldom quoted on survey data, to demonstrate that apparently trivial changes are quite marked. It is usually very hard to reach statistical significance levels with survey data because of the random 'noise' or error terms caused by, *inter alia*, question wording effects. All the results mentioned here as statistically significant by the application of a difference of means tests are significant *at least at* the 5% level, most at *better than* the 1% level.
34. Robertson, *op. cit.*, chapter 2. This shows that breaking down the electorate into twelve groups according to sex, a dichotomous class model, and three age groups produces a very high x correlation between change in average ideological score between 1974 and 1979, and change in vote preference between those years. Only one of the groups (middle class, middle-aged men) did not shift to the right in terms of mean ideological scores. They were the only group to show a small swing away from the Conservatives.
35. It can be argued that the Labour party, in its 1983 conference, has already started to move back towards a competitive, more right-wing position. For example, the deliberate obfuscation of its policy on nuclear weapons, and its abandoning of a clear-cut commitment to leave the EEC. It is entirely a matter for interpretation as to whether the election of the Kinnock–Hattersley leadership ticket does or does not signify this.
36. This was Barry Goldwater's slogan in the 1964 Election. At the time, as my diagram would confirm, he was seen as the most right-wing Republican candidate for some years.
37. Robertson, *op. cit.*, chapters 7 and 8.

Index